Win Win
Resolving
Workplace
Conflict

12 Stories

Endorsements

"Once again, Clive Lewis has given us a powerful presentation of why mediation matters. It should be read and acted on by anyone who is serious about competent management."

Alison Brimelow,
former President, European Patent Office

"Not your usual kind of 'text' book – reading the case studies or 'stories' (as Clive refers to them), made me feel as if I was reading a series of short novels that I didn't want to put down. You can't fail to be moved by the characters as their histories unfold, sometimes somewhat shockingly so."

Alison Middleton,
Head of Employee Relations and Reward, Baker Mackenzie

"Reading these 12 stories of conflict it is impossible not to recognise similar situations and similar individuals in your own back catalogue and you wonder if a different approach could have got you a different outcome."

Dave Smith,
Director of HR and OD, Gloucestershire NHS

"This much needed book provides many practical examples of how building better relationships produces better results in work and life. It's invaluable."

Lee Golding,
Executive Vice President, Human Resources, Travelport

"Changes are causing increasing levels of conflict, with huge financial and emotional costs to business and public services. This is a rare book that brings together learning that will not fail to help leaders make a difference."

Dr Noorzaman Rashid,
Director Board and Leadership Services, Harvey Nash

"The stories really brought to life the experience of the mediator and it was a memorable way to learn from Clive's experience and it confirmed to me how the mediation process can resolve conflict and re-build productive relationships in even the most difficult of situations."

Leigh Lafever-Ayer, Corporate HR Manager, UK and Ireland,
Enterprise Rent-A-Car UK Limited

"This book is timely and provides many practical examples of how people in the NHS can build better relationships and produce better results in work and in life. It's invaluable."

Liz Gambrell,
South East Coast NHS

Win Win
Resolving
Workplace
Conflict

12 Stories

Clive Lewis

RoperPenberthy Publishing Ltd

RoperPenberthy Publishing Limited
Springfield House, 23 Oatlands Drive, Weybridge, Surrey KT13 9LZ

Text copyright © Clive Lewis, 2011

Also by Clive Lewis:
The Definitive Guide to Workplace Mediation
and Managing Conflict at Work.
Difficult Conversations –
10 Steps to Becoming a Tackler not a Dodger.

This Edition published 2011

ISBN 978 1 903905 70 8 (paperback)
ISBN 978 1 903905 69 2 (hardback)

Cover design by Audri Coleman

Printed by Bell & Bain Limited, Glasgow, Scotland

Dedication

To my mother and in memory of my father

Contents

Author's note

"It is better to be alone than in bad company." – *George Washington*

When I was in my late teens I attended the funeral of an uncle. He hadn't been particularly active in maintaining an ongoing relationship with the family and had become somewhat isolated. Outside the church, prior to the funeral service, some of his children and step-children were openly struggling to cope with the news of his death. A small scuffle broke out as words were exchanged. It was rather tense. I stepped in and suggested that the parties calm down and think about the day in a way that didn't include aggression and hostility. After a few moments the arguments did indeed subside, and one or two of the onlookers accompanied one of the parties to a side street to have a cigarette. On observing what had happened, one of my brothers came over and congratulated me in my role as peacemaker.

Many years later I was appointed as a Human Resources (HR) Director. At least, I believed that was all I was. After an episode involving a management dispute however, I was attributed an additional role. The dispute involved three of my director colleagues and an email that one had sent to the other two. We had been in an enclosed room for around two hours with me trying to find a resolution to end the disagreement. When we eventually surfaced one of the secretaries came over to me and, grinning from ear to ear, embraced me with these words: *"Kofi Anan does it again!"* I thought it was hilarious, and we all had a good chuckle about it.

I thought no more about it until the following week when I was aboard a 12 hour flight to the west coast of America. About an hour into the flight I started to reflect on what she had said. I reached for my red A4 note book and started to write. The thoughts flowed continuously. I couldn't stop writing. I was making a note of all the themes that were cropping up in my mind in relation to conflict resolution, mediation and managing disputes. I was familiar with the concept of mediation but had never thought about it in any great detail. Furthermore, I had no idea that I had been wearing a badge at work with the word 'mediator' inscribed on it. Something had been unlocked in me. Little did I know that I was about to immerse myself in the field of conflict resolution and that it would take over a substantial part of my life.

Shortly after my return flight from the US, I researched the area of mediation and discovered a whole world that I previously knew nothing about. I decided to invest in myself and trained to become a commercial mediator. Throughout the course, the feedback from my assessors suggested that I had a natural leaning towards this discipline. Following the training, I immediately began looking for opportunities to mediate and subsequently founded the Globis Mediation Group, a company that specialises in mediating commercial, employment and workplace disputes and training mediators which I still run.

I have now personally mediated somewhere in the region of 250 disputes. I continue to be amazed, fascinated and astonished at the power of the mediation process and its ability to be able to transform lives.

Other events that have drawn my interest in the principles of conflict resolution have been:

- Those with whom I have experienced my own conflicts
- Working as a corporate executive for many years
- Managing people for nearly 20 years
- Nearly 20 years of marriage and seeing the effects of divorce on many of my friends and acquaintances
- Failing to learn from my own mistakes of the past
- Working in roles to which I was not always suited
- Witnessing the health problems of those in conflict
- Mediating, consulting, coaching, team building and facilitating for many large public and private sector organisations across three continents
- Attempting to be a better husband, father, friend, line manager and human being
- Trying to apply higher morals in business

Some time ago I started to write a blog. I wanted, in some way, to share with others what I could of my experiences in the mediation field. My first book, 'The Definitive Guide to Workplace Mediation', was published in 2009 to coincide with the new Employment Act that encouraged employers to strike up dialogue with embittered employees rather than resort to the litigation process. I wrote most of my first book on train journeys and in hotel rooms on the way to mediations, training sessions and seminars. The same has been true of this one.

All parties involved in a dispute have a story to tell, and this is mine. I decided to write it to help others learn about how mediation and alternative dispute resolution processes help resolve conflict. I also wanted to promote the many benefits of collaboration and productive relationships.

The book is in two parts. The bulk of the book is about stories of conflict and what this has meant to those involved. The second and much shorter part focuses on the role of Alternative Dispute Resolution, particularly mediation. It explains what it is, how it works and why its use continues to grow throughout the world. All the stories contained in this book are true, although due to the confidential nature of mediation and dispute resolution I have changed locations, sectors, ages and in some cases genders in order to protect the identity of those involved in the original story.

The introduction that follows is intended to shed some light on the topic of conflict, the theme around which all of the stories are centred, and the impact of the constantly changing world of work. It will also help provide some context for the stories that follow. I invite you to join me on a journey and exploration into a fascinating and exciting area.

Clive Lewis April 2011

Foreword

This is a book of stories. Stories have an effect on the imagination. Aesop and Hans Christian Andersen knew this. I learned it, too, when I was introducing what is now called diversity training into the judiciary 20 years ago. *"We know we are missing things through ignorance"*, they said. *"But we do not fully understand what we are doing wrong. Tell us some stories about things that have gone wrong."* I spent two years listening to people, and then the five true stories I told in the Eighth Kapila Lecture in November 1993 went round the world. In all of them serious injustice was being done in courts of justice, unwittingly.

The stories Clive Lewis tells in this book are also true. He has had to take steps to conceal people's identities, although I cannot help thinking that many of the subjects of these stories would welcome their inclusion in this book. For they tell how mediation has the power to change people's lives in a way in which litigation never could.

"Workplace mediation" means mediation undertaken at a stage before relationships at a place of work have broken down irretrievably. It may be conducted by an in-house mediator or it may be undertaken by an external mediator, hired for the day (or the week, or the month) to help to resolve deep-seated differences.

Some of these stories are about what we call *"employment mediation"*. This takes place when a job has been lost or a person's confidence shattered by discriminatory acts or omissions and all that may be achievable is a more civilised, less stressful exit from a total breakdown of relations. This is a form of mediation I sometimes undertake myself, and I too, like Clive, have witnessed scenes when two people, locked in conflict all day, hug and kiss through sheer relief that the issues between them have been resolved. Sometimes I get kissed, too.

This is a book about the power of mediation when conducted by a highly skilled mediator. All new mediators are taught the art of active listening, of reflective pauses, of asking open questions, of "playing back" what they have heard, of securing both sides' trust at the outset and keeping it through what may be a long and tiring day. This book contains examples of all these techniques - and many more. I commend it to everyone looking for better ways of resolving stress at work and all that this entails for human dignity.

Sir Henry Brooke, former High Court Judge and Chair of Civil Mediation Council

Introduction

"I look for three things in hiring people. The first is personal integrity, the second is intelligence, and the third is a high energy level. But, if you don't have the first, the other two will kill you." – Warren Buffett

We can all learn something about how to manage conflict and relationships better. The number of disputes being encountered in UK places of work is building at a staggering rate. Cases going to Employment Tribunals are growing by about 50% per year, with unfair dismissal, redundancy and breach of contract cases making up a large part of the increase. Around 600,000 cases are lodged in the UK Employment Tribunal system at any one time. This level of increase in industrial disputes is unsustainable. The statutory dispute resolution system wasn't designed to cope with such high levels of fall out and is cracking under the pressure; the financial cost of our collective industrial relations failure is running to nearly 30 billion pounds per year, with the cost to our health and emotions likely to be just as substantial. Something has to change. It is unlikely that the human race can go on living this way without running the risk of engendering some irreparable damage at some point in the future. Thousands of working people are watching their lives slip by whilst conflict, turmoil, tension and anguish takes its toll.

Part of the impact of globalisation, the information age, constant change, higher unemployment, increasing longevity and employment legislation has been the proliferation in the complexity of issues related to managing the workforce. The world of work has changed beyond all recognition in the last 20 years, with the concept of a *'job for life'* becoming a thing of the past. The phrase *'work until you drop'* is becoming much more poignant and multi-national workforces have become the norm. The UK, along with most other countries in the developed world, is still recovering from one of the worst periods of recession in the post-war era. The recovery period has brought uncertainty and paranoia as cuts, particularly in the public sector, start to bite. There is, of course, also a link to the home. The tough economic conditions that developed towards the end of the first decade of the 21st century have brought:

- Higher unemployment with around 7.8% of the UK working population out of work
- More people claiming job seekers allowance
- A 220% increase in the number of companies going bust
- A 19% increase in the number of personal bankruptcies
- A 51% increase in the number of men contacting the Consumer Credit Counselling Service as a result of being hit hardest in the recession

The combination of these aspects and others not listed is that the workplace is increasingly becoming an arena where employees arrive each morning weighed down with concerns about their families and loved ones. This also puts pressure on management level staff to become more attuned and aware of employees' personal pressures, requiring increased levels of people skills and sensitivity in order to keep positive employee relations intact.

In my day to day life I work with many HR professionals and recall having numerous conversations with those unhappy and unsettled with aspects of their work. For most this was because their respective organisations were embarking on a major period of change. Change in itself isn't a new phenomenon for the HR professional, but the difference in most instances was that the HR function was heavily impacted by these adjustments. The result was that those normally required to provide leadership on related projects were themselves psychologically disengaged as they were thinking about whether they themselves would be affected and if they would be able to provide for their families in a few months time.

One of the challenges that people in the HR function have had to deal with has been the burgeoning amount of employment legislation. This has led to an increase in disputes in the workplace as some disgruntled employees see more hooks on which to extract compensation from a current or former employer. The Employment Tribunals service, as we have seen, is struggling to keep up with demand. I recall one senior HR person telling me that two years previously his organisation saw 18 cases go to an Employment Tribunal. Two years on, that figure had increased to 127.

Employment Tribunals

Every five years, the Survey of Employment Tribunal Applications (SETA) is published. It is a fascinating read – to me anyway! The latest survey covers the period up to the end of December 2008 and runs to more than 250 pages. Here are some of the highlights from two of the categories – 'characteristics of the parties' and 'mediation'.

Characteristics of the parties
- 60% of claimants were men
- 82% of discrimination cases were brought by women
- 86% of defendants were white as were only 15% of those involved in race discrimination cases
- Employment Tribunal applicants were more likely to be aged over 45
- The median pay for claimants in full-time permanent positions was £20,000
- 25% of claimants were a member of a trade union
- 27% of cases were from organisations with fewer than 25 employees, 9% had 25-49 employees, 19% had 50-249 employees and 45% had 250 or more employees
- The private sector accounted for 72% of Employment Tribunal cases, the public sector 19% and the non-profit sector 8%

Mediation
- 23% of claimants reported that before they put in the Employment Tribunal application someone suggested that they should use mediation, compared with 15% of employers
- 9% of claimants had undertaken mediation
- The most commonly cited reason for not taking part in mediation was that the other party did not want to
- The initial discussion about the possibility of the use of mediation was most common in large employers and those in the private sector
- 27% of employers used an in-house mediator
- Amongst claimants, trade union/staff association members were less likely to say that they would use mediation in the future, as were those aged 55 or over
- 36% of claimants said that the case had caused them stress and depression

2009/10 Employment Tribunal Statistics
Here are some of the findings from the tribunal statistics of 2009-10:
- Between 2008-09 and 2009-10 there was a 56% rise in claims to Employment Tribunals
- There was a 17% increase in the number of tribunal claims associated with unfair dismissal, breach of contract and redundancy
- As of 31st March 2010, the caseload outstanding was 628,800, with three fifths of this being for multiple claims to the Employment Tribunals
- The 75% target was not met against a climate of increasing workloads
- 71% of customers said that they were satisfied with the overall service from the tribunals service

Dealing with the effects of disputes takes up team members' and managers' valuable time, often meaning that they have to postpone working on value-add areas to do so. Most of our waking lives are spent at work, and as a result many conflicts take place there too. In an excellent prose poem written by Killarney Clary she describes how many people feel at work:

"Because the ones I work for do not love me, because I have said too much and I haven't been sure of what is right and I've hated the people I've trusted, because I work in an office and we are lost and when I come home I say their lives are theirs and they don't know what they apologise for and none of it mended, because I let them beat me and I remember something of mine which not everyone has, and because I lie to keep myself and my hands my voice on the phone because I swallow what hurts me, because I hurt them – I give them the hours I spend away from them and carry them, even in my sleep, at least as the nag of a misplaced shoe, for years after I have quit and gone on to another job where I hesitate in telling and I remember and I resent having had to spend more time with them than with the ones I love."

In recent times, the shift in employee relations thinking has moved across three areas from:

1. The post-war era – The nation recognised the need to work collectively to rebuild the country's infrastructure and get the economy back on its feet. Most people acknowledged a sense of sharing responsibility in doing what was necessary to recover and recuperate from years of collateral damage.

During this period, trade unions served their members well to protect employment rights and prevent manipulation and exploitation as businesses competed for market share or greater efficiencies.

2. Political and economic change of the 1980's and beyond – The government of the day worked hard and fast to promote capitalism and secure Britain's future as a major player on the global economic field. We began to see a rise in collective disputes and the government clashed with unions as it (the government) tried to pursue change quicker and faster. As privatisation emerged with the sell-off of institutions such as British Gas, we saw employees revolt where executives such as Cedric Brown were awarded double digit increases in remuneration packages. At the same time the impact of European legislation began to come forth with the signing of the Maastricht Treaty which opened the gates for numerous types of employment rights to begin to flood through.

3. The credit crunch – We are now witnessing the effects of the increases in both individual and collective rights. Similar to the post war era, there is a need to help get the UK back on its feet. This time the war we are recovering from is one based on the collapse of the financial markets and loss of confidence. We are living and working in a period not created by the recession but tested by it. One of the ways employees are coping is to accept short term sacrifices in return for long term security. Periods of austerity bring with them a reduction or absence of choices for many people. As psychologist Abraham Maslow postulated, we must first attempt to satisfy survival-based physiological needs, and only afterwards do we seem to satisfy higher level personal and social needs, such as aesthetics and self-actualisation.

In order to surface successfully from this current period the labour market will need to pursue employee relations strategies based on:

- Consensus rather than conflict
- Developing positive attitudes towards change
- Building transparency, communication, honesty and reliability
- Encouraging openness from line managers
- A willingness to promote employee flexibility
- Clearing the way for the employee voice to be heard
- Promoting a fair balance between employees, trade unions and employers

It is not possible to simply mandate good employee relations. To support the above it will also be important to develop a legal framework where the law and market work in harmony and common sense solutions are favoured.

The economic argument for conflict resolution principles

Today in most organisations there is an ongoing tussle for allocation of resources. For years those in the mediation and conflict resolution industry have had difficulty in getting organisations, particularly in the private sector, to give priority to conflict resolution. I, and many others, have spent countless hours wondering how to change this. For a practitioner like me it seems so obvious. Time and time again however I have witnessed the negative effects of disputes on those involved.

I recall a dispute I was asked to mediate upon early in my career which involved two women in the healthcare sector. Amongst hundreds of other cases I have mediated on since, this dispute remains vivid in my mind for three reasons which will be detailed later. The original spat between these two, Gill and Sue, had begun six months earlier during a team meeting. Gill said something to Sue in the midst of the meeting which Sue found highly offensive and somewhat embarrassing, the result being that she stopped speaking to Gill. For six months their exchanges took place through third parties and, despite their requirement to work together in the same department, Sue refused to engage in dialogue. Eventually Sue became ill and was signed off work due to stress; she lost a lot of weight and her hair was starting to fall out. During the one-to-one pre-mediation sessions both expressed an interest in putting the issue behind them with Gill assuming that it was her comment during the team meeting that had created the tension, although she couldn't be totally sure.

On the day of the joint mediation session I commenced by giving the main mediation opening remarks, followed by a request to hear the pre-prepared opening statements from both sides with Sue to go first. Sue began to cry almost immediately. In between the tears she told Gill how she had felt embarrassed, outraged and incensed by the comment made at the meeting, to the point where she seriously contemplated some sort of revenge. She then went on to describe how and why she was unable to talk to Gill – just the sight of Gill made her feel sick. She only realised how much she had been affected when she lost her appetite and was unable to sleep at night. She also retold a story where she spotted Gill whilst out shopping with her husband on a Saturday morning and, horrified, dragged him into a nearby shop for enough time to let Gill pass by. During Sue's tearful discourse, Gill began to fidget noticeably and looked continually surprised at Sue's revelations.

When Sue finished I asked Gill if she would like to give her comments. Gill responded by saying, *"Sue, I'm so sorry. I had no idea that my comments had had such an impact on you."* There was genuine concern and sorrow in her comments. We then spent the next half an hour or so documenting the learning points to prevent reoccurrence and we were finished. That was it. The mediation session was over. We had been together for less than an hour. This is the first reason why this case remains clear in my mind – the speed with which everything was concluded. I said goodbye to both parties and proceeded to make my way to the car park. I reached my car, started it up and was about to pull out of the car park when I saw in my rear view mirror that Gill and Sue were in close proximity and still talking. I didn't realise at the time how momentous this event was, but instinct told me it was a rare thing indeed and hence it has also been vividly retained.

Two days later I was just pulling into a hotel when my phone rang. It was Sue. We exchanged greetings before she said she wanted to thank me. I said that it wasn't a problem and that I was pleased to help them out. Sue then said something that brought a lump to my throat. *"No, Clive,"* she said, *"I really want to thank you. For the first time in six months I have just had two sound nights of sleep. I feel so much better."* It was a very emotional moment. Through the phone

I could feel her sense of release of the anguish and pain that she had been carrying for so long. I have experienced instances like this since, but the first is always the most memorable.

The outcome of this case gave me a great sense of job satisfaction. The unfortunate aspect however was the waste of time, reduction in productivity and costs of absence that the organisation and individuals suffered as a result. Another glaring shortfall was that the organisation lacked the skills that were required to bring two people together and facilitate a discussion that could have nipped this situation in the bud months before. The costs associated with this dispute must have been staggering.

Some years ago, I stated that the management of conflict represents one of the biggest untapped areas for competitive advantage and organisation cost savings, something I still hold to be true. However, because most of the costs associated with conflict are unseen or indirect, it rarely becomes a priority area. In the table below I list some of the impact areas of conflict.

Table 1.0

Conflict impact areas	
Increases	**Decreases**
• Customer complaints • Employee turnover • Sickness • Absence • Legal fees • Risk	• Productivity • Project delivery • Employee attraction • Employee engagement • Health & Well-being

This type of scenario though can be taken one stage further. Disputes of this nature often provide a glimpse of the culture of the organisation. It is rare that such incidents occur on an isolated basis. Some time ago, we conducted some research with an organisation employing 18,000 people. One department of 30 was encountering rising levels of tension and conflict as well as embarking on a significant amount of change. Over a six month period of mediation, facilitation and team building with us, the department was able to report a 93% reduction in sickness absence and a 60% reduction in labour turnover and associated costs. These reductions were calculated at an annual value of £143,000. We took the basis for this work to calculate what the overall cost of conflict might look like at organisational level. We took a multiplication factor of six (which represented the number of directorates across the organisation) and assumed that similar occurrences were happening in each directorate.

We used minimum number levels i.e. 1% of the population of the organisation to help illustrate the point. In reality, it is likely that the number would have been much higher. The result was an annual indicative cost of just under £1m for the organisation. One would think that this type of example makes the return on investment argument easy to win. For a relatively small investment, mediation is highly likely to bring a large percentage of difficult and potentially costly situations to an end. On average, around 85% of the cases that go to mediation result in a satisfactory settlement for the parties. There are few other processes where hard pressed line managers and finance directors would be able to predict such a high rate of return against the organisation's financial resources.

I have a few thoughts on why the mediation and conflict resolution industry has failed to persuade business leaders on the business case for conflict resolution at work and why there continues to be a degree of reluctance. Here are some of them:

- It can be easy to ignore, avoid or simply put off dealing with conflict. It is one of those matters that require a large amount of energy and effort to deal with. It is often much more convenient to do something else
- Acknowledging that conflict is present can be seen as recognition of failure. Few people, if any, want to be associated with failure
- Some problems can go away quickly if you throw money at them. This is far easier to do in the private sector and probably explains why the public sector accounts for around 75% of revenue related to the workplace mediation market. It also probably demonstrates why 75% of disputes going to Employment Tribunals are linked to the private sector
- There is a lack of understanding in the boardroom about how the impact of conflict affects the bottom line
- Conflict situations are not always identified as a risk and included in the risk register alongside issues such as health and safety

Table 2.0 begins to show how the tool of mediation can be utilised at both operational and strategic levels.

Table 2.0

Mediation at the strategic level	
Operational Level	**Strategic level**
• Solves disputes • Gives line managers their time back • Improves customer service • Reduces absence • Improves team work	• Helps organisational learning • Helps form succession planning • Improves productivity savings • Increases the likelihood of achieving organisation objectives • Enhances competitiveness • Improves employee engagement • Improves organisational health and well-being • Can be linked to operational and financial reviews • Compelling business case for corporate and social responsibility • Reduces business risk

Tension exists at board level too. It can be a prerequisite that part of the criteria for becoming a boardroom member is that individuals aren't backward in coming forward. The added dimension about conflict in the boardroom is that it can spill over and affect various parts of the organisation. For example, if team members get wind of the fact that their boss is engaged in conflict with a colleague it can mean that they take sides with their leader. In extreme cases, silos may develop as whole functions may refuse to collaborate with each other out of a sense of loyalty. At board level, there are so many exciting developments that can happen linked to managing conflict, for example the summarisation of the outputs of a year of mediation cases could be used as a framework for organisational learning.

Case study

Pursar Technologies is a FTSE 250 global business. A dispute had developed between its Marketing Director, Customer Service Director and Chief Technology Officer regarding an email sent by the Customer Service Director to the Chief Executive with a proposal on direction for the company. The Marketing Director and Chief Technology Officer were also copied in to the email. The Marketing Director replied to all parties asking the Customer Service Director to explain why he had proposed an idea about how the company should be adjusting its marketing strategy without discussing it with him first. The situation was then made worse when the Chief Technology Officer indicated that he wanted to adopt an alternative marketing strategy to the other two. There followed a big falling out, which the Chief Executive decided was best left to the three of them to sort out.

This decision backfired, and eventually relations became so strained between the three that not only did they stop talking to each other but also stopped making joint visits to customers and collaborating on organisational initiatives. Customers then began to be negatively impacted by this turn of events and the sales pipeline started to slow down. Three months of this led to the Chief Executive realising that something needed to be done and engaged the services of a mediator. The mediator was locked in a room with the three executives for three hours and by the time the parties emerged they had agreed to put the dispute behind them. Apologies had been exchanged and it was back to business as usual. The Chief Executive was astonished that three months of stand-off could be settled with a three hour conversation. He also realised that the organisation had paid a huge price for pontificating over a dispute that could have been settled as soon as the original email had been sent.

Mediation in this instance, as with many, served a double purpose. Not only did it achieve its direct aim of getting the senior executives talking again but it also had a knock on effect of allowing them to build organisational capability, reduce organisational risk and increase competitive advantage. Mediation in any organisation is unlikely to be highly successful unless members of the board understand its benefits and are willing to engage in mediation themselves when trouble strikes.

Great companies
In his ground breaking research of the late 1990's, Jim Collins and his team identified the six key traits that all great (rather than good) organisations possess. The research had a sample size of 1435 companies from which only 11 made the grade that allowed them to be defined and categorised as great rather than good. The set of six traits is listed below, all underpinned by disciplined thought, disciplined action and disciplined people.

1. Level 5 Leadership – Jim Collins and his team were surprised, shocked really, to discover the type of leadership required for turning a good company into a great one. Compared to high-profile leaders with big personalities who make headlines and become celebrities, the good-to-great leaders seem to have come from Mars. Self-effacing, quiet, reserved, even shy – these leaders are a paradoxical blend of personal humility and professional will. They are more like Lincoln and Socrates than Patton or Caesar.

2. First Who...Then What – Jim Collins and his team expected that good-to-great leaders would begin by setting a new vision and strategy. They found instead that they first got the right people on the bus, the wrong people off the bus, and the right seats – and then they figured out where to drive it. The old adage

"People are your most important asset" turns out to be wrong. People are not your most important asset. The right people are.

3. Confront the brutal facts – Jim Collins and his team learned that a former prisoner of war had more to teach them about what it takes to find a path to greatness than most books on corporate strategy. Every good-to-great company embraced what they came to call the Stockdale Paradox: This was that you must maintain unwavering faith that you can and will prevail in the end, regardless of the difficulties, AND at the same time have the discipline to confront the most brutal facts of your current reality, whatever they might be.

Great companies recognise that having tough and crucial conversations can be vital. This aspect represents yet another reason to support the business case for the introduction of conflict resolution principles within the workplace. The aspect that I think applies in particular to the topic of resolving conflict is *'confront the brutal facts'*. All organisations have situations which they would rather disappear forever. This rarely happens though.

In this context, confront the brutal facts could mean:
* Following through on information about inappropriate behaviour by a line manager given at exit interview
* Addressing issues of conduct which are out of line with the organisation's values
* Having a difficult conversation with a top performer
* Introducing new ways of working
* Saying 'no' for business reasons to an individual or group of influence
* Taking the decision to exit the company from a declining market based on analysis of past performance

Whatever the topic, addressing brutal facts can make the difference between survival and extinction. Great companies recognise that dealing with difficult situations is an essential ingredient in success.

4. The Hedgehog Concept (simplicity) – To go from good to great requires transcending the curse of competence. Just because something is your core business – just because you've been doing it for years or perhaps even decades – does not necessarily mean you can be the best in the world at it. And if you cannot be the best in the world at your core business, then your core business absolutely cannot form the basis of a great company. It must be replaced with a simple concept that reflects deep understanding of three intersecting circles.

5. Culture of Discipline – All companies have a culture, some companies have discipline, but few companies have a culture of discipline. When you have disciplined people, you don't need hierarchy. When you have disciplined thought, you don't need bureaucracy. When you have disciplined action, you don't need excessive controls. When you combine a culture of discipline with an ethic of entrepreneurship, you get the magical alchemy of great performance.

6. Technology Accelerators – Good-to-great companies think differently about the role of technology. They never use technology as the primary means of igniting a transformation. Yet, paradoxically, they are pioneers in the application of carefully selected technologies. Jim Collins and his team learned that technology by itself is never a primary root cause of either greatness or decline.

Trust

Today's executives work under the spotlight more than ever before. A number of recent research projects have indicated that trust is at an all-time low. Peter Drucker once said that organisations are no longer built on force, but on trust. In organisations where trust is high, there are likely to be fewer situations of conflict. In a low trust organisation you are likely to see behaviours such as the following:

- People manipulating or distorting facts
- People withholding and hoarding information
- Low energy levels
- People making excuses for their many violated expectations
- People tending to over-promise and under-deliver
- People pretending bad things aren't happening or in denial about them
- Most people are involved in a blame game i.e. bad mouthing others
- An abundance of water cooler talk
- People spinning the truth to their advantage
- Getting the credit is very important
- New ideas are openly resisted and stifled
- Mistakes are covered up or covered over
- Many non-discussable issues

In a high trust organisation however, you are more likely to observe behaviours such as these:

- Palpable vitality and energy among workforce
- People are candid and authentic
- There is real collaboration and real communication
- People are loyal to those who are absent

- The culture is innovative and creative
- There are few *'meetings after the meetings'*
- People talk straight and confront the real issues
- People share credit abundantly
- Transparency is a practised value
- Information is shared openly
- Mistakes are tolerated and encouraged as a way of learning

I recall reading an example about what can happen when trust is high. It related to Warren Buffett, CEO of Berkshire Hathaway and generally considered one of the most trusted leaders in the world. He completed the acquisition of an organisation called McLane Distribution for $23bn from Wal-Mart. As public companies, both were subject to high level market and regulatory scrutiny. Typically, a merger of this size and scale would take several months to complete and would cost several million dollars or pounds to pay for accountants, lawyers and auditors to validate and verify all kinds of information. But in this instance, because both parties operated with high trust, the deal was made with a single two hour meeting and a handshake. In less than a month it was completed. In a management letter that accompanied his 2004 annual report Warren Buffett wrote, *"We did no due diligence. We knew everything would be exactly as Wal-Mart said it would be – and it was."* I accept that this example might appear to be an example of trust at the macro level. Here then is another example from *'The Speed of Trust'* written by Stephen M.R. Covey.

"Jim, a vendor in New York City, set up a doughnut and coffee shop for passing pedestrians as they went in and out of their office buildings. During the breakfast and lunch hours, Jim always had long lines of customers waiting. He noticed that the wait time discouraged many customers who left and went elsewhere. He also noticed that, as he was a one-man show, the biggest bottleneck preventing him selling more doughnuts and coffee was the disproportionate amount of time it took to make up change for his customers. Finally, after much thought, Jim simply put a small basket on the side of his stand filled with change, trusting his customers to take their own change. One might think that customers would, either accidentally or intentionally, count themselves out the wrong change. Jim however found the opposite, that most customers responded by being completely honest, often leaving him larger-than-normal tips. Using this method he was also able to move customers through at twice the pace because he didn't have to make up change. In addition, he found that his customers kept coming back because they liked being trusted. By extending trust in this way, Jim was able to double his revenues without adding any new costs."

This story illustrates the theory that a low level of trust results in a decrease in speed and a rise in cost and vice versa. People want to be trusted and respond to trust. Trust is a function of two things: character and competence. Character includes aspects such as integrity, motives and intent whilst competence includes capabilities, skills, results and an individual's track record. With increasing focus on ethics in our society, both of these aspects, but in particular character, are becoming critical. You might think that a person is sincere and honest but you won't trust them if they don't deliver results. The opposite, again, is also true; a person might have great skills and talents and a good record, but if they are dishonest you won't trust that person either.

Authenticity

Authenticity is closely connected to the character aspect of trust. I recently attended a management meeting with a group of senior professionals, and as our meeting progressed we reviewed progress in a number of areas. As the agenda moved on to a new topic, the Chair of the meeting invited the Senior Manager concerned to update the meeting on progress against a particular item. There hadn't been any progress. The Senior Manager had realised a short while before the meeting that he hadn't set up the measurement mechanisms that would allow progress to be tracked. This was a problem and should have been an area that we had full knowledge and control of. His response surprised all of us in the room. We were all so used to hearing comments of self-preservation and bottom covering amongst the group that when he said, "We have no data on this theme and it's entirely my fault, I'm so sorry, I am to blame," the room fell into a kind of shocked silence. After a few seconds the chair punctuated the silence with a light hearted comment that translated into veiled praise for the Senior Manager's honesty. Everyone in the group saw the funny side. Assuming others in the audience felt the same as me, the Senior Manager had, in one moment, sealed the long term respect of his peers. It was a simple but honest acknowledgement of an error and slip up, yet it made such a big impact. He was being authentic.

Sometimes entire cultures are held hostage by a downward cycle of spin and posturing. This reduces trust and creates additional unnecessary problems such as people withholding information. As a result, companies often require three meetings instead of one. These are the pre-meetings to prepare and position, the meeting itself where very little discussion of the real issues take place and the post meeting meetings where the really detailed discussions take place.

This is not of course all there might be to authenticity. Being authentic has much more to do with being true to oneself and being 'you'. Authenticity is played out when we grant ourselves the freedom to be who we really are and forego the urge to be like someone we might admire or become someone the organisation might want us to be. When we attempt to be someone we are not, people will in most cases see right through it. This is detailed further in the story 'United by death'.

The reason for focusing on trust and authenticity for this brief moment is to recognise the part it plays in the industrial relations arena in the 21st century. Organisations that want to be progressive and embrace new thinking will grab the notion of trust with both hands and incorporate it as a key competency for those in the leadership team.

Chapter 1
The power of storytelling

"Men build too many walls and not enough bridges." - Sir Isaac Newton

My father sadly died in 2006. For most of his life he was a Church Minister and as the youngest of five children I had no choice but to accompany my family to Sunday School. As time went by I learnt a few tricks to get out of going, but not enough to keep me away every Sunday. A memory that has stuck with me from this period of my childhood is of being in a class with about 20 other children hearing stories from the Bible. I can even remember the name of our teacher - a lady called Hermin Barclay. Ms Barclay told us how Jesus regularly used parables in his teaching sessions, and indeed it seemed to me that he in fact had a story to describe almost every situation.

Later in my life, as a corporate executive, I attended an advanced presentation skills training course, during which we were encouraged to tell our own stories as part of giving our message. The trainers suggested that stories have a way of gripping the attention of the listener. They commented that human beings have an innate interest in hearing about the life experiences of others. As we practised and rehearsed this principle during the course the word *'parable'* was never mentioned, but images of Hermin Barclay and her teaching came flooding back to me.

In the last 20 years storytelling has become a key tool in the kit bag for executives, comedians, politicians, speech writers and speech givers. When we tell stories, we share our heart. We become vulnerable as we relive experiences from our past. These stories might be sad, funny, distressing, regretful, long or short. Anyone who has experienced conflict will have embarked on a journey and will have a story of their own. In some cases the journey may have come to a successful end – some individuals and their opponents work out differences on their own or with the help of a third party. Other journeys may have ended in a more negative manner or may still be continuing. In some cases the journey could continue for years, as some never quite manage to find a resolution to the situation that has separated them and their adversary.

Recently, I saw an example of how the latter can be played out. I was invited to give a presentation on mediation and conflict resolution to some head teachers and other education professionals. There were about 60 people in the room. The session was going well, with many in the audience engaging with me in verbal and non verbal means. At around the halfway stage in the presentation, my eyes locked onto a delegate who was sitting a few rows back from the front on my left hand side. I felt uncomfortable. I sensed that he hadn't connected with me in the same way that many of his colleagues seemed to. I continued, providing many stories of my own as the presentation progressed. By the end of the session he was still looking at me but showed no signs that he wanted to make a contribution. When the session had finished I was having coffee and speaking with a few members of the audience who had formed a small queue in order to speak to me. Out of the corner of my eye I saw the gentleman join the queue and then leave it. Later, when I was on my own, he finally approached me. I wasn't sure what to expect but began to prepare myself for what he might want to say.

He broke the ice by asking me a few questions about myself. After I had answered him, there was a short silence. He then started to tell me a story. Now in his mid-fifties, he had been a high flier some years back and had been appointed as a head teacher before his fortieth birthday. Soon after being appointed he began the process of making his mark on his new school, aiming to root out any poor performers. He found one employee he deemed such and spent very little time planning how to remove her from his team. He told her in clear terms that he didn't see a role for her in the school and spent about six months focusing much of his energy on making her feel uncomfortable, to the point where their relationship, unsurprisingly, became strained. Eventually she resigned after finding a job at another school. The head asked his secretary to arrange the purchase of a leaving gift for her and to plan a small farewell ceremony. His secretary made the arrangements but the employee didn't turn up.

About one year later the head and the ex-employee bumped into each other in the supermarket. Both were initially lost for words, but the ex-employee, before she moved on, told the head how awful he had made her feel as a result of how he had treated her. She didn't mince her words. It was difficult for him to hear. Now, over 15 years later, and much wiser, he was still carrying the pain of the unresolved conflict with his former colleague. Tears came to his eyes as he told the story. He was now starting to think about retirement, but this event so early on in his career was still causing him much anguish. I asked whether it was too late for him to find his former colleague and try to sort their differences out. He said he didn't think so and that he would consider attempting to reconcile things with her. It is unlikely that his journey will be completed until he does.

There are probably thousands of people with stories that might sound similar to this one. If this book allows one person to pause, reflect and seek restitution with unfinished business, it will have been worthwhile writing.

Sharing our experiences

When we talk about our life experiences, we invite the listener to enter into our world and share the experience that we have lived. Telling stories encourages communication below the surface and promotes community, kinship and unity by bringing people together.

As we tell our stories we become vulnerable. We can expose our weaknesses, failures and prejudices as we recount the history of what happened. We might tell a story about dragons, drawbridges and men with arrows and bring it to life as we tell it to our children. The same process takes place when hearing stories about conflict. Every conflict story tells a tale of one or more dragons and how the dragon might or might not get slaughtered, silenced or put to sleep. In some cases the stories might reveal that the dragon lost the ability to exhale fire years ago, although everyone still thought that it could.

Most parties in conflict, on hearing what the other side has to say about the dispute, are likely to find it difficult to suspend disbelief and spend time examining the story for its deeper truths and hidden meanings. In the first instance, the party is unlikely to feel empathy towards their opponent and stretch out a hand to discover more about the difference that divides them. Closing the divide takes time.

Every authentic story will strike a chord within us. When we hear authentic stories we imagine ourselves in the sequence of events that unfold and imagine how we would feel if we had been the storyteller. Storytelling can carry both the listener and the storyteller to a deeper relationship level and help to form a bridge over the choppy waters keeping parties apart.

Conflict stories can also be a recognition of failure, a cry for help, a confession or a request for forgiveness. Because people feel powerless in conflict situations, they look for ways to be able to justify their behaviour or to have it endorsed by an ally. If there is an opportunity for an ally to respect them as a decent human being who didn't deserve the treatment they received, people will take it. Opponents may be characterised as evil, wicked and malicious people who want to do harm. This explains why the storyteller was unable to do anything to prevent or resolve it and puts them in a better light. In these ways, conflict stories can embellish what actually happened during upsetting events and divert attention away from obvious weaknesses on the part of the storyteller. The listener's attention is diverted to what the perpetrator did. The perpetrator's treachery is exaggerated in order to maintain the illusion of the storyteller's innocence.

Conflict stories can be parables that describe how someone brought a crisis into the life of the storyteller. The storyteller can elicit sympathy from the listener, as they are seen as powerless and helpless in the face of the wrongdoer.

The objective of listening to conflict stories

Conflict stories are made up of a whole myriad of things including fear, embarrassment, shame, jealousy, inability to forgive and deceit. The goal of a mediator and conflict resolution specialist is to uncover what lies beneath the surface of what is reported by the parties in dispute. In order to do this, the mediator (or rescuer) listens deeply and with empathy to connect with the storyteller and to prompt them to say more.

A second objective is to try and look for the truth. Every conflict story has more than one side. I learned many years ago never to form a judgment about a dispute after listening to one person's version of the story. Often someone might tell their story relating to the conflict situation they have encountered and, while doing so, portray the perpetrator as a demon. On meeting the so-called demon, however, you might discover that the label has been inappropriately applied to them. They may have been misunderstood, but to be classed as a demon is often somewhat out of perspective. The hope is that through the mediation process the first storyteller (or the accuser) may also discover this.

In the book 'Narrative Mediation', John Winslade and Gerald Monk indicate that every conflict story represents a 'true' story about what happened and a 'false' story in the sense that it minimises other stories that are equally true. Every conflict story then is an arrangement or connection of facts in a pattern that reveals the storyteller's deeper meanings, and communicates to the listener how the storyteller would like them interpreted.

Winslade and Monk show that in addition to negative harmful stories about conflict, there are:

• Positive, acknowledging stories people can tell regarding what their relationship was like before the conflict began
• Things they did to try and resolve it
• Aspects they might have done differently
• Things they still respect about each other

- Ways they tried to reach out and communicate
- Examples of how they tamed their desire to escalate and strike back

A third objective is to see whether the storyteller might be willing to look at what happened from a different perspective. We can do this by asking a series of questions such as:

- Why do you think things unfolded as they did?
- How would you have liked X to have approached you?
- Was there a particular reason why X acted in this way?
- What do you hope will happen as a result of this conversation?
- Has X ever acted in this way before?

We can ask questions that help the parties search for sources of disagreement or invite them to find out what their opponent really experienced, thought or intended.

The hidden story

In every conflict story there can be three separate threads which run throughout. First is the external story which is suitable for public consumption. Beneath this can be an internal story which is designed to protect the ego. Beneath that there is a third core or hidden story which explains why the storyteller found it necessary to invent the other two stories.

In telling the external story, the storyteller focuses on putting the other person in a bad light and articulating what they have done wrong. These stories are often rehearsed in anger and irritation. In internal stories, the focus is on trying to separate oneself from the contribution we may have made to the dispute. In doing so, we seek to justify our actions and hide our guilt, shame and embarrassment. In the third type of story, the storyteller removes their mask and reveals who they really are. These stories are likely to be much more open, honest and authentic. It is this type of story that the mediator will attempt to get to. It is this aspect of the mediator's job that can be the most difficult, yet the most fulfilling. Reaching the heart of a story can become the tipping point in getting parties back on the road to reconciliation. As people who have been engaged in conflict tell their core stories to each other and not just to the mediator, bridges are built which allow empathy and understanding to travel across.

Listening for the hidden story

When conflict stories are told, deep issues, feelings and needs are revealed. All stories speak to us directly through emotion and spirit and bypass our otherwise rational thought process. I remember reading a story about a mediation session centering around a claim for sexual harassment involving a man and a woman who had worked together for several years. At first they were unwilling to speak to each other about what had happened and instead sat frozen in silence. The mediator asked the man to listen with empathy and an open mind, without being distracted by thoughts about how he was going to respond when his turn came.

Instead of describing this man as evil, the woman spoke honestly about her fears and the pain she felt when she went to her car and found his unwanted love notes and requests for dates. She spoke graphically of her aborted efforts to tell him she did not want to see him. She described his silent staring and persistence in following her around the building where they worked, painting a clear picture of his harassing behaviour and her feelings of being hounded by him. She also acknowledged her ineffectiveness in communicating her desire that he stop. Finally, with the mediator's assistance, she turned to the man, told him she was miserable and, in tears, asked him to stop.

At the end of the story, they both cried. The man, for the first time, understood the pain he had caused and was profoundly ashamed of his behaviour. He apologised from his heart, saying he knew he could never make up for what he had done. He said he had fallen in love with her and admitted not noticing her fear or registering her rejection. He thanked her for opening his eyes and promised he would respect her wishes. He said he would never speak to her again unless she spoke first. In response she told him she understood his anguish and accepted his apology, even though his behaviour had been totally inappropriate and unacceptable.

With authenticity and emotional honesty, each party was able to hear what the other felt and, on that basis, resolve the conflict. They were both released from the burden of carrying their stories alone and from the hostile external stories of evil and fear that they had created. They were also able to transcend the internal stories they had told themselves in order to exonerate their own behaviour. The woman, for instance, had told herself that she was justified in not directly asking the man to stop because he was so insensitive that he probably wouldn't have listened. She admitted wanting to keep her feelings of fear and revulsion to herself because in her culture it would have been highly inappropriate for a woman to speak directly to a man. The man, in turn, had told himself that he did not need to acknowledge the woman's subtle signals, because she was behaving so politely towards him. He admitted being unable to hear the word 'no' and placing his need for affection over her need for safety. As they each revealed their hidden stories and mistaken assumptions, they were both able to see the events and actions that these assumptions had precipitated, and were also able to acknowledge the anguish and pain they felt as a result. Through their tears, they told each other that they finally understood each other in a genuine way and could now begin to repair the damaged relationship. The healing process accelerated as they created a new, third story – not of fear and pain, but of learning, listening and improved understanding.

Hearing truth

Oscar Wilde wrote in *'De Profundis'*, "*To speak the truth is a painful thing. To be forced to tell lies is much worse.*" Having mediated hundreds of disputes, I recognise that the role of the mediator is a privileged one. As the mediator builds rapport with the parties, all sorts of information might emerge as parties finally get the chance they have been waiting for; their opportunity to be honest and express what has been happening in their conflict filled lives. The revelation of truth can, to the listener, seem shocking. Three stories come to my mind.

In the first, I was mediating a dispute between an employee and his line manager. As the story of the dispute unfolded, the employee revealed that he was living three hours away from his family home in order to hold down a job. During the week, he lived on his own in a caravan, and once a month he would take a long weekend and take the three hour drive back to his wife, two sons and two daughters. All his children were under ten. Whilst living in the caravan, to help the hours pass when he couldn't sleep, he would send emails at 3.00am to his colleagues raising questions on various matters. These emails were, in most cases, a replacement for what should have been an open and honest face to face discussion. He saw communicating with others when he couldn't sleep as a way of sharing and spreading his own difficulties. His actions led to a whole series of adverse reactions from the recipients of his emails.

In another case, I heard about a situation where a man was working with a female colleague. They got on well, to the point where he thought their relationship strong enough to grant him licence to put his hand up her skirt and into her underwear. When she slapped him across the face objecting to his advances he lodged a grievance against her for slapping him. As part of the grievance he omitted to state what action had prompted the slap from his colleague. It was a year and a half before the matter was openly discussed between them as part of a mediation session. During the session, the female employee told her colleague how he had violated her dignity and made her feel used and dirty. He apologised and said that he had badly misread signals that he thought she had given him.

The third and perhaps most vivid example I recall is when I was mediating an alleged race discrimination dispute. The black female employee who had accused her white female line manager of racism was represented by a white female. The representative was strident in stating the reasons why her client felt as if she had been discriminated against. In mediating hundreds of disputes, I can count on one hand the number of times that one of the parties has walked out of a joint meeting. This was one of them. The representative seemed to have taken on her client's case with the personal drive and determination to see justice done. I had some difficulty in persuading her to stand back and take a more objective view. The case didn't settle on the day but did so a week or so afterwards through dialogue over the phone. Both parties agreed that an ongoing working relationship would not be viable and the employee left the organisation. A month or so after the mediation session I met with the representative on an unrelated matter, and we found ourselves discussing our backgrounds over coffee. I told her about my history and shortly afterwards she reciprocated. Her story was fascinating. She told me that she was Jewish and that most of her family had been killed in the Holocaust, with her mother passing on the story of these terrible events.

She had also read about and studied the Holocaust in great detail and, as a result, had set herself a mission in life – to ensure that any form of discrimination was stamped out. She had signed up to become an employee representative specialising in discrimination cases so that she could fulfil her ambition. This information had failed to surface during the mediation session but I had somehow managed to retain enough rapport with her to prompt this outpouring of her story. I now understood much more about the rationale behind her behaviour during the mediation session the month before. Reading these types of stories might shock the uninitiated, but they can be an everyday occurrence in the life of a mediator.

In a mediation session, not to mention life in general for some, it is difficult to keep a secret. In all of the cases above the parties had kept truth hidden from their colleagues. In the first case, the organisation was not aware of their employee's living arrangements for three years. In the second case, the gentleman in question held back on admitting that his hand had wandered out of bounds. In the third case, very few people knew about the representative's family background and history. When we as listeners react to hearing truth with shock and horror, it suggests to the storyteller that we disapprove of their actions. Our disapproval can mean that the storyteller clams up and refrains from continuing on their path of honesty. The mediator therefore becomes similar to a priest hearing a confession. In the same way that a priest would hear about all kinds of misdemeanours without passing judgment, the mediator also listens neutrally.

Everyone wants their story to communicate not only the hard logical facts but also the soft emotional truths of what they experienced – the heartfelt desires their story was designed to conceal. For these reasons, the best way to listen to conflict stories is to be deeply empathetic without being harsh, judgmental, pitying or sentimental. It is a tough act to walk side-by-side with the storyteller without accepting the literal truth of what they are saying.

Every conflict story falsifies and distorts the events it describes, if only by insinuating emotionally charged information into unbiased depictions of the facts. Yet, if every conflict is false, it is also an effort to communicate a deeper, more powerful truth. In a sense, all conflict stores are false, not merely because they are factually and emotionally distorted, but because they ignore the humanity of the perpetrator. In addition, they minimise responsibility for what the storyteller did and did not do and fail to recognise the possibility of resolution, forgiveness and reconciliation.

At the same time, all conflict stories are true because they contain verifiable facts and because their exaggerations allow a careful listener to intuit the perpetrator's humanity and prior victimisation, whatever the storyteller did or failed to do, and genuine desire for resolution, forgiveness and reconciliation.

While all good storytellers have a strong desire to be emotionally compelling at the expense of factual accuracy, at a deep, heartfelt level, they would rather their stories end in resolution, forgiveness and reconciliation than in enmity, impasse and recrimination. They can be supported in achieving these ends by mediators who do not desert or silence them but pay close attention to the emotional subtexts of their story and attempt to elicit its deeper meanings.

Truth in conflict experiences can be inherently subjective and uncertain. Conflict truths are partly defined by:

- Biased senses
- Distorted sensory perceptions
- Faulty intellectual frameworks
- Untested ideas
- Inadequate memories
- Differing moods
- Contradictory feelings and desires
- False expectations, complex systems and relationships
- Inconsistent attitudes
- A mixture of all the above

Just as there can be more than one truth about anyone there can be more than one truth about conflict. There is, for example, the truth that people want to communicate their pain not by talking about it directly, which might make them feel vulnerable in the presence of someone they do not trust, but by telling a story that hurts their opponent in the same way they feel hurt. If someone insults us, we can either tell them how painful it feels to be insulted or insult them right back, communicating more safely, powerfully, and pleasurably the experience of what it felt like to be insulted by them.

Yet by doing so, conflict stories provoke irrational responses and escalating actions, including defensiveness and rationalisation, aggression and counter-attack, cynicism and distrust, prejudice and stereotyping and escalation and revenge. These responses and effects stimulate counter-stories that cascade until every anecdote becomes a self-fulfilling prophecy, bringing forth behaviours it was intended to prevent.

Chapter 2
Stories of losing control

Proverb: "We should put out a fire while it is still small." – Kalenjin

As we have discussed, the concept of storytelling is one of the most important elements in the entire mediation process. For the mediator it is a method by which he or she can shape and direct the resolution of the conflict, but storytelling is just as important to the individuals involved – if not more so. We should never underestimate the sheer relief that an individual can experience when they feel that they are finally being listened to, especially by someone who can help affect a change. The emotional outpouring that accompanies a verbal one can, as these stories show, be an incredibly moving thing to witness. In some cases the bottling up of emotions makes up a huge percentage of the embitterment the individual feels toward their opponent.

The cathartic effect of finally being able to put one's point across to someone who can actually do something about it, often the mediator but sometimes, in rare cases, a member of the opposing camp, allows a bond of trust to develop between the two parties and often results in a less guarded individual more open to negotiations. Often the details of the story have become blurred over time, with individuals more likely to recast themselves as the embattled victim who did no wrong and similarly cast the other side as evildoers who show no mercy. They defend themselves to the hilt and can put excessive blame on their perceived aggressor, demonising them for their attitudes and actions, occasionally omitting facts that don't work in their favour until raised by the other side, after which admissions of guilt and apologies are usually forthcoming. Detecting and splitting the truth from the fiction is obviously essential before any remedial work can begin, and it is amazing how quickly the erected barricades can fall once a comparatively small admission of partial guilt is aired.

Whilst the content of an individual's story is of course important, it is the opportunity to offload the weight of the issues the individual has carried around with them that affects the most profound change. They have probably told the same story to all their friends and family dozens of times, or at least had to update them and constantly relive it. So by the time it comes to mediation (or any series of events that will lead to a final conclusion) it is not the retelling of the story itself that has the most profound effect but the release that accompanies such an action. Once they have had their say, be it a three hour phone conversation or a half hour invective in a mediation session, and the release of emotion has been achieved, the process of separating truth from embellishments can begin and the individual is usually able to think much clearer about their goals for the mediation session from that point onwards.

Usually the mediator is the listening post, but in one of the following cases the individual had a close friend who still worked in the company with which she had the grievance. The simple act of allowing this company representative to hear and see how their actions (he himself was uninvolved as far as the case was concerned) had affected the individual, rather than just my faceless toing and froing between the two camps, allowed the real impact of the actions to be transmitted effectively and lead to a speedy resolution.

This isn't always possible, but a face to face meeting can really bring home the truth to both sides if handled appropriately. Interestingly, it is not always the story of the affected individual that can carry weight. For example, one of the following stories outlines how the one individual's husband frequently attempted to shift the focus from his wife's unrelenting demands to how the process as a whole was affecting their life together. I'm sure he was originally there to offer moral support, but his constant reminders of the stress that the ongoing battle was having on their marriage was something that his wife had simply not noticed in her fight for equality and justice. Her single-minded attempts at retribution against her company was putting her most important relationship under threat and she had simply not seen it. Sometimes a third party, especially one so closely involved but also relatively detached, can offer some much needed perspective.

An issue that ties in directly to the idea of storytelling, from the point of view of the individual, is that of control of loss – the focus of this first selection of stories. Anyone who becomes embroiled in conflict runs the risk of losing control, both in the sense of allowing their emotions to get the better of them and also surrendering control of their conflict to a third party, such as a lawyer, advisor or family member. The three stories in this section illustrate the dangers of both these facets of control loss, showing clearly the potentially damaging effects that can be borne if bad advice is given, especially to those in vulnerable situations. These stories also demonstrate the points raised above, in that the simple act of listening to someone tell their story can assist in resolving disputes more than almost any other factor.

A loss of control in the most basic sense, i.e. allowing our subconscious feelings and emotions to overrule our conscious thoughts, is most common on the part of the party who feels most aggrieved by the situation that has arisen – typically an individual disputing the actions of a company or colleague. The continual ignorance or dismissal of grievances and concerns usually encourages frustration and anger to fester within the affected individual, which, as these stories attest, is often the first step on a dangerous path; the negative reactions caused by the brick wall constantly being encountered are all retained internally and can lead to anything from minor stress to serious depression, which affects not only the individual but their loved ones too.

It is no surprise then that when the individual finally gets their chance to air the grievances that have caused them so much tumult over the weeks, months or years during which these battles have been fought, they have great difficulty in holding back the tide of emotion that has been steadily growing with each occasion that they have not been listened to; thus what should be a clear and concise statement of their case turns into a barrage of anger, recriminations and tears.

It is our job as mediators to ensure that any such outpourings are kept as private as possible and that we remain professionally detached during these often moving scenes of passion. We are frequently seen as the ear that has been needed for so long. One act of storytelling allows all the frustration and bitterness to be dispelled with, leaving room, hopefully, to focus on the facts and, most importantly, a potential resolution.

If misappropriated or mismanaged, loss of control can be embarrassing and potentially damaging for the individual concerned, leading to potential ridicule from those whom they are desperate to appear strong in front of. On some occasions this can strengthen resolve, but more often than not it has a negative effect on the individual and negotiation from that point onwards is an uphill struggle.

Losing control in the sense of surrendering it to a third party is a decision that individuals shouldn't take lightly. Any involvement of a third party represents a de facto loss of control, as the individual is no longer the sole governor of events. This can be a perfectly harmless notion, but occasionally the third party can take over the agenda and drive it in their own direction without the client always knowing what is happening or being able to stop it. The relationship an individual has with their representative is very much like any other relationship – it relies on trust, honesty and doesn't always end well.

In one of the upcoming stories, a representative who was supposed to be acting for a vulnerable woman put his own interests before that of his client. In ensuring he was going to be properly remunerated for his time and work before fully committing himself to his client's cause. In cases such as these, it is important to gain an insight into the representative's thought process before deciding whether it is worth trying to speak to the client alone without that barrier. A manipulative representative, just like a manipulative partner, may, wittingly or unwittingly, push their client in the wrong direction and it is important to ensure the advice being given on both sides is fair and in the parties' best interests. However, a trusted representative can be a very useful ally as they can be the more rational and decisive face of an over-emotional client. They can offer professional guidance in situations where an untrained individual may feel out of their depth as well as offering hope and optimism to a demoralised client. However, for these to work effectively there must be absolute sincerity and selflessness on the part of the representative, absolute truth on behalf of the client, and honesty and openness throughout the entire process.

It can sometimes be awkward when working with a representative, either an elected representative in a formal mediation/grievance setting or an unelected representative such as a close colleague in a simple workplace dispute, but it is important to detect any ulterior motives, whether intentional or unintentional, early on and alert the individual if necessary.

Removing any wall to pave the way for a private face to face meeting with both parties can be a very good way of allowing the individual to get their point across, but it is important to ensure that the individual has the wherewithal to deal with what could be a very emotional and trying meeting. Losing one's cool in situations like this can lead to the inability to think straight, make groundless accusations and potentially become completely incomprehensible through sheer emotion.

Whose dispute is it?

"Every violation of truth is not only a sort of suicide in the liar, but is a stab at the health of human society." – Ralph Waldo Emerson

Some time ago I was asked to mediate a dispute for a large organisation in the public sector involving one of their professional workers, Sylvia. Sylvia had been with the organisation for some five years when she raised an issue regarding what she considered to be malpractice amongst some of her colleagues. After declining to obtain the backing of her manager the claims were dismissed and she quickly became cut off from her colleagues who accused her of lying. The situation gradually got worse and, feeling increasingly isolated, Sylvia's productivity levels plummeted and she was signed off sick from work for two months.

The employee representative
As the situation degenerated, Sylvia made more enemies. No one trusted her. Eventually she raised a grievance because she felt that her situation had not been acknowledged and dealt with properly. She then raised another grievance relating to her performance review assessment. A third grievance was raised linked to her being questioned about sick leave upon her return to work. Sylvia then received a phone call from a man offering his services as an employee representative. The man, Bob, said he had significant experience in the industry, had legal training (I was later to find out that he had trained as a mediator too) and that he had received a tip off about Sylvia's case. This was a welcome call for Sylvia; at last she had found someone willing to listen to her story and take her side.

Together, Bob and Sylvia decided to take on the organisation. They began to communicate with Human Resources and the in-house legal team, with Bob insisting that all communication was via email, resulting in lengthy and numerous correspondences. Sylvia then took another six months sick leave, indicating the cause to be work related stress. For the organisation, this dispute became their number one employee relations issue and mediation was recommended to Sylvia and Bob and, although they took some time before they agreed to it, a session was arranged about three months later.

During the protracted mediation session, agreement was reached in principle and Heads of Terms were drafted for a compromise agreement, including Sylvia agreeing to leave the organisation. I was not the mediator myself, but I knew the mediator involved had a good reputation. A compromise agreement was scheduled to be drafted soon after, but difficulties soon arose and prolonged the signing of the agreement, by which time the key staff involved in the mediation had moved on. It was now some five months since the mediation had taken place.

It was at this stage that I was called and briefed on what was happening, including the wish by the organisation to commission a fresh mediation session. After some further debate from Sylvia and Bob, this second mediation was agreed. Part of the reason for the procrastination centred around a discussion in the first mediation in relation to fees for legal advice. Bob wanted to ensure that a fee ten times the normal amount for such matters was included as part of any further discussions.

The phone call

Having been given the green light to begin dialogue with both parties, I spoke via telephone with the organisation and with Sylvia and Bob independently. One of the reasons that this case remains so vivid for me is the length of time taken over the initial call to Sylvia and Bob. It is quite normal for pre-mediation discussions to take somewhere in the region of 30 to 60 minutes, and so with this call starting at midday I expected to be finished by 1.00pm at the latest. I didn't put the phone down until 3.45pm. Apart from the odd *"yes", "okay", "I understand"* and a few audible noises to demonstrate that I was still on the line, I said almost nothing. I just listened. I'll come back to this later.

Sylvia talked and talked and barely came up for air. The situation reminded me of a little doll my sister had when she was a girl; the doll could be wound up and when fully coiled would talk and sing until the motor wound down. It was during this marathon telephone conversation that I learned of other baggage that Sylvia was carrying. Firstly her sister had been diagnosed with cancer and had only a few months of her life remaining, with Sylvia and other members of the family providing around the clock care. Secondly, Sylvia was a woman working in a male dominated environment, fulfilling a role usually undertaken by men. She felt that this was constantly held against her and that she had to perform twice as well as the men to achieve the slightest form of recognition.

In a separate phone call with Bob, I discovered that his legal training didn't permit him to sign off the s203 clause in compromise agreements. This is the document in which employees sign away their statutory rights to take any future legal action against their former employer. I was also to discover later that Bob had history with the organisation in question. He had worked there many years before and left following a falling out with hierarchy, but he still had connections in the industry.

Right up until the day of the mediation, Sylvia and Bob remained demanding. I must have had no fewer than ten separate telephone conversations with each of them as they asked questions, sought clarifications and requested assurances about the process we were about to engage in. The day of the mediation was the first time that I had met the two sides' representatives, and things with Bob didn't get off to a good start. He began by suggesting an alternative room layout, requesting tea and coffee to be on tap and which side should go first in the joint session. I had to politely but firmly decline these suggestions, realising at once that my mediator skills were to be really put to the test in this case.

The mediation session
After about an hour of mediation, both sides had agreed on the key issues. There were four or five main points and these were principally based on where the previous mediation session had ended. After about two hours, and during the private sessions, I noticed that Bob had calmed down and was finally beginning to work with me. It was a welcome change. However, Sylvia still wanted to hold on to the past and seemed reluctant to move ahead. It soon became clear that part of any settlement should include a provision for legal fees for advice relating to reaching a conclusion and signing the compromise agreement. It soon became apparent that Bob was concerned about receiving compensation for his time and energy, requiring an upfront assurance that he would be appropriately compensated.

Once this was agreed in principle, his focus and attitude seemed to change for the better. I found it incredible that Bob had held up his client's dispute while he took care of his own arrangements first.

A major stipulation of the organisation was that Sylvia would not return to them, and the question seemed to be more about what they would be willing to put on the table to secure her exit. Sylvia herself was repetitive in outlining how she had been treated over the years by her colleagues and employer, seemingly unable to get past this area. By lunchtime however we were clear about all the key points. There was though a protracted discussion taking place about the overall financial compensation figure.

The mediation at this point was being mainly conducted in private sessions. I shuttled from room to room to explore where there was room for manoeuvre. A flurry of activity took place in the afternoon after Bob indicated that he had to leave just after 4.00pm with Sylvia indicating that she didn't want to stay and complete the mediation without representation. I saw danger. It had taken months to get the parties back round the table again for a second mediation session and I was concerned that if Sylvia left at 4.00pm we would not have an agreement in principle and we would have to start from scratch all over again. I asked her to consider staying on alone and, to my surprise, Bob encouraged her to do so. We spent about half an hour together talking it through before she eventually agreed to stay on.

We broke for lunch and soon after I began my conversation with Sylvia once more, knowing that time was of the essence. We then moved into a joint session but the repetitions of mistreatment soon surfaced again to the point where I had to ask Sylvia for a quick one-to-one chat. The representative from the other side duly left the room and I pulled up a chair in close proximity to Sylvia. I glanced at her for a few seconds before I pointed out that this dispute was about her and if it didn't settle she would have to continue to carry it with her, along with her external issues. I asked her to put any comments made by her representative to one side for the time being and imagine waking up tomorrow morning with the dispute behind her. My eyes didn't leave hers and I spoke clearly and slowly. My objective was to engage with her at a deeper level.

Sylvia spoke about the commencement of the trouble, about how she thought she was doing the organisation a favour when she tried to warn them of wrongdoing and malpractice. She spoke of the hurt she felt when her concerns were not taken seriously and how she was the one made to feel that she was defrauding the organisation. She spoke about how, as a woman, she had been made to feel inferior to her male colleagues and as a result she hated men and would never work in a male dominated environment again if she had the choice. She then asked what I thought about the way she had been treated. Was it fair? What would I have done? Was she being taken seriously? Had I experienced a similar case before? The questions kept coming, and to each one the same response – silence. I could give no answer without compromising my neutrality.

It was clear that Sylvia was still hurting, but I could sense that I had got her attention. I left the room for ten minutes while I went to see the other side, asking her to reflect on what we had just discussed. The HR spokesperson for the organisation said that they had now reached the limit that they had come to the mediation with. I asked if there would be any difficulty with this. I didn't get a response.

A discussion then ensued which excluded me. Realising that the organisation had some thinking to do, I left them to get on with it. I returned to my own room, away from both parties, and waited.

Some 20 minutes later the organisation's legal representative came through to my room and asked if I could rejoin her colleagues. I agreed, but asked if she would give me a few moments to quickly update Sylvia on the situation. I did this and then met with the organisation's representatives. When I arrived at their room I was told, in confidence, that the matter with Sylvia had to be settled whatever it took, but that the settlement had to be sensible. Eventually we achieved breakthrough with the compensation amount, and what remained was to work through the detail of the agreement of this and other non-financial matters. I had to call Bob again to offer some advice to Sylvia on areas she appeared to be struggling with. It was as if I was dealing with a new representative. He was both positive and helpful.

It was 9.00pm by the time the summary settlement agreement was acceptable to both parties, the delay down in part to Sylvia continuing to pontificate over the detail. After 11½ hours of mediation the organisation finally signed. I took the document to Sylvia. She deliberated again and asked more questions. Finally, at 9.15pm, she signed the document. I was unprepared for what happened next. As soon as Sylvia signed, she put the pen down, looked at me and then burst into tears. She sobbed uncontrollably. It was as if the symbolic ritual of signing the document represented bringing to an end years of trouble, conflict, anguish and hurt, that it offered the closure that Sylvia had longed for but hadn't been able to articulate. Up until that point she had remained relatively composed for the whole day, which made it even more of a shock. Thinking that we had now finished, one of the parties from the other side walked in during Sylvia's outpouring. She saw what was happening and walked straight back out again.

After about 15 minutes, as Sylvia was drying her tears and we were preparing to leave, she thanked me for listening to her on the phone the other day. I was briefly stumped, then recalled our marathon pre-mediation phone call. I hadn't realised the high value that Sylvia had placed on having someone to tell her story to. After all, I had just listened. The security staff at the venue were now beginning to indicate that we had outstayed our welcome, and as we left I couldn't help reflecting about the issue relating to Bob and his fees. It seemed to me that Sylvia's troubles were multiplied by Bob ensuring that he would be taken care of first and foremost. In mediating hundreds of disputes, I have never encountered a situation as overt as this. On the whole, representatives play a very useful and constructive role in helping the people they represent to use the mediation process to achieve a satisfactory settlement without interference. I'm not sure whether Sylvia would invite Bob to represent her again however.

Observations

Early in my mediation career, I recall adopting a rather lukewarm attitude towards employee representatives. My impression was that their presence would only serve to hold up the mediation process and limit the chances of reaching settlement. With the benefit of experience however my stance has changed to become far less dubious and much more welcoming. The story in this case study is in fact in the minority and quite unusual. On balance, employee representatives play a valuable role in the mediation process. Representatives help parties:

- Think through options for solutions
- Consider a position in the event that their dispute goes to law
- Define acceptable settlement terms
- Feel less isolated
- Maintain a sense of objectivity
- Offer perspective on a position they may be holding
- Engage in dialogue about legal matters with the other side
- Maintain a sense of optimism

Given the choice now, in employment mediation (rather than workplace) I always recommend that employees attend mediation with a representative, particularly if the employer is represented. This is more likely to give a sense of balance and help the parties move towards resolution more swiftly. In the case of Sylvia, her choice of representative meant that she found someone who would take her side and share the burden. The choice also meant that Sylvia's battle became initially dwarfed by Bob's pursuit to secure remuneration for his time. Bob's transformation and willingness to co-operate only came to life once he was sure that he had secured a sufficient fee for his services. Only then did Sylvia's dispute become the focal point.

Disputes normally start off between two people, but as the dispute continues more people become involved as the parties share their story. Tens, hundreds or even thousands of people might then have something to say about the issue. Irrespective of the final number of people who eventually became embroiled, the immediate effects of the dispute remain with the two original disputants. I acknowledge that there can be occasions however when new disputes start as others get the chance to express comments about something or someone as part of the proceedings. There are also occurrences of team or departmental disputes and, to go one stage further, collective disputes. The core issue is that disputes that start off as our own will remain our own until their conclusion.

One of my objectives during Sylvia's mediation session was to try and shift the focus from Bob and his interests back to those of Sylvia and the organisations.

Although in my mind I questioned Bob's motives, I knew that his knowledge, history and personality would give him influence. Once we had reached an agreement in principle to Bob's demands our attention could turn to the person he was representing. Both the organisation and Sylvia were after the same thing – settlement and closure.

The first mediation session had gone some way to unlocking the issues but the parties, particularly Sylvia, needed more time to reach the latter. The mediation required a combination of patience and resilience; patience to allow Sylvia and the organisation to reach a settlement that was acceptable to them and resilience to withstand Bob and how he fulfilled his role at the start of the day. Sylvia's final outburst was a sign that the process had finally succeeded in granting a release from the emotional block that had developed over the period over which the dispute had been running.

Mediation is a process that can help parties reach both settlement and closure, but it is important to stress the differences between them. An Employment Tribunal can help parties to achieve settlement where one will win and one will lose. Mediation addresses the flaw in the litigation process by allowing the expression of fears, anxieties and past hurts as part of the negotiation. It is the ability to be able to talk about what some refer to as 'soft issues' that helps parties to reach the closure stage. Personally I see these aspects much more in a 'hard' rather than a 'soft' sense. Soft implies, fluffy and of little or no value. I am sure the organisation and Sylvia would disagree with this notion. Mediation allowed both parties to move on and focus on the future and not waste any more time dealing with the issues that separated them. It is difficult to think about how this was soft in anyway.

Stabbed in the back

"The price of anything is the amount of life you pay for it." – Henry David Thoreau

Olivia Taylor had worked as the Head of Communications in the children and families department of a local authority for 15 years. She was highly regarded but had resigned from her role some ten months previously claiming constructive dismissal and unlawful discrimination based on her sex and disability. The case was due to go to an Employment Tribunal in one month's time. At the time of her resignation she was a senior manager leading a team of 32 staff. Her role involved working on all aspects of internal and external communication including the media, publicity and marketing activities, event management, internal and external website and corporate messages.

The department had recently gone through a very difficult time following the death of a child who was in care with a family which came under their jurisdiction. The untimely death had then become a matter of public interest as there was speculation that the child had been mistreated. Olivia handled all the public relations activity associated with the unfortunate death. The role was demanding and often involved working long hours and weekends without additional remuneration. In accordance with medical advice Olivia spent her last year of employment on sick leave, citing stress, anxiety and reactive depression. She was prescribed anti-depressants and other medicines to help her cope with her panic attacks. The condition caused Olivia to suffer sleeplessness, specified agoraphobia, loss of confidence, and a severe drop in self esteem. Olivia claimed that her medical condition was caused by the treatment she received from her line manager.

Olivia's story
One morning, Olivia had had a discussion with her line manager, Simon Cooke. She was concerned that she had received a letter giving notice that her job title and the name of her department had been changed without any consultation. Added to that, she also felt that the new title and department name did not accurately reflect their respective roles. This was, according to Olivia, both demoralising for her and the members of her team and also confusing for internal and external stakeholders. In addition, she raised the point that her salary and grading was the lowest in her peer group of senior managers, the majority of

whom were men. Over the next year Olivia continued to raise the issue with her line manager both in meetings and by email. She received no response and so lodged a formal grievance.

The external consultant

During a series of department related meetings, Simon quizzed Olivia about the proposed content of key messages that were to be communicated in forthcoming publications. He asked her to think about further opportunities for developing internal and external messages, and it was Olivia's belief after the meetings that she would work up some ideas for new content and review them with her boss over time.

A few weeks later, without warning or consultation, Simon informed her that he had met with a recruitment agency with a view to engaging a consultant to consider a corporate communications strategy for the department. He advised Olivia that any further work on key corporate messages should be put on hold until the advice of the consultant was sought. Olivia was surprised and concerned at Simon's actions because the provision of such advice had always been a fundamental part of her role. Despite her concerns, Olivia expressed her wish to co-operate with the process if it was in the best interests of the department. Olivia subsequently met with Simon and the recruitment agency, postponing her holiday to ensure that she could attend the meeting. During their discussion, Olivia raised concerns with Simon saying that the proper tendering process was not being followed. Subsequent to Olivia raising this concern, the HR department sought tenders from two other headhunting companies.

As part of her role, Olivia also advised on many policies and projects, in particular where the organisation's corporate image, communications or reputation was involved. On one occasion the organisation was undertaking a number of key projects under the management of an over-arching strategic project management team, of which Olivia was a member. The project was named Cyrus. The main aim of Olivia's role was to ensure uniform and professional internal and external communications of projects, together with any new or revised policies that emerged from them. At a Project Cyrus meeting, Olivia was tasked with drawing up a communication and corporate identity strategy. Simon maintained an overview of work that was going on under the Cyrus banner and was informed that Olivia had been tasked with this piece of work.

The task of drawing up the Cyrus strategy required considerable discussion and research with individual project team leaders. In light of the importance of the Cyrus strategy to the organisation, Olivia conscientiously gave an entire weekend over to preparing a presentation to be delivered at a meeting of the project board early on a Monday morning. Copies of the strategy were circulated to the group of senior colleagues and the presentation was very well received. At the meeting, Olivia was asked whether she had heard anything more about the appointment of an external consultant. When Olivia confirmed that she had not, the general consensus was that Simon had changed his mind about making the appointment.

Immediately following the meeting, Olivia attended the senior manager's forum, chaired by Simon's line manager, Christine Smith, herself the Managing Director of the local authority. Christine introduced Olivia to Annette Golding, advising her that Annette had started work under a consultancy contract that day and had been brought in to draw up a communications strategy for the project. This seemed strange to Olivia, as it was the very same piece of work that she had just completed. Olivia had not been informed of, or even consulted about, Annette's appointment and was absolutely devastated to have been treated in this manner. She felt completely humiliated and, as some of her colleagues came over to express their own surprise at what had happened, she was finally reduced to tears. No one had spoken to Olivia about the issue, despite previous assurances that Olivia would be fully involved in the selection and appointment of any external consultant, as well as having the key role in directing the communications project.

Subsequent to Annette's appointment, the organisation stripped Olivia of her responsibilities in relation to the communications strategy and gave them to Annette. Annette was also instructed to conduct a review of Olivia's department, which, Olivia believed, was in fact an investigation of her. A few weeks later, Olivia took a telephone call from a colleague seconded to her department who had just returned from a meeting with Annette. The colleague warned Olivia that, in her view, Annette was seeking evidence on which to remove Olivia from her post. Olivia's feelings of being undermined, isolated and arbitrarily subjected to an investigation were further exacerbated by the organisation's repeated refusal to clarify the terms of reference for Annette's appointment. There was confusion as to Annette's exact role and reporting lines and it was some considerable time before any form of formal contract brief was put in place.

Relationship with Christine Smith
Olivia felt that Christine's appointment of Annette had undermined her and was therefore in no doubt that Christine was the one driving the agenda. Olivia found this particularly odd because she had always enjoyed good relationships with senior management, to the point where other senior managers sometimes turned to her for her guidance in dealing with extremely difficult and sensitive media and communications issues. Christine had by now also limited Olivia's input and

attendance at the weekly executive meetings, effectively removing her strategic input in that arena.

Olivia was mystified by Christine's approach and attitude towards her. To her knowledge there had never been any performance issues with her work. Consequently, Olivia felt that she had become subject to victimisation by reason of her asking about the way in which Annette had been brought in through the back door. Most of Olivia's colleagues felt unable to support her publicly for fear of the effect it would have on their careers. Olivia said the appointment made her feel like she had been stabbed in the back.

Grievance

As she had never received any response to her informal approaches, Olivia sent a letter to the HR Director, Lucy Trindell, documenting her various grievances. She didn't receive a reply. Three months later, still having received no reply, she wrote to Simon formally invoking the organisation's grievance procedure. Olivia asked Simon to address her concerns which in summary were:

1. The appointment of Annette and the manner in which it was handled
2. Annette's review/investigation of Olivia's department and the effect it had on Olivia
3. Olivia's salary, grading and job title and the organisation's failure to address these issues
4. The Managing Director's treatment of Olivia and the effect that it had on her position within the organisation

Olivia and Simon held a grievance meeting a few weeks later. As Olivia began to explain the details of the grievance, Simon started to challenge her, questioning why she believed she had the right to have a view on the Managing Director's activities and decisions, or to have been consulted on the appointment of Annette. Olivia was surprised as Simon became argumentative, belligerent and confrontational, to the extent that Olivia voiced her concerns about the appropriateness of his behaviour. Olivia questioned whether Simon was in a position to resolve the grievance, considering it so closely involved the Managing Director.

Olivia received no formal response to the grievance hearing. A few weeks later she was scheduled to meet with Simon and a few colleagues to discuss issues relating to the project. In the course of the first meeting it became apparent that Annette had presented an initial strategy report to the Managing Director and that a decision had been made to pass the report on to others to review and progress. Olivia was extremely surprised that this task had not been given to her and asked why the work had been given to someone else. Simon responded by saying that Olivia had *"neither the experience nor the skills to take that plan and turn it into a programme of work that would deliver what the authority needed"*. Simon's response left Olivia feeling completely humiliated, particularly since it was made in front of the other attendees, one of whom was a junior member of her own team. This decision to give the work to an employee from another department was taken while Olivia was still performing her duties.

Olivia eventually received a written response to her grievance which acknowledged that Annette's appointment was handled badly, but did not fully or adequately address Olivia's grievances. Two days prior to writing a further appeal letter about her grievance, Olivia was signed off sick by her GP due to work-related stress and depression. At this stage she was finding matters increasingly difficult to deal with and so decided to put all correspondence in the hands of solicitors. The organisation's continual failure to respond fully to Olivia was beginning to adversely affect her health. Subsequently, the organisation wrote to Olivia suggesting mediation to try and resolve matters. Olivia considered that she had no option but to resign.

Medical condition
Olivia sought treatment with her GP and was regularly prescribed with anti-depressant medication. In the doctor's reports he gave his opinion that the trigger for Olivia's illness was work-related and gave a guarded prognosis for recovery. He expressed considerable concern with regard to her condition, saying she was very fragile and anxious, that she was experiencing nightmares and panic attacks and was unable to go out of her house alone. Olivia was later referred by her GP to a community mental health team.

Olivia availed herself of the organisation's welfare service. The Welfare Officer visited Olivia at home on a number of occasions to offer support and advice on coping strategies for the physical, mental and emotional difficulties she was facing. The organisation's Welfare Officer later reported that Olivia was suffering from a reactive state, loss of confidence and self esteem, panic attacks, faintness and agoraphobia. It was his opinion that Olivia's medical condition would not improve until her grievance was dealt with.

Unfair dismissal
Olivia's solicitors were extremely concerned about her worsening health and repeated attempts were made to bring matters to a conclusion, but to no avail. The solicitors wrote a final letter to the organisation seeking a resolution to the situation. The authority was given a deadline of five days by which to respond. When the authority failed to reply or even acknowledge the letter, Olivia resigned with immediate effect. Olivia said that the matters detailed in her grievance, as

well as the organisation's failure to properly hear her grievance over a period of more than 11 months, amounted to a repudiatory breach of her Contract of Employment, entitling her to accept the breach, resign and claim unfair and constructive dismissal pursuant to the Employment Rights Act. Furthermore, Olivia contended that the treatment she received was connected to the protected disclosure she made in respect of failure to follow the recruitment policy and, as such, her dismissal was automatically unfair.

Sex discrimination and equal pay
Olivia's job was classed as senior manager (SM) level within the organisation. In the peer group there were ten members of staff at the same level (eight males and two females). Olivia believed that the two females (of whom she was one) received the lower salaries of the group, with Olivia herself receiving the lowest salary of all. In common with the other senior managers Olivia was a head of department. Olivia was concerned that she only learned about the salary review once it had been completed. Having had no discussions with anyone about her actual role and day-to-day responsibilities, which equated in terms of authorisation, decision-making, strategic responsibility, planning, resource and budget responsibilities with those of her male peers, she assumed that the salary review was based on job descriptions alone.

Disability discrimination
Olivia's solicitors contended that she suffered from a disability within the meaning of the Disability Discrimination Act in that she had been diagnosed as having a mental impairment lasting for 12 months. The effects of this condition had a substantial impact on her ability to carry out normal day-to-day activities.

Summary
In summary, Olivia would be claiming for:

- Automatic unfair dismissal
- Notice pay and any accrued but untaken holiday pay due
- Equal pay for like work, or in the alternative for work of equal value and/or arrears of remuneration as appropriate
- Less favourable treatment for a reason that relates to her disability (such claim to include an award in respect of injury to feeling, personal injury and aggravated damages)
- Failure to make reasonable adjustments with regard to her disability

About ten months after leaving the organisation, Olivia received notification that a three day tribunal hearing had been scheduled to begin in six weeks time.

Mediation

A few days after receiving the notification from the Employment Tribunal, Olivia received a letter from the organisation indicating that it would be willing to attempt mediation prior to the tribunal taking place. She contacted her solicitors, who advised her that at this stage, mediation would be a good idea. The mediation session was arranged.

On the day of the mediation Olivia arrived with her solicitor, her assistant and her husband, also an employee of the local authority. The local authority was also represented by a solicitor and two senior managers, one of whom was Harry Scholes, the Deputy Managing Director. Olivia and Harry got on very well together and had had previous contact both in and out of work. Olivia knew that Harry was aware of what had been happening with her situation but also that he had no involvement in the matter.

During the joint opening to the mediation session, both sides indicated their willingness to achieve settlement. At this stage the dialogue was solicitor to solicitor. Following the joint opening session I went to spend some time with Olivia, her husband and her representatives. I asked Olivia's solicitor what she thought about the opening session and she responded by saying that the organisation seemed not to be accepting any blame. She did say however that it was positive that they were interested in achieving settlement. I asked Olivia how she was feeling about the process and what her thoughts were. She looked at me and then burst out crying.

The impact of the ongoing difficulties with her former employer was clearly continuing to take their toll on Olivia. She reached for her bag and pulled out a picture of her and her husband, a picture she said had been taken five years ago. She asked me to look at the picture and identify anything that looked different. Straight away I could see that she was but a shadow of her former self; her previous long blond hair had been reduced to thinning, much shorter locks and she had lost weight. The picture I was looking at showed a radiant, healthy, smiling woman, whereas the woman I was engaged in the mediation session with was thin, sad and cheerless. The strain of the dispute had taken an evident physical toll. Her picture gave me the impression that she once used to turn heads. Now my thought was that if heads did turn it would be for very different reasons. It would have been unkind and crushing for Olivia if I had articulated these thoughts, so I merely mentioned that I could see the damage that had been caused by her turmoil. Her husband replied by saying, *"That's an understatement."*

When Olivia had composed herself she began retelling the story as it happened. She talked for nearly an hour, her comments continually interrupted by her tears. At the end I asked if she was ready to think about the settlement she would like to achieve through this mediation. She was unsure, but wanted her former colleagues to know about the effect the situation had had on her. I acknowledged what she had said and asked her, if she were able, to start thinking about what she would need in order to achieve settlement and move on.

My preliminary talk with Olivia over, I went to see the representatives of the local authority. I asked what they thought about the opening session and what their thoughts were on achieving settlement. Harry had noticed the obvious effect of the dispute on Olivia, commenting that he hardly recognised her. He went on to say that the organisation knew that they had done some things incorrectly but they didn't have a bottomless pot of funds to throw in Olivia's direction. Harry said that financial settlement was possible but that he had strict guidelines on what he could and could not deliver. A prerequisite for any settlement was that the organisation would not make any contribution towards Olivia's legal costs.

This Henry Kissinger style shuttle diplomacy carried on for the next few hours as I shuffled from room to room. We seemed to be making good progress, or so I thought. Just before lunchtime I was speaking with Olivia about the terms on which she would be willing to settle, but it was as if I had hit a brick wall. Olivia still wanted to talk about the events that led up to the mediation. I realised that continuing to press Olivia for settlement terms would be futile, but it struck me that, after a morning of separate rooms, Olivia might benefit from talking directly to Harry about the way she felt. I also felt that it would be beneficial if this could be done without legal representation. I told Olivia what I was thinking and I asked if she would be willing to talk to Harry alone.

She agreed on the condition that her husband could accompany her. I went to see Harry and explained my suggestion and Olivia's condition. The organisation's solicitors were nervous about the suggestion, but agreed.

The meeting
What happened during the meeting was remarkable. Olivia started the conversation and explained to Harry how she felt the organisation had treated her and the impact it had had on her. The tears began to flow again as she recounted experiences that had lasted a few years. It was difficult for anyone in the room not be moved by her account. Harry in particular, who was hearing much of the story for the first time, was visibly moved. He was clearly shocked, surprised and astonished at some of the things he was hearing. But he listened, without interrupting, asked questions for clarification and then, critically, apologised for the way his former colleague had been treated. His apology and the body language that accompanied it were congruent. Upon hearing this,

Olivia shed more tears. She articulated how she felt that the organisation had let her down, expressing discontent at how the organisation had worked hard on defining and publishing certain values that were clearly not practised by the senior figures who signed them off. How could they, given the despicable way in which they had treated her? This ambiguity was something that Olivia struggled with and eventually led to psychological contact with the authority being broken. Finally however, the chance for Olivia to express herself and be listened to had finally arrived.

Her story finished, Olivia asked Harry what he thought about the series of events. Harry didn't know what to say. The meeting ended soon afterwards and the parties went back to their separate rooms where they could summarise what had happened to their solicitors. A critical hurdle to the mediation moving forward had been Olivia being afforded the opportunity to express her emotions and feel listened to, an opportunity she had finally been afforded.

As soon as Olivia gave me a sign that she had breached this barrier and was ready to start looking to the future, I seized the moment by asking questions that would help her get what she wanted. These included questions such as:

- What did you have in mind to put this behind you today?
- What amount of compensation would help you start to move on?
- If money alone won't address the issue, could you outline what a settlement package might look like for you?

The mediation moved quickly on from this point and terms for settlement were reached and drawn up by 5.00pm. After a 9.00am start it took until 8.00pm to draft and agree all of the settlement documentation, some financial and some not. Once the documentation was signed I went to each of the parties' rooms to say goodbye. Olivia was noticeably happier. She had reached the finish line. Something in her manner and the situation prompted me to do something rather unusual; I asked if she would like to say goodbye to Harry. She considered the idea, looked at her husband and then agreed. I extended the same invitation to Harry, who also accepted. As Olivia entered the room her eyes connected with Harry and, once again, she broke down and cried. This time Harry came over to comfort her and they hugged. The crying quickly turned to laughter and they exchanged warm words. At this point I left the room. We had been able to reach settlement, forgiveness and reconciliation from a marathon session that had left me exhausted.

Observations

Sybil Phoenix says, *"If one is honest one has to admit that there can be no reconciliation without forgiveness."* To achieve that twin aim in this case it was vital that Olivia was given the chance to express her emotions and feel that she had been heard, with Harry also emerging as a critical cog in the settlement machinery. In tandem with this there are two other aspects of this story that I would like to highlight – dealing with emotion and the mediation timeline.

Dealing with emotion

Parties are likely to come to mediation with carrier bags stuffed with emotions. Some of the emotions that these metaphorical bags will contain are anger, fear, shame, jealousy and embarrassment. Quite often, parties coming to the mediation table will not have seen their opponent for some time. If they have seen them, they probably haven't spoken to them. Now they come face to face with the person causing them to carry this baggage. The challenge for the mediator is to create the right environment and give enough space to each of the parties to express how they feel. The ways in which different people deal with conflict should not be underestimated. To some, the emotional burden of the affair is not very strong and they can move on to other issues after a quick recapping of their story. Others though may have been affected on a deeper level and may need longer for expression. The mediator needs to use patience, etiquette and endurance to keep working with each party until they (the parties) feel as if they are ready to move on.

In my book *'The Definitive Guide to Workplace Mediation and Managing Conflict at Work'*, I outline that in the mediation process the mediator attempts to help the parties work through a mediation timeline which encompasses three main stages:

1. The past history – At this initial stage the mediator explores areas such as *'What has happened? How did you arrive at this point? How did it make you feel?'* It is during this stage that emotional feelings are likely to emerge. Parties who feel that they have not had sufficient opportunity to talk about the past are likely to find it difficult to move to the next stages.

2. The present situation – During this stage the mediator will move on to discuss current feelings and get a sense of what might be required to address emotional needs before looking at the future.

3. The future possibilities – At this final stage the challenge for the mediator is to explore what needs to happen in order for the parties to move on and to prevent similar issues from surfacing again. In particular, in cases where there will be an ongoing working relationship, what behaviour does the opponent need to be wary of that might infringe the feelings of their colleague once more? Part of the role of the mediator is to help paint a picture of a new beginning in the minds of the parties. In some cases, the mediator may need to adopt a firm approach to help parties move to stage three.

The mediation timeline

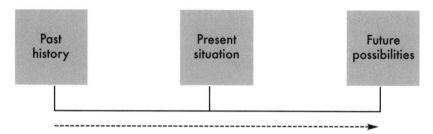

The other aspect to highlight in this case is that whilst the mediation process can work at a surface level to reach settlement, it can also work at a much deeper level and help parties reach closure with a dispute that they have paid for with so much of their lives. In this sense, mediation can work at both a transactional and transformational level. In the case of this story the mediation may also have arrived at a satisfactory conclusion with the joint session between Henry and Olivia shortly before lunchtime. There was no requirement to invite Olivia and Harry to say goodbye to each other as settlement had already been achieved. Mediation was partially used as a hard negotiation tool to reach financial settlement, whereas its chief function was at a humane, compassionate and benevolent level to help Olivia move on with her life. Every mediator has a different style and conviction about how the process should work and not all mediators would sign up to using mediation in this way. Having mediated hundreds of disputes, I can count on one hand the number of times that a mediation session has ended in this profound way. It was very unusual. Although Olivia's dispute was not technically with Harry, he represented the organisation that she felt had treated her inequitably.

Asking the parties to say goodbye like this was not planned but was instinctive. In that sense, it is a tribute to the mediation process that there is room for flexibility, uniqueness, innovation and imagination to be applied in this way.

A question of advice

"Give me a fruitful error any time, full of seeds, bursting with its own corrections. You can keep your sterile truth for yourself." – Vilfredo Pareto

Solicitors, Turner Norman acted for Ms Rose Sweeting in a claim she made against her employer, Swimming Pool Services Ltd ("SPSL"). Rose brought proceedings in the Employment Tribunal against SPSL for unfair dismissal, wrongful dismissal and unlawful deduction from wages (failure to pay holiday pay and sick pay). In a judgment sent to the parties, the claims for unfair dismissal, wrongful dismissal and holiday pay were dismissed, the claim for sick pay was allowed and SPSL were partially successful on the counterclaim and were awarded £18,159. Ms Sweeting appealed to the Employment Appeal Tribunal ("the EAT") and SPSL cross-appealed. Both appeal and cross-appeal were later dismissed by the EAT.

Ms Sweeting duly served a detailed mediation position statement in which she set out her criticisms of Turner Norman. Turner Norman accepted that they owed Ms Sweeting a duty to exercise reasonable skill and care, but also stated that Ms Sweeting would only be entitled to damages if they had been found to have breached that duty. A mediation session was arranged between the parties. Ms Sweeting attended with her husband and legal representation whilst Turner Norman also brought Counsel as well as their insurers.

Mediation
Turner Norman were confident of the merit of their position, but at the same time they recognised that Ms Sweeting was not satisfied with the service they had provided to her. Turner Norman therefore approached mediation with an open mind and were hopeful that through the mediation process the dispute could be resolved without the need for, or the expense of, court proceedings.

Meeting with Rose Sweeting
Rose Sweeting had been employed as Managing Director of SPSL for five years before she had been suspended from her position. She first consulted Turner Norman about the suspension and they advised her continuously from then onwards in all legal matters relating to her employment including the disciplinary hearing, her subsequent dismissal, the appeals process, her application to an

Employment Tribunal, the tribunal hearing and the Employment Appeals Tribunal. As has already been noted, Rose was unsuccessful in her application to the Employment Tribunal and her appeal to the EAT was rejected.

Turner Norman had invoiced Rose the sum of nearly £60,000 in legal fees. During the early stages of the case, and prior to the Employment Tribunal, SPSL made a *"without prejudice"* offer to Rose under a compromise agreement of £32,000.

This was rejected on the advice of Turner Norman. Once Rose had made an application to the Employment Tribunal, SPSL issued a counterclaim. The tribunal found in favour of SPSL's claim and their decision was upheld at the Appeals Tribunal. Rose was ordered to pay damages to SPSL amounting to £28,000.

The total financial costs to Rose Sweeting and the losses suffered by her were:

- Loss of settlement   £32,000
- Cost of legal fees   £60,000
- Cost of counterclaim   £28,000
- Loss of earnings and damages to
  career in period   £27,000
  Total loss suffered by Rose Sweeting   £147,000

In initial dialogue with Rose during the mediation session it transpired that at the time her case was heard at the Employment Tribunal, the maximum level of compensation available was around £59,000. The cost to Rose in legal fees incurred in pursuing her case against Turner Norman exceeded the maximum possible level of settlement. These losses were also compounded by the counterclaim awarded against her. However, Rose had swiftly recognised her duty to mitigate the loss suffered due to her lack of employment and had commenced work on a consultancy basis immediately following her dismissal.

Rose asserted that Turner Norman failed to exercise their duty of care to her and that, as a result of this failure, she suffered punitive financial losses, material and irrevocable damage to her reputation and career prospects, and significant detriment to her health. Turner Norman had initially been retained by Rose to advise her in their capacity as specialist employment and personal injury lawyers. As such they had a duty of care to assess the issues of her case and to advise her as their client so as to safeguard her position, maximise her chances of success and preclude or minimise any potential losses. Her new legal advisors contended that the repeated and cumulative failings on the part of Turner Norman throughout their handling of this case constituted irrefutable evidence that they fell significantly below the standards expected of a reasonably competent law firm. Rose and her new legal advisors pulled out a summary of key failings from the six weighty lever arch files that they had brought to the mediation session. They were outlined as follows:

Summary of key failings on the part of Turner Norman:

Rose's new legal team contended that Turner Norman were in a position from the outset to assess the strengths of their client's case, to advise on the likely prospects of success in bringing a claim and to estimate the realistic levels of any settlement which could be made, should her claim succeed. Multiple failures of advice during the initial period following the suspension of Rose Sweeting included the following.

Failure to conduct early assessment of the case:

Given the information available from the very early stages of this case, the allegation was that Turner Norman were in a position to assess the likely value of any claim and to advise their client accordingly. Furthermore, once the letter confirming the dismissal of Rose was received by Turner Norman, it should have been absolutely clear that their client faced an uphill struggle with any claim (on the grounds of both unfair and wrongful dismissal) and that, even if the claim were to succeed, the maximum compensatory settlement Rose could achieve was likely to be around £40,000 (approximately six months' salary). Rose's new lawyers stated that this assessment and analysis of the case should have been paramount in informing and determining Turner Norman's advice and strategy from this point onwards.

Failure to advise Rose Sweeting to resign from her position as Managing Director:

The SPSL disciplinary hearing for Rose was held and the decision to dismiss her from employment was communicated in a letter a few days after this meeting. In the weeks following her dismissal, Rose pursued the opportunity of work on a consultancy basis with some locally based contractors, including direct competitors of SPSL. Turner Norman were aware of this throughout and specifically aware that Rose was to attend a meeting for the contractors at which SPSL were also due to be present. Despite this, Turner Norman failed to advise Rose that she should resign as a Director. As a result of the failure, SPSL's lawyers subsequently claimed that, in working with a competitor whilst still a Director of SPSL, Rose was in breach of her fiduciary duties as a Director. This was a major factor in the failure of the *"without prejudice"* severance negotiations which were well advanced and nearing agreement at this time. Arguably it also weakened Rose Sweeting's position and damaged her standing at the subsequent Employment Tribunal.

Incorrect and inaccurate advice on the prospects of success:

During the early stages of the case Turner Norman advised Rose that she had a 70%-80% chance of success with her claim to tribunal. Later on, this estimate was reduced to no more than 60%. At the final stages, Turner Norman advised Rose that her prospects were not good, and the figure was adjusted to 50%. Rose's new legal advisors would further assert that Turner Norman's failure to accurately assess the merits of the case and its chances of success led to Rose failing to agree the settlement offer of £32,000 that had been tabled and to her consequent cumulative legal costs and tribunal losses.

It was at this point that I noticed the actions of Rose's husband. He seemed disengaged and a little preoccupied with his BlackBerry. It was not convenient to say anything to him at the time but I lodged the behaviour I was seeing from him in the hope of hearing his thoughts about the dispute as the day unfolded.

Failure to define a clear strategy and to conclude a severance deal under a compromise agreement:

Turner Norman were aware both of the allegations against Rose and of the fact that she had begun work on a consultancy basis for a competitor. Rose's legal team argued that Turner Norman were also aware that once it was known to SPSL that she had taken up this consultancy position, the scope for a severance deal under a compromise agreement would disappear. Rose said that at this point, given the very limited prospects of success, and with a maximum compensation deal at stake, Turner Norman's strategy should have been to agree a negotiated severance deal under a compromise agreement if at all possible.

During a six week period, compromise agreement negotiations took place and SPSL made an initial offer and two subsequent offers. Turner Norman did not respond to these offers at first, and then advised Rose to hold out for more money. Despite the scope for a deal to be negotiated and the pressure for this to be secured ahead of the meeting where SPSL and the consultancy would both be present, negotiations broke down. The immediate loss to Rose of this failure on the part of Turner Norman was at least £24,000. This initial loss was subsequently compounded by the legal fees and counterclaim costs. Once SPSL became aware of Rose's consultancy work all offers of settlement were rescinded.

I thanked Rose and her legal advisors for outlining their position with such clarity and asked their view on what level of settlement they would be willing to accept during the mediation. One of Rose's legal advisors said that they would be looking for at least £65,000 plus a contribution towards costs. I asked them to also consider what their bottom line position might be in the event that they were unable to secure what they had just expressed to me.

As I left the room, Rose's husband followed me in order to use the bathroom. I asked him how he felt the day was going, to which his response was that he just wanted to put the whole thing behind them. He said that he had advised his wife not to pursue any legal action against her former employer, and then revealed that it was putting their relationship under great strain. He relayed his desire for this to be the last day that they would have to devote time, energy and money to discussing the case. He seemed resentful, embittered and angry that this issue had taken up so much of his time. He also added that the costs associated with pursuing the claim were beginning to outweigh common sense and that he could not sustain funding the action for much longer (they had recently sold one of their buy-to-let properties to allow them to continue funding the claim). The whole episode was now at the stage where their pillow talk circled around one thing – the claim and legal action. He remarked how this had made him feel hostile towards the whole thing but that he would do his best to support his wife in whatever way he could.

Meeting with Turner Norman
After explaining to Turner Norman that Rose wanted to do everything possible in order to reach a settlement, Linda Cowell, the barrister representing Turner Norman, began by telling me that the initial advice Rose had been given had been based on an early assessment of her case using information provided by Rose. She said that Rose's instructions were that the disciplinary proceedings against her were a sham and that the charges against her were trumped up because one of the Directors wanted her job as Managing Director. Linda continued by saying that it became apparent that there were weaknesses in Rose's claim, namely that her acts or omissions could amount to gross misconduct and justify summary dismissal.

Indeed, the Employment Tribunal ultimately found that Rose had been guilty of gross misconduct and that her dismissal was indeed fair. Further, Rose seriously damaged her credibility by stating untruthfully through Turner Norman that she had destroyed her company diary. This fallacy came to light when the police raided her house at SPSL's instigation. Rose also put Turner Norman in a very difficult position, according to Linda, by telling the police, again untruthfully, that she had retained other documents which were the property of SPSL, on Turner Norman's advice. She added that Turner Norman recognised that Rose's strategy from the outset was to achieve a settlement of her claim and they worked towards this. She made reference to an attendance note in her file which was made following a telephone call. The note said:

"She said they were in financial difficulties when she arrived. They were overstretching the company and they were making too much out of the company

and it was always going to cost them to sack her and now all she is asking for is three months' gross pay plus sick pay, plus the car. That needs to be the bottom line and needs to be agreed within 48 hours or she wants to go to tribunal. RB (Rachel Barker – the lawyer advising Rose on behalf of Turner Norman) in discussing that in reality not advised to go to tribunal, expensive and rocky road. RB also concerned about this meeting this Thursday which could scupper any negotiation talks because she will be exposed as working with competing consultancies. She is saying can RB put a time limit on it? She understands that we may have hit a brick wall. RB saying she has been as bullish as she dare to say no, we are walking away from this unless they come up with something better but RB does not want her to walk away from possible money on the table."

A second telephone attendance note of a further conversation a month or so later records that Rachel explained to Rose that the potential offer "never solidified" and had since been contradicted by another member of staff. The note concludes:

"RB saying that unless they are prepared to negotiate we cannot take it any further and appear to have hit a brick wall with an offer now despite all our best efforts."

A few days later, Rachel sent Rose an email in which she set out her advice in detail. She said that she remained pessimistic and believed that it was unlikely that SPSL would raise their offer above the £18,000 currently on the table, and that if that was the case then she would advise Rose to "seriously consider the benefit of accepting a settlement payment now." The email added:

"Although I remain optimistic that your chances of success in the Employment Tribunal are good, I can also advise you that there will be considerable further cost involved in pursuing such a claim."

She estimated the cost of a one day hearing at £5,000 to £6,000. She also said that there was a possibility that, if successful, her compensation might not exceed £22,000 and might be reduced "substantially" if SPSL successfully argued that any pay in lieu of notice would be no more than three rather than six months, and that as Rose had lined up new employment at a similar rate of reward the compensation she would obtain through the Employment Tribunal might, when she had paid all costs and taken into account her time in preparation and attending, be similar to the £18,000 on offer.

She continued that Rose was therefore wrong to state in her mediation position statement that she (Rachel) failed to advise her to accept the offer of

£18,000 and that she advised her instead to hold out for £21,500. On the contrary, Rachel said she advised Rose repeatedly to accept the offer, but the latter did not do so. Indeed, it is clear from the quote from the attendance note relied on in Rose's position statement that when Rachel referred to £21,500 she was not advising her as to the amount she should accept, but was explaining the negotiating position she had taken. Unfortunately, the increased offer failed to crystallise, and then the lower offer was withdrawn.

I interrupted at this point and asked whether Turner Norman were ready to give me an idea of a settlement figure that they might accept throughout the course of the day. Linda Cowell said she was disinterested in discussing any potential settlement – although Turner Norman admitted that there were one or two things that they might do differently next time, they maintained their position that they had provided high quality advice to their erstwhile client. Linda wanted to outline their position to me in full and for me to inform Rose that they were resolute in their stance. I asked further whether Linda might be willing to meet with Rose's lawyers to discuss legal points of detail to help us move forward. She declined. She hadn't been impressed by Rose's lawyers during the joint opening session and she did not want to cause them embarrassment by pointing out what she referred to as the obvious weaknesses in their case. I pressed, but realised that my proposal did not readily recommend itself to her. Linda asked again for the option to outline the summary of Turner Norman's position. In fact she didn't ask, she suggested that she complete her summary before we take any next steps.

According to Linda, Rose ignored Turner Norman's advice about attending the meeting with SPSL's competitors and, precisely as they had feared, this brought the negotiations to an end. Rachel Barker advised Rose as to her duties as a Director and the risks she was running in connection with prospective consultancy work for SPSL's competitors. Against this background, Linda said it was unfair of Rose to seek to blame Turner Norman for her own failure to take any step to resign as a Director or to seek further advice as to whether she should do so.

Linda made a series of further points before concluding, and I summarised what I believed to be the key issues. It was now around 11.30am. I spent the next four hours shuttling between the parties, exploring whether any settlement offers would be forthcoming. They weren't. At 3.30pm one of the representatives from Turner Norman, Robin Hartle, agreed to meet with Rose. Rose was keen to talk about how she had felt let down by the organisation she had retained to advise her. The three of us met in a compact yet informal room, conducive for honest conversation. Mr Hartle expressed regret that one of the company's clients should resort to taking legal action against them. Although he listened intently, he was careful not to say that he thought his organisation had failed in the execution of their duties. At this stage of the day Rose was feeling worn down, to the point where she was crying as she put across her opinion. I remember the scene vividly. She was wearing a blue silk blouse which was slowly becoming more soaked as her tears continued to flow. It was difficult for one not to be moved by Rose's quandary. She pleaded with Robin to see the substance and sagacity in her argument and compensate her for her inconvenience. Robin was experienced though, and although he empathised with his former client he was evidently under strict instructions to ensure that he didn't give any ground in our private meeting.

I asked whether either of them might be prepared to say what they would be willing to settle for. Rose said that she wanted £65,000. Robin replied by saying that this was some way off from what Turner Norman had in mind. He indicated that he would struggle to pay any compensation in excess of £20,000. His rationale for this was that Turner Norman acknowledged one or two deficiencies in their handling of the case but nothing substantial enough to warrant compensation at the level Rose was suggesting. This was the first time that Turner Norman had given any indication of what they might be willing to settle at or indeed whether they might be willing to settle at all. Robin said nothing further and I ended the private session, inviting both to go back to their respective rooms in order to update their colleagues.

20 minutes later I went to see Turner Norman. I thanked Robin for his contribution in the private meeting, and was then surprised to see that he was beginning to prepare a settlement agreement. I asked if, based on the size of the gap indicated in the private meeting, he was optimistic that a settlement would be achieved in the region of what he had just indicated. It was now approaching 4.30pm. Robin gave me a wry smile and said he was sure that settlement would be forthcoming.

I went to see Rose. As I walked into the room Mr Sweeting said, *"So, they're playing games then? I knew they wouldn't come clean and say that they messed up."* I asked what he meant and he explained that he thought that, judging by what his wife had said, Turner Norman weren't taking her case seriously. I asked Rose's team what they wanted to do based on the size of the financial gap that had been indicated at the last meeting. Rose believed that it was worth holding out for them to increase their offer, but her husband was less optimistic, suggesting to his wife that she take what was on offer and allow them to get on with their lives, adding that if there was a chance that they could wake up tomorrow morning with the whole thing put behind them then they should take it. I asked again what they were prepared to do in terms of the financial gap. Mr Sweeting turned to his wife and said that the whole thing should never have been allowed to get as far as it had, to which Rose responded by protesting that she had no idea it was going to get this far. They started to argue, which made uncomfortable viewing for both myself and the legal advisors. I quietly excused myself from their room and went back to see Turner Norman.

As I entered the room I saw Turner Norman's insurance underwriter packing his things away and threatening to leave. They had a signed agreement on the table consisting of £25,000 and the writing off of any legal fees, but that was their bottom line. I swiftly returned to Rose and informed her of this final offer, adding that the only two options were to either accept the offer of settlement or continue fighting the legal battle. Mr Sweeting, now seemingly calling the shots, said that they would sign, but Rose dissented, saying this was still way off from what she wanted. Her husband argued that he had had enough of the battle and was determined to take the offer. Again they argued, but this time I sat and waited as both struggled to be heard over the other.

When a moment of silence finally returned, I asked again for some direction on where they wanted to go. Mr Sweeting repeated his stance.

The discussion went back and forth for another 40minutes before Rose asked me one more time whether I thought that Turner Norman might increase their offer. I said that based on my last conversation with them it looked unlikely but would check if she wanted me to – if they were still in the building. I waited for a reply. Mr Sweeting didn't have to say anything – his look said it all. Rose eventually told me not to bother and said that she would take the offer on the table.

Within about an hour the terms had been agreed, settled and wrapped up. The session had taken nine hours. Unlike the parties in the 'Stabbed in the Back' case, neither of the two sides was willing to say goodbye to each other. In fact Mr Sweeting said that he would need restraining if he came close to anyone who had anything to do with Turner Norman ever again. He said that what they had put his wife through was appalling and shocking and that he had been left to pick up the pieces. Rose, the real claimant, was now very quiet. Turner Norman were stoical and said that they had learned from the experience but wouldn't say any more.

Observations

Disputes rarely remain between two people. Parties involved in a dispute usually need someone who they can confide in, and rarely keep the story of their fall outs to themselves. As their story spreads, friends and associates will often sympathise with the storyteller because of their affiliation with the speaker and a desire to ease their pain. In this case, Rose's husband took control of bringing the rumbling legal wrangling to an end. The way that the dispute had taken over their lives had upset and frustrated him. It didn't seem that his idea of intimacy and sharing a quiet moment with his wife was to have dialogue about who may have been right or wrong or the spiralling costs for ongoing legal fees. Mr Sweeting wanted to protect his loved one from any further pain that would come as a result of her continuing on the path that she had been treading for so long.

There is always a fascinating dynamic for the mediator to work with when the parties involved in the mediation include an individual and a corporate body. The individual carries with them the emotion, feeling and sensation of the hurt they have felt over time whereas the corporate body will usually be represented by someone somewhat detached by comparison. Although they might empathise with the anguish and suffering of the current or former colleague the sense of hurt or distress is likely to be on a different, much lower level.

In cases where the organisation has arguably failed in its corporate and social responsibility, the representative might be powerless to act because of restraints that the organisation has placed upon them. It is always critical that the mediator is ultimately engaging with the person who is not only able to empathise with the opponent but has the gravitas to effect real change and sign off a solution that fits with the expectations of the other side.

One of the most poignant parts of this mediation was the face to face dialogue between Rose and Robin. Robin was hearing for the first time what his former client really thought about the way she had been treated. It is a strength and testament of the mediation process that the letter of the law can be suspended for a moment while adult conversation laced with feelings and passion takes place.

As indicated in the table below, in some cases the mediation process can bring advantages to the process of litigation for this very reason. Mediation works because, unlike other dispute resolution processes, it fully addresses emotional needs. Whilst the opportunity might be given to discuss aspects such as injury to feelings in the litigation or grievance process, the opportunity is rarely given for the disputing parties to discuss emotional issues in detail with each other. In an Employment Tribunal, for example, where the employee wins the tribunal claim, although a judgement may take account of the emotional effect that the dispute has had on someone, it is unlikely to result in full closure for 'winner'.

Three aspects of a dispute

Physical (two or more people)		Mental (point of dispute)		Emotion (anger, fear, shame, embarrassment)	
Litigation/grievance process	✓	Litigation/grievance process	✓	Litigation/grievance process	x
Mediation	✓	Mediation	✓	Mediation	✓

The fact that mediation addresses emotion should not be interpreted as being a process that is soft and fluffy. This case gives an indication of how mediation is a pragmatic, commercial tool that can bring an end to years of costly, time consuming litigation.

Chapter 3
Stories of difference

"We will have to repent in this generation not merely for the vitriolic words or actions of the bad people. We must come to see that human progress never rolls in on wheels of inevitability. It comes through the tireless efforts and persistent work of men… and without this hard work, time itself becomes an ally of the forces of social stagnation. We must use this time creatively, and forever realise that the time is always ripe to do right." – Dr Martin Luther King, Jr.

We are all unique. Variations in eye, hair and skin colour, height, weight, religious views and sexual preference are just some of the hundreds of ways in which each individual is different from the next. Unfortunately with these variations come prejudices – pre-existing notions of a person or class of people often rooted in anything but fact or experience. As the world has seen on too many occasions, prejudice can act as the starter pistol for hatred, murder and genocide, but thankfully this is the far end of the scale. Much more common are the judgements that prevail in many modern societies, or more accurately individuals or small groups within society. Different societies have different issues to tackle, but it is perhaps not surprising, given humanity's instinctive nature not to trust *'outsiders'*, that prejudices are still problematic in countries that claim to welcome all nationalities, religions and abilities, such as Britain. A country that does this relies on its people to be accepting of change, but as history has shown, and continues to show, this is not always the case. These culture clashes are never more evident than in the workplace.

To address the varying and more complex nature of workplace disputes arising from issues relating to differences, the Equality Act of 2010 was introduced in order to establish nine key areas that the British Government believed were at the heart of such problems. These were:

- Age
- Gender
- Disability

- Sexual orientation
- Religion and belief
- Maternity
- Civil partnership
- Race
- Gender reassignment

The introduction of this legislation recognised the changing shift in attitudes towards minorities and added layers of protection for those who were victims of more modern types of discrimination (e.g. civil partnership and gender reassignment). Britain has come a long way from the days of 'no Irish, no blacks, no dogs', but divisions still exist and, in areas of high migrant populations, are growing. These divisions, and the tensions that come with them, can't help but spill over into the workplace.

It is not surprising when we look at the history of the British workplace that bigotry and prejudice became, and still are, a problem. A history of slavery, most notably during the heights of the British Empire, along with government intervention (such as the 1905 Aliens Act which practically institutionalised the idea that immigrants alone were responsible for rapidly deteriorating workers' conditions at the time) set the scene for such attitudes. Two World Wars did little to bridge the divide, despite those foreign to Britain playing a huge part in Allied successes, after which Britain enjoyed a huge boom in manufacturing. This required instant, cheap labour, for which hundreds of thousands of migrant workers were recruited, despite attempts by the incumbent government to avoid the burden of these workers' families settling in the UK afterwards.

Many employers took on this migrant workforce purely to have them perform the most menial and undesirable tasks, therefore instantly creating a segregation effect that can be seen in action in one of the following stories. Racism was openly rife in Britain at that time, aided by politicians making damaging, baseless comments about the intentions and behaviour of immigrants which only served to inflame tensions. The achievement of upward mobility in the workplace by immigrants incensed bigoted colleagues who complained and fought against these small victories, occasionally violently. These violent protests have since largely made way for political pressure, but so far have only been successful in small pockets of the country.

Immigration is one of a number of examples I could have used to illustrate minority groups having been unfairly and unjustly persecuted because of bigotry and unsubstantiated viewpoints – in the workplace everything from gender, age and ethnicity to computer literacy and dress sense can be cause for discrimination. Of course we don't want to turn into a country where no one can take what is clearly meant to be a joke, but there is a definite line between innocent horseplay and instant, irrational hatred. If you also consider that because of legislation like the Equality Act workplaces are now more diverse than ever, supposedly with no gender, class or race barriers preventing employment and upward mobility, individuals who hold bigoted or prejudiced views now work with, or even for those for whom they harbour a dislike or a hatred. The reactions of these individuals can be many and varied, but very few who have these opinions hard-wired into them will be able to set aside their differences and work together harmoniously, which has consequences for both themselves and the target of their animosity. These individuals, if dismissed on the grounds of discrimination, will almost always hold the target of their hostility at fault and will not recognise that their actions and beliefs are the real cause of their downfall.

Alongside this pre-existing discrimination is another more recent type – positive discrimination. This variation is different than the example above because it generally involves previously liberally-minded workers finding themselves becoming prejudiced because of marginalisation at work on behalf of certain groups or minorities. For example, if a company publicly announces a drive to recruit more women (possibly by virtue of new government targets on workplace equality) and then picks a female candidate for a job instead of an equally suited male one, the male candidate will perhaps suspect he has been discriminated against on the grounds of his gender and may make a formal complaint. If this particular individual were then to experience a similar occurrence again, he may start to foster resentment for female competition in the workplace.

His missed opportunities for employment or promotion at the hands of women may be solely down to suitability for the job, but it is easy to see how such prejudices can be built up, erroneously or otherwise.

So in the war of differences we have two camps – those who have pre-existing prejudices that they exercise on colleagues and those who form prejudices based on negative workplace experiences at the hands of certain groups – and with multiculturalism both in society and the workplace knowing no bounds, it provides ample opportunity for such views to be unfortunately aired. Considering the amount of people in employment such cases are comparatively rare, which shows that the majority of people are happy to work with those of different races, cultures and religions – provided that everyone is treated fairly. The media are quick to decry any governmental decisions that favour ethnic groups for fear of being branded racists, which, for those who have little exposure to the people concerned, only helps paint a portrait of a section of society whose sole aim is to impart their beliefs and values onto ours. This ignorance, fuelled by certain parts of the media and a refusal or inability to connect with those involved, will inevitably lead to tensions in the workplace and beyond.

Cases involving those with unsubstantiated prejudices, perhaps passed down through the family or a circle of friends, can sometimes prove difficult for a mediator to work on – especially if the individual is not willing to admit any fault on their part or see reason. This can prove problematic for two reasons. Firstly there is the obvious issue that someone not willing to share their story or give any ground will be very difficult to work with and will be less likely to work towards a compromise, and secondly the mediator can occasionally want to play the psychologist and delve into the roots of an individual's irrational hatred of a particular person or group of people.

These subconscious driving forces are what we refer to when we talk about the 'core story'. Everything we do, whether we realise it or not, is driven by our core values and desires. These may have been instilled through childhood or only relatively recently formed, and in mediation sessions they may take some time and digging to uncover, but in cases where a party is clearly holding back or is not even willing to discuss the matter in depth, we need to find out why this is. We don't want their innermost secrets, but deep-set attitudes towards a particular person or group of people need to be identified if a successful resolution is to be reached. Incidents that reach the stage of mediation don't often spring from nowhere, rather they are dictated by the actions of one person or a particular group of people with similar core values. These instances were evident in the last batch of stories and are starkly evident in the ones to follow.

As we've seen, it is of course possible for liberally-minded people to have prejudices thrust upon them following a series of unexpected but, to them at least, linked events, but many incidents involving the areas we have discussed have a history of sorts behind them. In these incidents the core story can prove invaluable and, as you'll see, lives can be changed when they are revealed and discussed.

The case of race

"If there is any great secret of success in life, it lies in the ability to put yourself in the other person's place and to see things from his point of view – as well as your own." – Henry Ford.

Cobra Systems, a technology company who have grown quickly over the last ten years, thanks mainly to the rise of lifestyle developments such as social networking and online marketing, appointed a new Chief Executive to aid their growth. His brief was to take the company from its entrepreneurial beginnings to a mature corporate organisation. Part of the strategy to do this was to appoint a number of directors to lead new functions such as marketing, HR and sales. A year after the new appointees were in place, the strategy seemed to be taking shape with revenue continuing to rise sharply.

One of the new directors, a black man by the name of Barry Trueman, was appointed as HR Director. Barry had come from a much larger company where he was the assistant to the HR Director but, despite doing very well, was regularly in the firing line taking the criticism for the change of direction the company was going in. The remaining eight Directors in Cobra Systems who reported to the Chief Executive were white males, as were all but 15 of the 3,000 strong workforce, all of whom worked in secretarial/administrative positions.

One afternoon, Barry was having a catch-up session with one of his team, Sue. At the end of the hour long session Barry noticed that his colleague looked nervous and twitchy, and so asked her if everything was okay. She responded by saying that there was something on her mind but she wasn't sure how to raise it with him. Barry assured her that she could speak freely with him. Sue said that it would probably be best to show him an email that she had been forwarded rather than explain it, although she was supposed to keep it to herself. She proceeded to open her folder and handed Barry a printout of the email to which she had referred. Barry looked at the document and started to read. Despite corrections in spelling and grammar, the following text is the exact content of the email:

"Dear Brian,

Good to see you at the pub yesterday evening. Very much enjoyed our discussion. I don't know whether anything can be done about the situation we find ourselves in. We may just have to wait until Barry Trueman leaves for his next job – or better still he is sacked for some misdemeanour that we can orchestrate. In my 15 years of working for the company I never once imagined that I would see the day when a nigger would be appointed to such a powerful position. How did this happen? It feels as if all my dad's years in the National Front movement have been in vain. We should have seen it coming. As soon as these monkeys had access to education, problems set in. They started to see themselves as equal to us. It seems that Mr. Trueman has had more access than most. I was in a meeting the other day and at the end of the meeting Sue thanked everyone for their contribution and then said that she would give our thoughts to Barry so that he could agree the way ahead. I felt sick. It seems as if the whole organisation now has to wait on a black man to make a decision. This is wrong. I saw him pull up in his Jaguar the other day and stay in the car while he was on the phone for about 15 minutes. I was tempted to do something to his car to make sure that he didn't get home safely. My colleagues advised me otherwise. I have also thought of leaving, but my wife talked me out of it. I see now that it would be silly to let the wog drive me out. I think that all we can do is wait for him to mess up. I'm sure he will soon. It is just a matter of time. Maybe you and some of your director colleagues can help with this?

By the way, what do you call a black man with a degree? A nigger…..lol Hope to see you down the Bull in Arms at lunchtime.

Justin"

Barry was shocked and saddened. He thanked Sue for bringing the email to his attention and asked if he could hold on to it. Brian, the recipient of the email, was the Marketing Director, a middle aged white man and one of Barry's peers who had been with the company for about the same time as Barry. The next day, Barry asked to see his boss, the Chief Executive. Barry updated him on a few business matters before handing him the email. The Chief Executive read it and was obviously embarrassed. Barry said that he didn't want to discuss the content of the email but would leave it to the Chief Executive to do what he deemed fit, feeling that because of his position as HR Director and given the subject of the email it would be inappropriate for him to be involved in any actions the company might want to take.

The Chief Executive sought legal advice and retained the company's employment lawyers for additional support. The company then invoked the disciplinary process and suspended Justin on full pay while the process got underway. The Sales Director, a peer of Barry's, heard the disciplinary and a few weeks later Justin was dismissed. He appealed the dismissal but the company upheld the decision, while no disciplinary action was taken against Brian. During this period, the relationship between Barry and Brian broke down with Barry concluding from the email that Brian concurred with Justin's comments.

Things deteriorated so badly that they ended up only speaking through intermediaries before the Chief Executive noted the tension and stepped in. During a weekly meeting with Barry he asked how Barry was feeling about the episode. Barry found it difficult to answer and asked whether they could have that discussion at another time.

A few weeks later, during an off-site executive team meeting, Barry gave a presentation updating the senior team on HR issues. During the question and answer session, Brian asked Barry a question about the organisation's HR strategy. Barry ignored the question and started to talk about something else. Everyone noticed that there was an atmosphere in the room. During the coffee break the Chief Executive took Barry to one side and asked him if he would consider engaging in mediation with Brian, seeing as the tension in the room just before the break indicated to him that the situation needed resolving. Barry agreed to think about it.

The following week it was brought to the Chief Executive's attention that a new employee had not been put on the payroll system. It transpired that Brian hadn't gone through the usual monthly 'head of function' sign off process – a process that would have required a face-to-face conversation with Barry. The Chief Executive summoned Barry and Brian separately and said that he had heard about the payroll issue and would be arranging for an external mediator to come in to help them sort out their dispute, advising them to accept the mediator's call when it came.

The mediation

A week later I made contact with both Barry and Brian independently. Both agreed to have a preliminary meeting with me for the process to be explained. The mediation session was arranged for two weeks later. On the day of the mediation, both Barry and Brian arrived on their own and without representation. I had also asked the Chief Executive to join the session at the beginning. He did so, thanking the pair for agreeing to be part of the session and wishing them every success in finding a solution to their dispute, and then left. I provided some narrative for the joint opening session and then invited Barry to give his thoughts on why the mediation had been requested. Barry said very little apart from how he hadn't realised that he was working with a racist. Brian responded in kind by saying very little apart from refuting Barry's allegation.

Quickly realising that we would make little progress in a joint session, I moved to private sessions. I first met with Barry who didn't say much more than he had done in the opening session. He did add one additional piece of information however, which was that he hadn't worked his way up to such a senior position and persisted with his further and higher education to become the subject of racist remarks. I asked him what he wanted to do and he replied by saying that the ball was in Brian's court as he thought that his acceptance and encouragement of racist views was inappropriate in the 21st century. He added that he wasn't sure whether it would be possible to continue working together. Barry asked me to go and spend some time with Brian and feed back on the discussion. Before I left the room I asked whether Barry would consider having a joint meeting again with Brian later on. He indicated that he might.

I met with Brian and attempted to engage in dialogue, Brian was unresponsive. I asked him what he wanted to achieve from the day, to which he responded that he wanted Barry and the rest of the organisation to know that he wasn't a racist. I offered Brian 15 minutes to think about what he wanted from the day after which I would return to discuss his thoughts.

Brian's story

When I returned, I asked whether Brian had had any further thoughts about the day's proceedings. He took a deep breath and began to outline his thoughts. He said that he was finding the whole process uncomfortable and difficult and that he had experienced a range of emotions over the months that the disciplinary process had been underway. He then said something which I hadn't expected; despite having the appearance of being white, he was actually mixed race and that his father was black. Not only that, his father had also left his mother when Brian was young. He described how throughout his working life he had been able to hide his cultural background from his work colleagues, how he hadn't planned to do this but that early on in his career he overheard a conversation amongst some colleagues which was laced with racist overtones. It would be best, he decided, to play down the fact that he was mixed race, putting his complexion and skin tone down to the man his mother later married and claiming him to be his father. Brian was resentful of his father's absence, so attempted to block out his existence. He described his anguish and explained that he found it difficult to identify with being black or white. When Justin started with his banter Brian again felt he had no choice but to go along with it out of fear of embarrassment of being acknowledged as black (or mixed race).

Once Brian had finished his story I asked if there was anything else that he wanted to add. Brian paused for a few moments before recounting an experience from junior school when he was about eight years old. His father and mother had already split up, and one day his father turned up unexpectedly to pick him up from school. The next day during morning break some of Brian's school friends started teasing him for having a black father even though he (Brian) looked white. They started calling him cruel names, and Brian lashed out, starting a fight with one of the ringleaders. He recalled how the experience brought him embarrassment, shame, disgrace and humiliation. He realised in that moment that it wouldn't be good for him to let people know anything about his black heritage. He asked his father never to pick him up from school again.

Brian now had his own family. He had married a white woman and over the years had had a few deep conversations with his wife about trying to re-establish a relationship with his real father. He was truly sorry for being a silent contributor to Barry's situation.

I thanked Brian again for sharing such personal information and asked whether he would be willing to share all or part of his story with Barry. Brian thought for a while and then said that he would be willing to, but wanted a break first. We had been together for nearly an hour. I went through to see Barry and explained that Brian wanted to talk to him about a few things and asked for all three of us to get together in 20 minutes time.

Joint meeting
The three of us met again. I explained again to Barry that Brian had a few things that he wanted to say and invited Brian to begin when he was ready. All mediators have a choice about how information is relayed between parties. I could have given Barry an indication of what Brian wanted to say, but this would have diluted the impact. My preference was to allow Brian to look Barry in the face and share his story with him. After all, it was his story.

Brian apologised to Barry for the situation that had arisen between them and for the part he had played as a silent contributor. He then began to recount his experiences in the same way that he had done with me previously. Barry listened intently and was visibly shocked. When Brian had finished his story silence settled upon the three of us. At first Barry didn't know what to say, but after a few moments he started to ask Brian questions about his background and upbringing, questions Brian answered openly. It was as if the two men had realised that they had something in common.

I remained silent while the two men talked. Barry asked Brian whether he had any idea how much unease he (Barry) had been through as a result of the email experience. Brian responded that he had some idea, but acknowledged how damaging his silence and implied participation had been. Barry asked Brian how long he planned to conceal the information about his background, to which Brian responded by saying that he didn't know but had been thinking hard about this aspect of his life for some time. This event had brought things forward.

Barry admitted that he could see Brian was experiencing a sense of anguish with his story and that he had no desire to make it worse. To this end he was happy to let Brian decide what to do and accepted his apology, but did stress how painful the whole experience had been for him. He described how he had worked and studied hard in order to make a better future for his family and thought he had escaped the curse of racism, but now realised that it must have existed behind his back for some time. He was sorry that society hadn't yet fully embraced diversity in every sense. He described how it felt to devote years to study and hard work, only to regularly feel like a second class citizen in some environments. He recalled a story of boarding a train at Birmingham International. As he boarded the train in the first class compartment a white man looked at him and gave a wry smile to his travelling companion. They then started whispering to each other. Barry articulated how it took all his strength to remain professional and dignified, despite his desperation to speak out and ask them what they were talking about. Barry continued to speak of the hurt he felt to be judged by his fellow passengers purely on skin colour.

I thanked Barry for his openness, and Barry replied that he felt better being able to express his thoughts. It was now lunchtime and I asked whether the pair would be willing for the three of us to have lunch together. Both agreed. Over lunch the conversation covered many topics, but no mention was made of the dispute that had brought them together. After lunch I asked to meet with Brian alone again and asked him what he wanted to do next. Brian said he was unsure and would have to think about what this experience meant for him before making any next moves.

I asked whether they might include saying anything to the Chief Executive. Brian added that he probably would but that he would have to consider the details first.

I then went back to Barry and asked if he wanted to take the day's proceedings any further. Barry said that the day had probably gone far enough and that Brian had much thinking to do, but that there was some unfinished business with the Chief Executive. He couldn't understand why, when the company had acted so swiftly in dealing with Justin, Brian hadn't been included in any of the disciplinary proceedings. I phoned the Chief Executive and asked if he would be willing to join the mediation session. He arrived about half an hour later and I detailed the progress that Barry and Brian had made. I explained that the session had had a particularly powerful impact on Brian, but stopped short of going into any detail as I hadn't yet had Brian's permission to do so. I made the Chief Executive aware that Barry wanted to have a chat with him about a few aspects concerning the investigation and disciplinary process, and he agreed to a private meeting.

Before facilitating the joint meeting between Barry and the Chief Executive, I had a private meeting with Barry. I explained that I hadn't told the Chief Executive about what Brian had revealed earlier and intimated that I thought it would be better coming from Brian. Barry agreed straight away. He realised that Brian was going to have to start facing up to his secret and that he (Brian) would be the best person to have that conversation with the Chief Executive.

The Chief Executive and Barry met. I invited Barry to outline his thoughts and Barry explained that it had been a useful day and that he and Brian had covered good ground. He continued by saying that there was nevertheless a piece of the jigsaw still missing in his mind regarding the absence of Brian in any aspect of the disciplinary process. The Chief Executive explained that it had been considered, but on the advice of the organisation's legal advisors, who were handling the process, they agreed not to take any formal action against Brian. A discussion had taken place with Brian with the conclusion that there was no indication he had been racist in any way. It was thought that Brian's naivety had been in remaining silent – a silence that indicated consent and participation. The Chief Executive acknowledged that in hindsight Barry should have been given a general update on how the disciplinary process was progressing. Barry expressed to his boss that he was starting to wonder whether he, as Chief Executive, was reluctant to support the matter because Brian was a senior manager. The Chief Executive recounted the process that had been undertaken and assured Barry that he was genuine in his desire for discrimination of any kind to be eradicated from the organisation. He went on to explain that he had recruited Barry based on merit and that the colour of his skin never registered as something he should be concerned about. He also suggested to Barry that as difficult as this experience might have been, he shouldn't take it as a signal that the whole organisation was racist. Barry accepted the Chief Executive's sentiments.

I went back to Brian's room and explained that the Chief Executive was now on site and had been in private discussion with Barry. I confirmed that I had not told the Chief Executive anything of what had emerged during the day about his background. I then invited Brian to join me, the Chief Executive and Barry in a joint session.

With us all in the same room, I began to say that it looked as if the day had run its course. I concluded that Barry and Brian had had a good exchange of words and had made a great deal of progress. Brian interrupted and said that he wanted to tell the Chief Executive his story, which he then did. The Chief Executive listened attentively and, like Barry, was shocked and surprised with what he heard, commenting that he would never have guessed Brian's ethnic background. He added that he could sense Brian's anguish and would be willing to listen further to anything else that Brian wanted to say. When Brian had finished, he summarised by saying that he wanted to take the evening and the weekend to think things through. We all shook hands and agreed to talk again on Monday.

The next stage

That evening, Brian went out for a meal with his wife. He talked to her in detail about the day's proceedings and how he had expressed his remorse to Barry. The whole affair he said had left him shaken and dazed and had knocked him for six. He felt as if this was a life changing moment and that he had found the experience so profound that he was thinking of resigning. It was time he started to be true to himself. His wife said that he should think things through, but that she would support whatever decision he made. They finished their meal and went home.

At 2.00am on Saturday the phone rang and woke them from their sleep. Brian answered and a woman asked to confirm if it was indeed him. Brian said that it was and the lady informed him that her name was Alison and that she was the girlfriend of Brian's real father. Brian was still half asleep and asked her to repeat what she had just said. Alison did, going on to explain that she knew about Brian's family history. Brian, now fully awake, asked why she was calling him at 2.00am. Alison replied that she was calling from a hospital and had some bad news – Brian's father had been taken ill on Friday with a suspected heart attack and had just died. Brian went quiet. Alison asked if he had heard what she had said. Brian said that he had and asked her which hospital she was calling from. Brian took the name, put the phone down and explained the phone call to his wife. As the news sank in he began to sob. Amidst his tears he recalled the moment when, standing by the school gates, he asked his father never to come back and pick him up again. It was as if these words had come back to haunt him.

On Monday morning, Brian phoned the Chief Executive to inform him of his father's death and that he had decided to tender his resignation. The Chief

Executive said that his father was the first priority and that they would deal with anything else when Brian was really ready. Brian attended his father's funeral and took some time off to reflect on recent experiences. Two weeks later he submitted his resignation in order to take some time to think about what to do next. With the mediation still on his mind, he phoned Barry and invited him for lunch. Barry agreed and over the meal Brian apologised once again for all the trouble that had been caused. He added that the last few months had been an incredible journey for him and had prompted him to think deeply about the direction his life was going in. The death of his father had proved to be the last straw, and he now felt as if he had no choice but to face up to reality, although what his next steps would be he didn't know. Brian and Barry spoke for hours and subsequently a friendship developed between them.

I was to hear later that Brian asked to withdraw his resignation, but did ask for two months off work while he thought some things through, a request to which the Chief Executive didn't hesitate in agreeing. His view was that Brian had been through a life changing experience and that the organisation was obliged to support him in whatever way they could.

Observations

The last 30 years has brought huge swathes of legislation changes in relation to diversity at work. Acts relating to race relations, equal pay and other aspects have been brought together under one umbrella with the Equality Act of 2010. It took four years to complete. It is expected that the UK workforce will embrace the concept of diversity and the nine protected characteristics and move in harmony with each other. However, the British media set the tone for the likely level of approval in some quarters with headlines like, 'The end of jokes in the workplace.'

Prejudice is our longest lasting, deepest and least resolved source of conflict. It can operate consciously and subconsciously and extends to all strands on the diversity spectrum. Over time, certain groups have become used to the possession of power, wealth and authority. Society has grown used to seeing a stereotypical person fulfilling certain roles or occupying particular positions. This can mean that when someone occupies a position that doesn't fit a particular stereotype, it can be seen as unusual and become problematical for some to accept. For example, the last 20 years has seen large increases in the number of women who take up senior positions, often at boardroom level. In this case, it was Justin who had difficulty working with a black HR Director.

Forming judgments about people regularly happens when we interact with those who are different to us. The difference could relate to the melanin content in our skin, a person's gender, sexual orientation, height, age and a whole raft of other differences. Tackling discrimination is something that needs to be given priority if an organisation ever wants to achieve its full potential. Research repeatedly demonstrates the enhanced value and richness that diversity brings.

Overcoming prejudice is difficult mainly because it is normally deep rooted. From our childhood, we begin to associate thoughts with people. For example, one may have heard one's parents say that anyone with a Scottish accent is likely to be tight fisted, or that all African businessmen are corrupt. We then grow up believing this and our perceptions become more difficult to shift as we get older. It can be complex and can operate on multiple levels. The truth is, of course, that there is good and bad in all people.

In 'Conflict Revolution' by Ken Cloke, he describes some options to diffuse or respond to prejudice. He suggests that to castigate, blame, or point fingers is not the only way to react when one might feel that they have become the victim of prejudice. He lists ways in which the victim can defuse prejudice by assisting those in its grip to:

• Develop a knowledgeable, confident self-identity and appreciate who they are without needing to feel superior to others
• Experience comfortable, empathetic interactions with diverse people and ideas
• Be curious and unafraid of differences and commonalities
• Feel comfortable collaboratively solving problems and negotiating differences
• Be aware of biases, stereotypes and discrimination when they occur
• Stand up for themselves and others in the face of prejudice, without becoming biased in return

There are many ways of confronting prejudice, bias and discrimination that allow us to amend not simply the overt statements and behaviours that express it, but the covert places in people's hearts and minds where it lies buried. To begin with, we can each acknowledge and speak openly about our own prejudices, how we have struggled to overcome them, and watched others do the same.

When confronting other people's prejudicial statements we can:

• Bring awareness to our emotional responses and calm ourselves before speaking
• Assume people have good intentions
• Try and understand where their prejudice has come from
• Discuss their statement one-on-one, privately, in a non-threatening way

- Request permission to offer feedback
- Be low key and non aggressive
- Don't shame, blame, attack or accuse
- Be friendly and accepting, yet assertive and clear
- Be hard on the problem and soft on the person
- Ask if the effect they created was one they intended
- Ask if they ever felt discriminated against or harassed for any reason, and get details
- Indicate what it feels like to experience prejudice using "I" statements
- Tell a story about prejudice to help them listen and learn
- Try and assess the cost of prejudice, offering examples from personal experience
- Suggest alternative phraseology, approaches, or perspectives
- State your disagreements openly and honestly
- Bring in a third party to mediate differences
- Ask for feedback on your feedback

Selecting to apply the law or company grievance procedures in cases such as the one we have just discussed is likely to result in a limited and narrow outcome. Justin's dismissal will have succeeded in sending a message to the organisation that racism is not acceptable and will not be tolerated. It falls short, however, in helping Justin, or any of his colleagues, address his prejudices and preventing any future reoccurrences. It could be argued that any learning has been limited to ensuring that any actions and thoughts should be untraceable and not reduced to email or any other form of written communication. This sort of message, if received by Justin and his former colleagues in this way, could simply drive such behaviour underground. An alternative approach would be to include a method of introducing conversation that may help uncover reasons for such behaviour. This would help Justin address what appears to be systematic discrimination and go some way to protecting him and a future colleague from a similar event.

One of the strengths of the process of mediation is that it gets people to talk. Once he started, Brian began to quickly reveal information about his history and background. It became clear that Brian was carrying years of unexpressed emotion and as soon as the opportunity was given to share his 'secret' he took it. The setting had to be right, including the fact that Brian needed to feel that he could trust me as the mediator to be able to be empathetic to what he wanted to say, and to keep this secret where required.

Mediation was also invaluable in getting both Brian and Barry en route to building a friendship and working relationship that was stronger than it had been before. Their deep conversations meant that a bond had developed between them and their future together had much more meaning than it would have had before mediation.

Finally, although not explicit in this case, is the fact that the organisation had the opportunity to learn from what had happened. The scenario had exposed an insight to a culture where racist undertones were at play. If it was demonstrated that Justin's behaviour was the tip of the iceberg, the Chief Executive and his colleagues could have put some behaviour and values training in place to begin addressing it.

The age divide

"For some people, becoming a leader can be a real power trip. They relish the feeling of control over both people and information. And so they keep secrets, reveal little of their thinking about people and their performance, and hoard what they know about the business and its future. This kind of behaviour certainly establishes the leader as boss but it drains trust right out of a team." – Jack Welch

Some time ago I was asked to help in a situation that had developed between a line manager, Sarah, and her direct report, Hilda, both of whom worked in the sales department of a company in the publishing industry. The problem had built up over the previous 18 months, the last six of which Hilda had spent on sick leave. She had been employed with the company for about 30 years and was proud of the fact that she had an unblemished employment record during that time. Prior to Sarah taking over two years previously, Hilda had only worked for two other line managers in her lengthy spell. Sarah had been with the organisation for five years and had been recruited as part of the company's strategic development programme. Hilda was 58, Sarah 27.

When Sarah took over the department she was given the brief by her line manager to *"sort things out."* It was believed that the department had the potential to perform much better than its history suggested. One of Sarah's first actions was to hold a series of one-to-one discussions with her new team of 12 people. As part of those discussions, she floated the idea of setting objectives and reviewing performance at regular intervals. Whilst this was common practice for her, it was as if she was speaking a different language to many of her team members. Hilda, in particular, was insulted that after 30 years with the company she would now be subjected to formal monthly discussions with her boss about her performance. Immediate relations were further worsened when Hilda told Sarah during an objective setting session that she was young enough to be her daughter. This did not go down well with Sarah, who was aware that in the company's 80 year history it had become quite paternalistic, whilst the new initiative of more female managers was a further sign of impending change. Sarah promptly told Hilda that her relative youth didn't mean that she couldn't run a department and proceeded to carry on with the discussion. Things didn't get any better over the first year of their working relationship with differences beginning to emerge in methods of communication, not helped by Sarah's preference for email and text compared to Hilda's more traditional approach of face to face conversations.

One Tuesday afternoon, Sarah took a call from an angry customer. The customer said that at the end of the previous Friday they had contacted Hilda who had promised to send them some information that they urgently required. The information hadn't arrived. Sarah said that she would look into it and went to Hilda to discuss the incident. Hilda explained that as the call had come through last thing on Friday she didn't do anything with it as she was about to leave for the weekend but also crucially forgot to pass the request onto her colleague, who would have to produce the information, to follow up. Sarah was extremely angry, publicly rebuking Hilda in the open office environment, demanding to know how she could have let the customer down and why she hadn't stayed later on Friday to sort it out. Hilda burst into tears and ran out of the office. She didn't turn up to work for the rest of the week.

The meeting

On Hilda's return to work, Sarah said she wanted to have a chat with her at 10.30am. Hilda arrived at the meeting room at 10.45am to find that Sarah was accompanied by a member of the company's HR team. Hilda was invited to take a seat after which Sarah, glancing at her notes at regular intervals, proceeded to tell Hilda that she was launching an investigation into the customer incident and that the result of the investigation could be some form of disciplinary action against Hilda. This was, understandably, a bombshell for Hilda. She was surprised and astonished. Her surprise quickly turned to anger, fury and rage, asking Sarah how she dared treat her in this manner. Sarah, in her textbook management style, informed Hilda that she would, of course, be treated fairly.

While the series of events were playing out between Sarah and Hilda, Sarah was also having battles with other members of staff. Two defected to competitors shortly after Sarah's arrival whilst another took early retirement after 25 years' service, stating that he could no longer face coming into work. The fact that he preferred to retire with a lower pension rather than remain with the company for his final two years and collect a full pension spoke volumes. In his view this was a price worth paying.

The investigation into the customer incident took a month to run, concluding in Hilda receiving a written warning. Sarah's decision was based on her position that to promise something to a customer and then fail to deliver was a cardinal sin. For Hilda, this was the last straw. She was bewildered that after 30 years of service she found herself in this position. It was even worse for her that the organisation appeared to be supporting Sarah. Hilda continued to come to work, but now refused to engage in any form of dialogue with Sarah apart from one word answers where absolutely necessary. Two weeks after the warning was issued Hilda was signed off by her doctor for work related stress. Her sick note indicated that she would be back to work in one month, but this was extended for another month just as she was due to return. This pattern repeated itself for five months until Hilda finally came back to work, only to be signed off again after only two weeks.

Sarah was beginning to grow weary of Hilda's absence. The organisation had a policy of paying employees full pay for the first six months of sickness. When Hilda came back for two weeks it effectively meant that she could take fresh sick leave for up to another six months on full pay. Sarah was beginning to wonder whether Hilda's sickness was genuine. Occupational health was asked to carry out an assessment. The report confirmed Hilda was genuinely ill.

Taking action
By this stage, Hilda's situation was being discussed at the highest level in the organisation. The Chief Executive knew Hilda personally, seeing as she had been one of the longest serving members of staff. The HR Director was asked to intervene. Mediation was proposed as a potential way forward for the situation. Hilda needed some convincing as she had never heard of mediation in a work context.

It took her two months before she eventually agreed. I met Hilda and Sarah for the first time on the day of the mediation. Hilda was accompanied by a male friend much younger in years, a businessman with some knowledge of employment law, whilst Sarah was joined by her husband who was also an employee of the company. A few things struck me from my first interaction with each of them. Firstly Sarah came across as a 'tough cookie', rigid in her views, seeing the situation as a business matter and determined that this fiasco wouldn't derail her fast stream career path. By contrast Hilda was unconfident and required reassurance, but was angry at the way she had been treated by what she described as 'this youngster'. Their age divide still posed a big problem for Hilda.

The separate and joint discussions got underway. Hilda wanted an apology and an assurance that if she came back to work she wouldn't be subjected to the same treatment. Sarah told me privately, all the while through her steely exterior, that she wasn't sure if she wanted Hilda to return. She maintained that things needed to change in her department and that all members of the team would need to work to the same principles – her principles. The conversation went back and forth. We had joint meetings, then private sessions, then more joint meetings. More information began to flow which only served to consolidate the fact that Sarah and Hilda saw things only from their own point of view, although the level of hurt on both sides was deep. By lunchtime both were starting to feel weary from the discussions. It was clear that they hated each other and that forgiveness was some way off.

The shock

Just before lunchtime I popped into Sarah's room while she and her husband were preparing to eat their lunch. I encouraged them to continue, given that it had been a long morning, stating that I merely wanted to find out how they thought things were going. Sarah put down her sandwich and started to give her thoughts on progress. She began to recount some of the history of the dispute, acknowledging as she did that there were flaws in some aspects of her management style. She said that she had been feeling the pressure of managing a growing team and being required to deliver results. Just as I thought I knew the direction the conversation was heading in, Sarah did something that I was totally unprepared for – she burst into tears. She sobbed uncontrollably, with her husband looking as taken aback as me. He clearly hadn't anticipated this either. The tears kept coming; tears through which Sarah was trying to talk but couldn't. Her steely exterior had cracked.

This display carried on for about five minutes but it felt like an hour. Sarah managed to get across that the experience had been affecting her badly outside of work. She had been unable to relax at night and was now on tablets to help her get to sleep, before stunning me by announcing that she had suffered a miscarriage two months before; an announcement that brought with it more tears. Her husband comforted her as she explained that she attributed some of the blame for this episode to the various work issues. I said that I was very sorry to hear of their experiences but said no more. This was a deeply personal moment for Sarah and her husband. I remained with them for another ten minutes while they consoled each other before leaving and saying I would come back later.

Reflections

I went to my own room to get some lunch and reflect on what had just happened. I thought about how Sarah and her husband must be feeling. It wasn't just Sarah who was experiencing difficulties, for her husband had been sharing the pain too. I was also reflecting on the change in Sarah's countenance. Her steely exterior had now gone, and it now felt to me as if she craved respite from wearing the mask of a hard-nosed commercial line manager. I began to wonder how many other line managers wore similar masks to work. The requirement to achieve and deliver results, coupled with increasing job insecurity, can sometimes cause people to act in a way they would not normally. This leads to a lack of authenticity that can have a twofold effect. Firstly, leaders may struggle to build fully engaged teams if they are not authentic themselves. This is because, as we touched on when discussing trust, people will follow someone they find to be genuine, that they can trust and believe in. It is easy for most of us to pick up on something that isn't quite right about a person who isn't being themselves. Leaders will never get full buy-in when this is the case. Secondly, it is difficult for anyone to keep up an act forever. It is likely that at some stage an experience or encounter will force us to reveal who we really are. This can bring a great sense of relief as the pretence and deception finally comes to an end.

The settlement

In the sessions that followed after lunch, it emerged that the assurance that Hilda was looking for would be unlikely to be forthcoming from Sarah. Despite her earlier emotional breakdown she still wanted to ensure that tasks would be achieved on time. We were now at a stalemate. Two of the options left to consider were for one, or both, to move to another department or leave the company. Sarah made it clear to me that she wouldn't be going anywhere. Hilda, however, seemed willing to engage in dialogue that involved a conversation about moving on. At this point, Hilda's friend became a key player in the process as Hilda was struggling to keep up with the practicalities of what leaving the company might look like. I also had to engage a member of the HR team to advise me on what the company would be willing to offer.

The settlement position was for Hilda to move on and be compensated for the equivalent of six months salary. As the reality set in, Hilda cried. She spoke about the years of service that she had given to the company, only for it to be prematurely brought to an end by this *"youngster"*. Her friend helped her to understand the detail of the proposal. He was excellent. Earlier in the day he had been giving me cause for concern by seemingly playing the role of quasi-solicitor. I ascertained that seeing Hilda go through the experience of many difficult conversations helped him to soften and move to a position of helping Hilda to be released from any further anguish.

It took a number of hours to complete the negotiated settlement. Once we had agreed, Hilda took legal advice over the phone and by 7.30pm we had finished. Independently both Sarah and Hilda told me how exhausted they were but that they were pleased to have arrived at a solution. The mediation had worked. I offered both the opportunity to say goodbye to each other but both declined.

This aspect was unfortunate but understandable. It was too soon for both parties to move on from the rawness of the exchanges of the day, to shake hands and 'forgive and forget' what had happened.

Observations

The main aspect to this dispute was the age gap. Sarah wanted to make change happen quickly whilst over the years Hilda had got used to things just as they were. This is a very clear example of how clashing styles and personalities can drag team performance down if they are not addressed immediately and appropriately.

My attempt to broker reconciliation between the two ran aground at quite an early stage in the day. One of the key aspects of mediation is that the parties remain in control of the solution to the dispute. As mediator, one might have initial thoughts about what a solution might look like. However, these thoughts have to be put to one side to allow the parties to find their own way. This was a classic case of a 'workplace' mediation switching over to 'employment' mediation. When workplace mediation is arranged there is an ongoing working relationship between the parties at the commencement of the mediation, whilst the opposite is true of employment mediation. It is possible however, as happened in this case, for a mediation to start out under the banner of workplace and then to switch to employment as it becomes apparent that there is likely to be a cessation of the employment relationship. This is one of the reasons why it is critical that mediators are appropriately trained to be able to handle any scenario.

The day with Hilda and Sarah took a number of twists and turns as it unfolded before ending with the final solution. The aspect that remained most memorable for me was the revelation about Sarah's miscarriage. By any level of measure, this was a shock. Somehow, the mediation process had made such an impact on Sarah that it had prompted her to talk not just about her issues at work but also her private and personal hurt. The fact that she had indicated a correlation between the dispute and the miscarriage was eye opening, and this part of the discussion instantly took the mediation to a much deeper level. The impact was not on Sarah alone, but also on her husband who had accompanied her.

Here is a second observation. One of the predictions I make about how the world of industrial and employee relations is likely to have impact in the 21st century is the age divide. In many organisations, ambitious 30 and 40 somethings are getting their hands on the levers of power and they like it. Along with shorter tenure, the average age of a CEO has steadily got lower over the past two decades. 15 years ago, the average age of a FSE 100 Chief Executive was 55. Now it is 52. In 1996 there were six FTSE 100 Chief Executives aged 45 or under. In 2008 there were 13 In this case, Hilda felt buffeted by her new ruthless 27 year old manager who wanted to come in, shake things up, make a difference and build her career.

Today's organisational leaders are faced with the challenge of managing four generations, the range of which is growing all the time. For example, organisations may face an influx of 18/19 year olds who opt out of attending university for fear of the size of the debt they might leave with whilst at the other end of the spectrum, lifting the default retirement age may mean for some that the term 'work until you drop' unfortunately becomes a reality.

The age ranges
The four generations are usually referred to as:
- Matures (born 1925 – 1945)
- Baby boomers (born1946 – 1964)
- Generation X (born 1965 – 1979)
- Generation Y/ Millennials (born 1980 – 1995)

Each group is, of course, different and generally favour diverse ways of approaching the world of work. The rapid acceleration of advances in computers and other technologies has widened the generational knowledge gap. A big change is taking place between the traditional workplace which might be recognised by the first two age generations and the new generation workplace, which might be recognised by the second two categories.

Traditional workplace
- Security from the institution
- Promotions based on longevity
- Loyalty to the organisation
- Wait to be told what to do
- Respect based on position/title

New generation workplace
- Security from within
- Promotions based on performance
- Loyalty to the team
- Challenge authority
- You must earn respect

Younger workers may prefer to receive instant messages rather than attend a company mandated workshop and share their own insights via blogs, wikis, or podcasts rather than talking to others through a procedure they've developed. Matures and baby boomers may prefer to learn via formal classroom instruction and printed texts. They may also tend to be more verbal than visually orientated communicators, choosing face to face or telephone conversation over email.

Those in the generation X category may show much more flexibility in their approach, but may prefer action-orientated learning that focuses on solving real problems.

As the first generation to grow up alongside the development of computers, their learning and work style can at times be more visual than verbal. This generation grew up during the 1980s at a time when the world was much more economically stable. Working with change became a key mantra for this group as organisations profited from emerging markets. Loyalty to oneself emerged and many in this category became used to recognising the inherent value in themselves and would be willing to move jobs in order to achieve personal objectives and goals.

Unlike their parents and grandparents, generation X employees do not plan on staying with one job or company throughout their career - nor will they sacrifice their family for their job. They grew up seeing their parents being made redundant. Many of them have grown up as children who have witnessed the effect of divorce. Therefore time for their family is very important to them. Generation X employees want, and expect, their employers to hear what they have to say. They want to understand the big picture for the company and how this influences their employment and growth. They can be creative thinkers, independent, results oriented and bring with them a healthy dose of scepticism.

The generation Y's/millennials were born into the computer age, where learning is a team process and occurs through a network and through connections. They prefer to do things their own way rather than be told how. This last point can lead to difficulties in itself. There are many disputes that are triggered by what those in the mature or baby boomer category might call 'a lack of respect'. There can be a clash of values, where those who are older may have been brought up to show respect to those who are older than them or have authority. If the same values aren't held or shown by generation Y employees, interactions with someone from the baby boomer category may cause tensions.

The challenge is for any organisation with a spread of employees from all four categories is to be flexible enough to adapt opportunities for learning, communication and career development for all.

Women and computers

"'We' and 'they' no longer exist. This planet is just us. The destruction of one area is the destruction of yourself. That is the new reality." – The Dalai Lama

Redmarley Ltd is a company that specialises in providing business services to the security industry. In general, they maintain properties, carry out mechanical and electrical installations and take care of overall infrastructure, employing about 1,000 people. Sarah Richards was employed by Redmarley as an IT Manager for three years in a department of ten.

Sarah's main area of focus was software support. Her main duties consisted of providing business support within Redmarley's bespoke software package by engaging users, identifying current and future requirements and assisting coordination across departments, including identifying areas for improvement, efficiency and training delivery. Two years after Sarah's appointment, Redmarley got involved in a joint venture with Baker Knowles. A few months after the joint venture, Baker Knowles requested that they take ownership of the entire IT process. This meant that following a strategic review the combined headcount of IT staff would reduce from 21 to 20. Sarah was put into a pool with other colleagues who were at risk of redundancy and, following a period of consultation, she was indeed made redundant. She appealed, but the appeal was turned down. She decided to take her former employer to an Employment Tribunal for unfair dismissal and sexual discrimination, believing that, as the only woman in the team, she had been unfairly selected for redundancy.

A three day tribunal was scheduled to commence in four weeks time. Redmarley proposed that mediation take place prior to the tribunal, an idea Sarah rejected at first but later agreed to. I was asked to be the mediator.

I was able to have a telephone discussion with both sides before the day of the mediation and knew that Redmarley would be represented by their HR Manager, Managing Director and legal representative. Sarah indicated that she would be coming alone, despite my advice for her to be accompanied by a legal or non-legal associate. Sarah said that if she needed advice there was someone she could call.

The mediation

On the day of the mediation I travelled to the location by train, a journey that took just under an hour and a half. The offices were located in a semi-rural area with no taxi rank at the train station, meaning that I had to use the station phone to call for a taxi. While I was waiting, the lawyer representing Redmarley, Elaine, also arrived at the train station and, after my explanation of the taxi situation, suggested that we share the taxi I had booked. A few moments later it arrived and we both got in. We arrived at the venue about five minutes later, as did Sarah, the HR Manager (Janet) and my assistant, Susan. We all greeted each other in the car park and then went inside.

Janet was kind enough to show us the three rooms that had been allocated for us. I settled in and began the process of having a private discussion with both sides to outline what was likely to happen throughout the day, starting with Sarah. Sarah said that although she had an open mind in relation to the mediation session she wanted to hear what the organisation's approach would be towards the day before she said much about her position. Her frame of mind was that she had spent much of her life over the previous year preparing for an Employment Tribunal. Now it was just around the corner she was looking forward to having her day in court if a decent financial settlement wasn't reached during the mediation session. She didn't seem to be as talkative as she had been on the phone a few days earlier.

Whilst I was with Sarah, I noticed some muffled discussions taking place in the room next door. Janet had allocated three rooms next to each other which wouldn't have been a problem if the walls hadn't been so thin that we could hear the voices of Sarah's former colleagues from Redmarley. I thanked Sarah when she had finished and, upon leaving, had a quiet word with Susan, who confirmed that she could hear the voices too and was equally concerned about the potential breach of confidentiality.

I had to try and do something to fix the flaw, so went through to see Janet and her colleagues to explain the predicament that had developed. Janet said that although the offices were sizeable most of the meeting rooms were in use, but popped outside anyway to check whether there were any alternative arrangements that could be made. I accompanied her and spotted a small unused office opposite. I enquired about its suitability and, as I did so, Janet seemed to have a mild panic attack. Before I could open the door and peer into the office, she explained that the office belonged to a certain person. She said his name. I can't divulge his identity for obvious reasons, but it's safe to say that he is a well-known public figure whose name would be known to most people. Janet explained that the person was a Director of the company who was usually in once or twice a week. She opened the door to show me the office space and the pictures inside proved it. I thought it was hilarious, but Janet was still in a state of shock and didn't seem to share my amusement. She talked of her fear that the user of the office might come in unannounced. I asked her to calm down and asked if she would be willing to find out whether it might be possible to use the room because of the sound proofing difficulties. She went to check with the office user's PA. Five minutes later she returned saying that it was fine to use the room as long as we left it as we found it. By now, thankfully, she was beginning to see the funny side. I rejoined Sarah and briefed her on what had been happening for the last half an hour, asking if she would be willing to change rooms. She said that would be no problem.

The room exchange sorted, I went into see Redmarley about their approach to the day. Elaine began to talk me through the company's position which was, in general, that they believed they could prove that they had undertaken a thorough and robust process that had led to Sarah being identified as the person that should have been selected for redundancy. Elaine explained in detail the process that had been followed.

She outlined the following:
1. They had written to the claimant advising that her role was at risk of redundancy. The claimant was invited to attend a consultation meeting a few days after the letter was sent. The claimant was reminded of her right to have a representative present.

2. The company met with the claimant for an individual consultation meeting. The meeting was chaired by the HR Manager, Janet. The claimant chose not to be accompanied. The company explained the reasons and rationale for the redundancy to the claimant. The claimant had a full opportunity to put forward any matters which she believed would mitigate the redundancy. The claimant compared herself to a number of other employees in the department and said that her specialist skills and knowledge in software development would be needed on an ongoing basis.

3. The company wrote to the claimant advising her of the consultation process and terms of alternative employment roles available.

4. The company met the claimant for a second individual consultation meeting. The claimant chose not to be represented. The claimant was reminded of the alternative employment roles available and asked to indicate if she wished to be considered. The claimant raised nothing material to alter the impending redundancy situation.

5. A few weeks later the company wrote to the claimant confirming the content of the second individual consultation meeting and reminding the claimant that she had one week to indicate if she wished to be considered for the alternative employment roles available.

6. The claimant advised the company in the appropriate timescale that she did not wish to be considered for the alternative employment roles.

7. The company then wrote to the claimant inviting her to attend a third individual consultation meeting. The claimant was reminded of her right to have a representative present.

8. The claimant then attended a third individual consultation meeting. The claimant chose not to be accompanied. Janet chaired the meeting. The company confirmed the claimant's dismissal by reason of redundancy. The claimant then raised submissions relating to other IT positions. The claimant believed she should have been pooled with other positions. The company said that other roles in IT were very different to the claimant's. It was the claimant's role that was redundant. The claimant submitted that her role also consisted of IT training, which was one of the alternative employment roles that the claimant had declined to express an interest in.

9. The company confirmed the claimant was dismissed by reason of redundancy. The claimant was paid one month's notice in lieu.

10. The claimant wrote to the company requesting an appeal hearing. The company agreed.

11. A few weeks later the claimant attended an appeal hearing. The claimant was accompanied by a colleague. The appeal was a lengthy hearing chaired by the Managing Director. The claimant was given a full opportunity to put forward all matters relating to her dismissal. The company adjourned the meeting at various points and subsequently reconvened and confirmed the decision to uphold the dismissal.

Elaine confirmed that the company denied the accusation that the claimant had been unfairly dismissed. The claimant, she said, was dismissed for a fair reason, namely redundancy. She also added that the company also rejected the idea that the claimant was dismissed for a reason relating to her sex, stating that the company would never give anyone less favourable treatment on the grounds of their sex.

Elaine's opening gambit lasted about 15 minutes. When she had finished I asked her why throughout, she had referred to Sarah as 'the claimant' rather than by her name. Elaine said that she did not want to become too familiar with Sarah as she was representing the company so thought it better to refer to her as 'the claimant'.

Private meeting
I left Elaine and her associates and headed back to Sarah's new room. She had made herself comfortable and, having worked for the company for some time, was used to the public figure that used the office. She had even helped this particular individual with one or two computer problems in the past, she said.

I asked Sarah if she would like me to run through how the mediation process would be working again. She said that she would but, at the end of my summary, she asked me a strange question. She asked me to confirm my neutrality. I consented but wondered why she had requested this of me. I then asked if she would be willing to outline her approach for the mediation session. She started by saying that she should not have been made redundant and that the process was a sham, designed to weed her out as the only female in the IT department. I asked whether she would be willing to continue with her claim for unfair dismissal and sexual discrimination if the mediation was unsuccessful. She replied in the affirmative with such haste that I had no need to ask if she was sure about it.

Sarah's story
I invited Sarah to outline the history of her situation. She said that there were a number of people that should have been put in the selection pool for redundancy and she would be referring to them by name at the Tribunal. She continued by saying that an IT systems development project had begun two or three weeks before she started with the company – a project the then MD wanted her to be involved in the implementation and training of. A presentation was conducted before him and the project's customer, but the IT team had failed to produce what was required with regards to having the system ready. Her contributions of programming a training rollout and course content were welcomed and appreciated by the MD however and he commented so during the presentation.

The MD expressed his disappointment however with regards to the contributions from other members of the IT team.

Following the presentation, one of Sarah's colleagues said to other members of the team, including the IT Director, that Sarah had "hijacked" the meeting. According to Sarah this was an attempt to undermine her by her colleagues but was thwarted firstly because someone recorded the entire meeting without telling anyone (of which she later obtained and transcribed a copy) and secondly because the MD stepped in and set the record straight. This incident caused a huge amount of furore behind the scenes and acted as the catalyst to get her out of the organisation.

Sarah then went on to list other incidents that followed soon after she joined the company. She sent an email to her line manager detailing a series of points that she felt needed addressing, but was unsupported in terms of not having the proper tools to do her job, namely a laptop. When she eventually received the laptop she was not given the correct username or password, which rendered it no more use than a rather expensive paperweight. Everytime she rang the computer service desk she was told to try different usernames and passwords until eventually she took it in to the IT hardware team personally, asking for the assistance of the computer hardware operations manager as she knew that he wouldn't encounter the prejudices she was facing from that department. He requested for a laptop to be *'built'* for her in a particular way. What she ended up with however was her line manager's old laptop that, it transpired, the operation manager had already returned earlier that week due to it being faulty. Sarah returned the laptop and was kept waiting as the department told her that it would be ready in a few hours. When she returned at the end of the day it was still not ready. It hadn't even moved or been taken out of its bag.

Sarah also made her line manager aware that a colleague who was a crucial link for her to be able to deliver what the contract required of her did not respond to any of her voicemails or emails. She said that the tone of emails from the department also began to change, and that they were now quite abrupt. In most cases there was no opening or closing greeting. The training equipment that she had been requesting was not ready, yet it was given to her under the pretence that it was. Later, Sarah said she was told by a colleague that the exact words overheard in relation to her request were, *"She can fuck off if she thinks she's getting that."* Sarah told me that she never received a useable laptop from the department the entire time she was in the company.

Sarah also heard, via a colleague, that a manager in the IT department had been overheard making sexist remarks, namely about women having no place in the IT department. The manager was regularly overheard saying that Sarah would be better off in the secretarial or HR team. The same manager was heard to call her a *"right little bitch"* because she refused to collect a tea and coffee order for the team one day seeing as she felt she was asked to do it more than anybody else. Sarah alleged that other more sensitive comments were made about her too; she had been asked more than once what colour underpants she wore to work and whether she was on her period when she displayed anger after being let down by a colleague.

Although Sarah was giving good background to her dispute, she seemed to be referring many of her responses to my female mediator rather than me. I wasn't quite sure why this was. Nevertheless, at least she was talking. She said that she was now the focal point of the department. The project was not going as well as it should and she was becoming the scapegoat.

A new coordinator was put in place on Sarah's project, a project that everybody knew she had built up and had put enormous amounts of work into, ready for the next release. A month or so later, Sarah heard that the Operations Director gave the new coordinator a special mention at a senior management team meeting. Sarah said that this spurning of her efforts hurt her as her colleague was receiving the plaudits for her drive and hard work through such adversity.

Sarah continued to list a range of other issues to indicate how badly she had been treated and why she was not able to undertake her work to the level she wished. She believed that a case was being built up against her. The final straw came when, at a project review meeting relating to a training project that she and her colleagues had been working on, everyone who had completed the course was given a certificate apart from her. At this point, Sarah said, she now felt very unequal, demoralised and unwanted by the business, treated as if she didn't matter to them anymore. She was left questioning herself as to why she was being treated differently to the others. She could sense that something was going on and her suspicions were confirmed the following week when she was put at risk of redundancy. She said that the joint venture with Baker Knowles provided a great opportunity for the company to dress her dismissal as legitimate redundancy, but she suspected that it was no such thing. Sarah mentioned that during an appeal meeting about the redundancy the MD made a remark that confirmed to her that the whole situation was planned and that, no matter what, they wanted her out of the business; when she raised the point that not all alternatives had been disclosed and that others should have been put at risk, the MD replied by saying, *"You wouldn't have got anything anyway."* It was clear, Sarah said, that the only option open to her was to leave.

I thanked Sarah for her candidness and said that I would like to have a discussion with both sides together. As I turned to leave the room she beckoned to my assistant. I continued to make my way out of the room, but a few minutes later my assistant came and told me what Sarah had wanted. It transpired that when Sarah saw Elaine and I arrive together she assumed that we were friends and that I would be biased. It hadn't occurred to me for a moment that our joint arrival would give this perception but I could understand it as soon as I heard it. I had learnt a big lesson and will never repeat this mistake again.

The joint meeting

We all met in the joint session room and I outlined how the day was designed to work. I asked both sides to provide some background for their case and both gave a summary of the key issues as they saw them. Although Sarah had declined to bring legal representation it seemed that she had spent much time getting to know case law and had prepared how to present her argument.

The meeting was tense. Those Sarah had accused of plotting her exit were now eyeball to eyeball with her. We stayed together for about half an hour while attempting to thrash out key points. Elaine was on good form, rehearsing how she might come across during a tribunal. Sarah didn't seem flustered however.

At the end of the joint session, both sides had a good idea of what they were up against. I decided to go and spend some more private time with Sarah. She said that she would not be backing down and that she was looking forward to being able to put forward her argument to a judge in a tribunal setting. I asked Sarah to talk more about one of the cases she referred to during the joint session. As she did, it became clear that she had formed the basis for what she might receive at a tribunal on a case that a judge hadn't yet announced a ruling on. The media had been following the story but at the time of the mediation the case had not yet completed its trajectory through the legal system. I reality checked this with Sarah and invited her to think objectively about basing a quasi-legal argument on media hearsay. This seemed to make some impact but Sarah's position didn't move much initially. She was expecting a financial settlement in the region of £300,000. Her salary at the time of dismissal was £35,000.

Towards the end of this second session with Sarah, I revisited the incident in the car park. I told her the full story and said that I had learnt a big lesson from it, assuring her that I was neutral and had no allegiance to either side apart from doing my best as a mediator to encourage both sides to reach settlement. It appeared, to me anyway, that our rapport was building.

The day continued with private sessions throughout, with opportunities to get both sides back into the same room not readily presenting themselves. We also ran into difficulties given that although the Managing Director of Redmarley was present, he had limited authority to settle the matter. Despite his assurance at the start of the day that he would be able to do whatever was required to bring an end to the dispute, he later revealed that any settlement over £20,000 would need to be signed off by his board. It transpired that as a result of the joint venture, the MD could not take any significant decisions without having a discussion with colleagues who represented both Redmarley and Baker Knowles.

By late afternoon, Sarah had indicated that she would be willing to come down to a settlement of £100,000. The MD made the call to his colleagues, inviting me to join them on the call. Although the mediation was taking place in the UK, we were joined on the phone by six of the MD's colleagues who were in three different continents. It was early in the US and late in the Far East, and it puzzled me why seven senior people from all over the world were required to sort out a situation regarding one disgruntled member of the IT team. I summarised nearly eight hours of talks into 15 minutes to provide the background, conscious that the people on the phone were senior business people and likely had much more important things to do with their time. I therefore spared them the minute pieces of detail as well as the more difficult, confidential and sensitive pieces of information that had unfolded throughout the day. Our phone conversation lasted for 50 minutes, the result of which was permission for the MD to increase his financial settlement by £5,000 to £25,000 – still only a quarter of Sarah's revised target figure; a gap I feared was still too large.

It was now 6.30pm and I was conscious of time running out on us. I took the revised offer to Sarah who simply laughed and got up to leave the room and to go home, claiming that she was clearly not being taken seriously. I attempted to offer her some perspective once more but my efforts were rejected. It was evident that as things stood we would not be successful in achieving a resolution today and at 7.45pm Sarah said that she could not devote any more time to the process. She thanked my assistant and I for our efforts and said that she would be continuing to prepare for tribunal. I asked for a few moments to see whether Redmarley were planning any last minute offers, but, upon checking, was told that they had already arrived at any final figure that they would be putting on the table. We concluded the day and I thanked both sides for their contribution. The mediation had succeeded in clarifying the key issues for all concerned, but had failed in its objective to help the parties reach final settlement.

I began to make my way home. It was late but I was hoping that the public transport schedules would allow me to get back to sleep in my own bed. I was on my train journey home and nearly dozing off when I remembered something which caused me to sit upright. I had left some notes on the flipchart in the public figure's office. I had captured Sarah's key issues throughout the day to help keep focus. Although no-one was named on the notes and there was no particularly sensitive or confidential information on there, I still broke into a cold sweat. It was late and there was no way that I could go back and get myself let in to remove the chart. I didn't sleep that night as I worried about what I could do to fix the situation. I considered going back early in the morning but wondered if I would encounter difficulty trying to gain entry so early. I decided to phone Janet first thing in the morning and explain what had happened.

At 7.30am the next day I called Janet on her mobile phone. She answered and I explained the situation. She calmed my fears, saying that she would go straight to the office and remove and dispose of the flip charts. At 8.35am she called me back telling me that her assignment had been successful. I breathed a huge sigh of relief and noted my near mishap. Two in one day.

The second mediation session

Two days later I received a call from someone called David. He said that he was the HR Director for the corporate parent of both Redmarley and Baker Knowles. He said he had been briefed by Janet on what had happened during the mediation two days before and asked if a second mediation session could be arranged, adding that he was aware that the MD's authority to settle may have prevented conclusion being reached on the day. He said that the parent company had given him authority to do what was required to reach a pragmatic solution and asked whether I would be able to ask Sarah if she would be willing to try again. I contacted Sarah and explained the situation. When she realised that David had contacted me she said that they must be serious, clearly recognising that David had sufficient clout to act. Another mediation session was scheduled for two weeks time.

On the day of the second mediation I was met by only David and Sarah – neither had brought representation. Strangely, we met at the hotel where Enoch Powell delivered his infamous *'Rivers of Blood'* speech in 1968. Within five minutes of meeting David for the first time, I knew he meant business.

The mediation got underway with a joint opening session. Sarah thanked David for getting involved and said she had attended the session with an open mind. Both rehearsed the key points of the dispute. These were:

• Whether redundancy was the real reason for Sarah's dismissal
• Whether the comments and actions of Sarah's colleagues amounted to sexual discrimination
• What financial or non-financial compensation Sarah would be looking for
• Reinstatement or reengagement
• Whether Redmarley had breached any processes at all

We spent about an hour and a half in joint discussion about the five key issues. Both had points to make and, importantly, both listened to each other. At the end of the joint session I suggested that we take a break and reconvene after about 15 minutes. 20 minutes went by. Neither David, nor Sarah reappeared. Another ten minutes passed and still no sign of either. I had no idea what was going on. I looked out of the window and into the pedestrianised area which was bustling with shoppers. Amidst the shoppers I spotted David and Sarah standing by a lamppost talking. David was smoking. I was horrified – not that he was smoking, but that they were talking together. I hadn't planned this part of the mediation process. I was just about to run outside to join them when I stopped myself. It struck me that the fact that they were engaged in dialogue was a good thing – my issue was that I hadn't arranged for the mediation to move along in this way. But this was an issue for me, not the parties. Another 20 minutes or so passed before both came back, whereupon I asked if they had a good meeting. They laughed and said that they had. At that moment, I knew that the likelihood of achieving settlement would be enhanced.

The mediation continued and moved to private sessions. The focus of the discussion had moved from who was right or wrong to achieving a pragmatic settlement that was acceptable for both parties. Eventually at around 4.00pm, settlement was reached which consisted of five parts:

- The company agreed to pay a financial settlement to Sarah
- An agreed reference was drafted
- David agreed to make contact with another company that were looking to recruit a person with Sarah's skills
- Redmarley would undertake training on equality and diversity management
- Sarah would be given the opportunity to talk to some of her former colleagues about how she felt as a result of their treatment

Two months after the mediation, Sarah called me to say that she had secured another job following the lead from David at the mediation. She had also received a verbal apology from the former colleagues who had contributed towards her experiences.

Observations

There are three points I will refer to in reflecting on this case.

i. Authority to settle

It is always important to have the right person in the room that has the authority to settle disputes. Mediators who are trained by reputable providers will be told about the importance of establishing who the person with the authority to settle is early on during the mediation process. David brought weight, gravitas, emphasis and focus to this case. The MD of Redmarley had indicated that he had the necessary power and influence to bring a satisfactory resolution to the dispute, but soon realised that what he had in his mind as a satisfactory settlement was some way off from Sarah's figure. A mediator can only take someone at their word if they say that they have authority to settle. Asking too many questions or asking for clarification in an inappropriate way could cause considerable harm and embarrassment. The good thing about this case was that when it was established that Sarah's expectations were significantly out of line with Redmarley's, David got involved.

The person with authority to settle can vary. Sometimes the power might rest in the hands of the parties themselves and on other occasions someone else might need to be identified. It is possible that an organisation's structure might prevent disputes being settled in a pragmatic, amicable and timely way. This can be because real decision making power is centralised, meaning that even very senior managers are required to refer up. I have found this to be the case across a range of sectors, in particular the education sector. In universities for example, Heads of Department can have a huge span of control but can have limited authority to sign off levels of relatively low expenditure. For the mediation process to work well it is the person with authority to settle who really makes things happen and makes the mediation process work.

ii. The mediator and continual learning

The second aspect of my reflection relates to my own learning. The taxi incident brought unnecessary embarrassment and a hurdle which had to be overcome later in the mediation process. I had not envisaged for a moment that sharing a taxi with Elaine would lead to difficulties. It confirms that the mediators' role of neutrality and impartiality is a privileged one but one that is precarious and can be broken and damaged in a moment.

In a dispute, parties look for help from someone who they believe will hear what they have to say and will be non-judgemental when they do. One of the main strengths of mediation is that of the neutrality of the mediator. In most other forms of alternative dispute resolution, methods such as arbitration, a person will take sides based on what they hear and form a judgement based on who is right or wrong or who has the stronger argument. The way in which a mediator leaves the parties to decide how they want to settle their dispute and refrains from becoming involved in taking sides, is a major contribution to its ongoing high success rate. My neutrality was questioned right at the start of the mediation process and it took a good few hours for it to be re-established. Thankfully it was, and progress could continue to be made.

A second personal learning point related to the second mediation session when David and Sarah were talking in the street. Although mediation has high levels of flexibility, mediators like to feel in control of the process. My first reaction after the shock of seeing David and Sarah talking was to hurry to the street and get involved in what was happening. It took a few moments for me to realise that I could 'let go' of the situation. One of the objectives of mediation is to get parties to talk. David and Sarah were doing just that, albeit not in the way I had envisaged. No single mediation session follows the same path. As mediators grow in experience they learn to follow their instinct and intuition. A phrase I often use when training new mediators is that outside the circle of the non-negotiable aspects, anything goes (the non-negotiable aspects are confidentiality, mediator neutrality and the ability to have non-binding discussions). The likelihood is that if ten mediators had been involved in mediating this dispute, ten different ways would have unfolded to help the parties arrive at an amicable solution.

iii. Mediation is more than trying to establish who is right or wrong

The third learning point is that as a reader of Sarah's story you may have experienced smoke coming out of your ears as you learned of her experiences. There are some who would find practicing as a mediator difficult. This is because mediators are taught to be un-shockable and deadpan even after hearing the most awful and frightful of stories. The traditional way of dealing with a case such as Sarah's would have been to allow the history to be played out in a tribunal setting. This would have allowed both sides to present their argument about what happened and establish the right and wrong.

In legal settings, although it may be possible to address past wrongs, the ability to apply a satisfactory remedy can be more limited. For example, if Sarah won her tribunal case, her victory may have become short lived because:

- Her health may have suffered as she prepared to take her case to tribunal
- Her reputation may have been damaged as the media brought attention to her case
- Her ability to secure another role in IT may have disappeared
- She may have attracted legal costs if she decided to seek representation at the last minute

In effect, resorting to a tribunal would have led to a *'lose-lose'* scenario.

It may always seem as if the best way to deal with situations like Sarah's is to make the individual or organisation pay for the damage that they have done. In the legal process, very few disputes can be identified with issues of right and wrong in such a clear cut way. The application of remedy may also be difficult and rigid.

In the discussion with David, he acknowledged that there had been shortcomings in how Redmarley had handled Sarah's employment. The strength of the mediation process lay in the fact that human to human interaction took place, allowing the expression and venting of emotion.

This is not to confuse the word emotion with something deemed to be soft and fluffy. It is difficult to think of another process that would have led to such pragmatic and sensible solutions being achieved such as:

- Agreeing a satisfactory reference
- Helping Sarah to find another employer
- Agreeing to provide training on equality and diversity issues
- Providing Sarah with the opportunity to talk to her opponents and perpetrators

Mediation may not be suitable for every case, but in those cases where parties decide to use it there is a high likelihood of achieving settlement, closure, justice and forgiveness as part of one process. Sarah was able to move on with her life and learn from her experiences whilst Redmarley were also able to recognise where issues could be handled differently in the future.

Chapter 4
Stories that cut deep

"Almost all conflict is a result of violated expectations." – Blaine Lee

As we have already seen, depth of feeling and emotion are huge driving forces behind an individual's actions, be it consciously or subconsciously. Sometimes as mediators we have to dig a little to uncover these core stories, but as the story of Brian in the last section illustrated vividly, occasionally conflict stories can bring out the most unexpected and unplanned revelations, to the surprise of all concerned. These can sometimes be an unwanted distraction but usually they move the resolution on much quicker than hours of toing and froing. In situations such as these we can say that the narrative is driving itself rather than the mediator pushing the agenda, which is something every mediator wants. Rarely do individuals head into mediation sessions desperate to get a huge secret off their chests, but sometimes the nail is hit on the head so cleanly that the dam simply breaks and they can do nothing else but let the river flow. This is more often the case with initially reserved or shy individuals than those who are open and forthcoming from the start. Sensing who has something to hide and who doesn't is a skill that only comes with practice.

These types of stories are core stories of a sort, but differ from the ones we have previously discussed as they aren't necessarily the driving force behind an individual's treatment of others but rather are present on the other side of the fence – affecting those who feel aggrieved. For example, if an employee who used to be bullied at school for being overweight starts to receive the same treatment at work it is very likely that all those feelings from the school playground will resurface, despite a gap of 20 or 30 years or more. This person's past doesn't influence the way in which they treat colleagues, but it does have an impact in the way they react. The aggressor probably has no idea about their target's background, a background that may only finally come out at a mediation session with all the emotion that involves. Of course the whole thing may have been the result of a misunderstanding or a backfiring prank, but, like many issues that end in court cases or mediation, it could have been avoided if it had been dealt with at the very start rather than being left to worsen over time.

Using this example, it is easy to see how, during a mediation session, a couple of simple questions on the issue can elicit a surprisingly emotional response. We have seen in past examples that these outbursts, if conducted in the presence of the perceived aggressor, can have one of two outcomes – either the aggressor realises the enormity of their actions and vows to make amends or the individual involved loses control of their emotions and therefore also the opportunity to get their point across, running the risk of weakening their position in the negotiation.

But what if two opposing factions find, through their stories, some common ground? The chances are that two people, say an employee and their line manager, who have been at loggerheads since day one won't have taken the time to learn about the others' interests, pastimes and background.

Instead they have spent their days adding layer upon layer of negative association onto that person, usually based on tiny, trifling matters, until they have a demonised caricature of that individual cemented in their mind which as we saw with the story of Sarah and Hilda, can be very far from the truth. It is therefore highly unlikely that any shared interests will be discovered before the mediation session.

Shared interests however can act as a very useful springboard to help overcome complete breakdown. They are not easy to achieve and, as the example in the following selection of stories attests, it may take something so traumatic as a death in the family to, if not unite two people, then certainly break down initial barriers. Again this can sometimes require some digging for core stories, but on occasion the protagonists lead themselves down these paths of their own volition, at which point the mediator can subtly utilise any newfound connection to bring the two parties a little closer to negotiation.

Occasionally an individual with a painful past, such as the bullying victim highlighted earlier, will not only find themselves in a position where their painful experiences are relived anew but will encounter huge resistance from their superiors when trying to combat it. The example given in this book is the church and the attitude of some of its members towards women. This is an institutionalised battle that has been going on for no short time, and is especially relevant in today's climate of equality and fairness. Despite legislation such as the Equality Act coming into force, it seems that it is getting no easier for female clerics to make headway in their careers.

In these instances, a mediator may find, as was outlined in the previous section, that certain individuals hold prejudicial views about a person or group of people that are hard-wired into them – in this case the older generation of church members who are resolutely against female clerics. Some in other industries will have what they consider to be solid reasons for their prejudices based on experiences, whilst others, particularly in the church, may feel that they have strict rules in place (i.e. the Bible) that prevent them from even countenancing the idea of apologising for their views and are determined to stick with their decisions and actions no matter what. Many of these individuals, through refusing to communicate with and educate themselves about those that fall under this umbrella, will see and treat them all as one and refuse to acknowledge that their actions may have much more of a significant impact on some individuals than others. For example, a female employee who has suffered either physically or psychologically at the hands of a male family member or partner may have a stronger reaction to male criticism and intimidation than someone who hasn't. The aggressor in this case will have no knowledge of these events, having refused to offer her equal billing in the establishment, which starts a spiral of decline that will only lead to negative outcomes. One occasionally encounters people like this, but we must remind ourselves that it is not the job of the mediator to try and educate or change this person's way of thinking (although of course this would be a great result), but to sow the seeds of change by trying to make them see the impact their actions had on the individual in question – to attempt to swap positions and see things from the other's point of view. This is of course a necessary step in the road towards a resolution, but it can also be a life changing experience for that individual when the session is over. For every one that has an epiphany however, another will just agree terms and move on with their views unaltered. This can of course be hard to take, but, as we have already discussed, it is not up to the mediator to play the psychologist. We are not qualified, or suited, to effecting personality changes.

It is not just the aggressor whose stubborn streak can cause problems for a mediator. An individual with a grievance can sometimes find that the entire chain of command in their workplace is against them and they may then feel powerless to do anything to stop what they see as unfair treatment. Often in these situations the individual may request a severance package as part of any mediation settlement, citing the fact that they can't work in such an environment, but for various reasons they can sometimes stand and fight, if not to try and regain their post then to make the public aware of this obviously deeply felt issue.

Weeks, months and possibly years worth of being confronted by brick walls, especially concerning issues that stem from past incidents, may have built up so many layers of defiance that the actual core of the conflict has grown out of all proportion and now reflects only a small percentage of a much bigger fight. This can undermine the efforts of a mediator to come to a settlement, knowing as this happens, possibly by admission or suspicion, an individual will be pursuing further retribution once the mediation has been completed. In these instances the opposing party feels no need to come to an agreement as they know that any settlement won't represent the end of proceedings and will just be a concession of ground before the next battle. Again, as we will see, all we as mediators can do in these situations is perform our function as best we can and try to convince the individual that further action will only prolong what may already have been an incredibly trying time and ask them to include all their demands in the mediation agreement. Sometimes this works and sometimes it doesn't, but it's important to recognise that we can only usually influence events on the day and not for the future.

The following three stories are also good examples of the variety of ways in which storytelling can feature in mediation. In one case storytelling from two opposing parties led to the discovery of common ground and therefore the creation of a new, more harmonious story for the pair of them; in a second the mediation was undermined by the determination of one party to pursue action against the other regardless of the outcome; and in the third a startling admission altered the course of one story and allowed both parties to find a positive way forward. In two of the three situations, the discovery and utilisation of elements of the individuals' core stories helped to forge new paths for the two parties, whilst in the third case the core story was, for one individual, so strong and unshakeable that nothing could sway her from her path of retribution. Two key elements that each party in a mediation session must accept are the willingness to negotiate and the willingness to draw a line. Any further conflict renders the mediation pointless, but as you are about to see, some issues cut so deep that resolution is more of a dream than an ambition.

I hate you

"In the end, all you have is your reputation." – Oprah Winfrey

Some years ago I was asked to mediate a dispute between an employee of Chepnet Council and an elected Council member. The mediation was commissioned by the Head of Legal Services. She and her team had spent many hours working on the case and were somewhat exasperated by the time the call came through to me. In preparation for the case I was given permission to speak with both parties and was provided with some written background information. As with all the stories in this book, names, locations and other similar information have been changed to preserve anonymity and confidentiality.

Problems within the Council had begun when funding was withdrawn from the Indian Leadership Council (ILC), although members made a decision that non-financial support should continue to be given to the organisation. This involved a manager being placed at the centre, selected and managed by officers in the Corporate Voluntary Sector Team (CVST). A secondment of a permanent employee from the Corporate Policy Unit to the ILC was made and members were informed of this action.

The seconded officer at the ILC had been in the post for a year and had been managed by the Grants Programme Manager, Pauline Holt, in line with a work plan which had been agreed by the Management Committee of the ILC. Because of the volatile nature of the relationship with the Council and the ILC the progress of the ILC had been reported on a regular basis to the lead member, Councillor (Cllr) Bailey, whose portfolio included the voluntary and community sectors. Cllr Bailey and Pauline are both of Indian descent.

As the decision by members to select and manage the worker at the ILC was left to the discretion of officers in the first instance, logic would dictate that any subsequent decisions regarding any personnel matters would follow the same principle and therefore be at the discretion of officers. As the officer tasked with the responsibility of managing the Centre Manager, it was the Grants Programme Manager's duty to give advice and recommendations based on reasoned opinion gathered through performance appraisal with the Centre Manager. This included determining if the Centre Manager was fit for purpose to deliver support to the organisation according to his work plan and his ability to carry out his duties as a Council Officer working within a community based setting.

Pauline discussed some concerns raised by the manager of the ILC through performance appraisals and an informed judgment was made to withdraw the present manager of the centre and another manager would be selected to take his place. This decision was reported to and discussed with the centre manager, the chair of the ILC and the lead member. A decision was then made by the lead member to call a meeting and inform the elected members that had been nominated on to the ILC committee of this decision. These members are Cllrs Smith and Timpson.

Complaint

A meeting was called to update members on the situation regarding the Centre Manager. In attendance were Cllrs Smith, Bailey and Timpson, Barbara Bryson (vice chair of the ILC), Mr Benson (chair of the ILC), Pauline Holt, Ashton Carr (interim Head of Business Strategy) and three managers from other departments.

Ashton opened the meeting by saying that he thought everyone knew each other, to which Cllr Bailey retorted quite sharply that, *"everyone here knows each other, they just don't know you."* This embarrassed Ashton. He began to cover the background and current situation, explaining why officers had made the decision to withdraw the current centre manager. Cllr Bailey became quite hostile and made comments along the lines of, *"this meeting is null and void as there is no minute taker. If you (pointing to Pauline Holt) had briefed your line manager (indicating to Ashton) he would have known how to conduct these meetings. I want the leader of the Council to be present to explain this decision."* Ashton explained that no minute taker was necessary as the purpose of the meeting was to inform councillors about the officer decision, adding that in any case Pauline was taking notes. Cllr Bailey informed Pauline that he did not trust her to take notes because she would simply write to reflect her own views and not what was actually said at the meeting. He also told the other attendees that any decision that officers made in respect to the ILC would be overridden by him and that if he'd had anything to do with it the Centre Manager would not have been withdrawn in the first place. He then asked that the meeting be closed and reconvene only when Cllr Ryan could attend. He then asked who the line director was for Pauline and Ashton. When Ashton informed him who it was, Cllr Bailey responded, *"Oh God."* Pauline and others assumed that he meant this in a derogatory way as Cllr Bailey rolled his eyes toward the ceiling while he spoke.

Pauline later described Cllr Bailey's behaviour as thoroughly inappropriate and frightening. She said that it was impossible to fully convey his actions on paper, commenting that his shouting, the vitriolic tone of his voice and his gesticulations showed a total lack of respect for the Council and its relationship with the voluntary sector. Pauline wanted it noted for the record that she found the councillor's 'personal attack' towards her and her colleague Ashton to be:

- Offensive
- Abusive
- Intimidating
- Undermining

Furthermore, she was shocked and appalled that his attack was in the presence of other councillors and members of the public (ILC).

An internal investigation, headed by a senior director of the authority, into what happened followed some months afterwards, during which Pauline spoke about the incident with a great deal of emotion and was clearly still upset about the situation.

She felt that Cllr Bailey, through his accusation that she was an untrustworthy minute taker, appeared intimidating and undermined her professionalism. She also felt that the meeting deteriorated further with Cllr Bailey's continued aggression.

In his investigative meeting, Cllr Bailey said that he believed that the meeting itself was misconceived and ill informed. He felt that decisions were being taken without the involvement of the ILC. He explained that he recognised that his tone and aggressive style of speech might be perceived as intimidating, but that was the way he was and people should understand he wasn't being intentionally aggressive or intimidating towards them. He felt that more senior or accountable staff should have been present to inform the ILC of the Council's actions. He also stated that he felt this was a personal attack as there were other councillors and representatives of THE ILC present who had not been named in the complaint. He believed these representatives and councillors had similar views to his about the reason for the meeting and the way it had been conducted. He added further fuel to his concerns of a personal complaint by stating that a number of comments attributed to him in fact were stated by others, and that he needed to consult his solicitor for advice on how he might proceed.

The investigator concluded that:
1. The meeting itself was obviously difficult and contentious. Council officers were giving important and controversial information to the ILC representatives, who were clearly unhappy about what they were being told. Emotions were obviously running high, particularly on the ILC side

2. Cllr Bailey's behaviour and tone of voice can appear aggressive and intimidating whether intentional or not

3. Putting issues one and two together, combined with the presence of an officer who lacks experience of working and dealing with Cllr Bailey on a regular basis, could lead to the perception that Cllr Bailey was abusive, offensive and intimidating

4. The complaint could be resolved by a clearing of the air meeting between both parties without the need for any further action

The investigator recommended that:

1. Both parties accept the conclusions of the investigation reached in the report.
2. The Cllr meet with Pauline to formally recognise his behaviour towards her was unacceptable. This would allow the following:

- Pauline Holt could tell Cllr Bailey how his actions made her feel
- It would give Cllr Bailey an opportunity to share his concerns about how he felt at the meeting with Pauline

The Head of Legal presumed as there were no further complaints in the weeks following the investigation that there was hope for reconciliation. Her hope was short lived however when her secretary brought the following letter to her attention.

Letter from Lewis Solicitors to the Chief Executive, Chepnet Council

Dear Sirs

Re: Councillor Stephen Bailey

We have been instructed by Cllr Stephen Bailey in regards to alleged defamatory allegations made by a council member, Pauline Holt, following a meeting of the Indian Leadership Council ("ILC") committee.

We are informed by our client that following a meeting of the ILC a complaint was made against him by Ms Holt. We understand that her complaint referred to our client's alleged behaviour in the meeting, which she openly stated was aggressive and threatening. The unfounded allegations of Ms Holt were then disclosed to members of the council and other professionals who work closely alongside our client.

Although an internal investigation was carried out by the Council, due to the flawed and inconclusive findings of the investigator the allegations of Ms Holt have continued to seriously harm our client's professional reputation.

The internal investigation was flawed due to the following:-

1. *The remit of the report was not clearly set out and it was not made clear to our client how the investigation would be carried out.*
2. *The investigation was not carried out in accordance with the Council's internal investigation procedures.*
3. *Only four of the ten people present at the meeting were interviewed as part of the investigation. The Council failed to interview key witnesses, who would no doubt have confirmed that Ms Holt's allegations were without foundation. It is clear that by failing to interview key witnesses the Council was unable to obtain an objective view of the meeting.*
4. *The internal investigation was fragmented. The selective interviewing of witnesses led to a number of damaging rumours about our client's professional reputation.*
5. *The officer conducting the investigation knew our client on a professional level. The report of the investigating officer made a number of unacceptable personal references to our client.*
6. *An inconclusive investigation report was published and disclosed to a number of members of the Council, leading to further rumours about our client's professional reputation.*
7. *The report of the investigating officer failed to give any firm conclusions, or confirm that the allegations made against our client were unfounded.*
8. *Conclusive findings of the internal investigation were not reported to the other Council members present at the meeting, leading to further questions about our client's professional conduct.*

We have advised our client that, in our opinion, the allegations and statements made by Ms Holt were defamatory and are highly damaging to his professional reputation. The allegations of Ms Holt therefore give rise to grounds for a claim of defamation. The flawed investigation by the Council has merely added weight to Ms Holt's defamatory accusations, as opposed to confirming to all members of the Council that they were without foundation.

We are now instructed to carry out further investigations and obtain witness evidence, following which time we will be advising our client in relation to a claim for defamation against both Ms Holt and Chepnet Council.

We now require your written confirmation that the following actions will be taken:

1. *Provide our client with a full written apology from both Chepnet Council and Ms Pauline Holt.*
2. *Remove the previous investigation report from all of our client's records and*

advise all members of the Council that the report has been removed.

3. Carry out a full independent investigation. This investigation should be carried out by a different and independent Council. A remit for the investigation should be provided to our client. He should also be provided with the opportunity to respond to the findings of the further investigation.

4. All members of the Council present at the initial meeting should be interviewed and statements taken.

5. Correspondence should be sent immediately to all those who have been made aware of the investigation. This correspondence should confirm the initial investigation was flawed and a further investigation is to be carried out.

6. If, as we have no doubt, the further investigation confirms that the allegations of Ms Holt had no foundation, disciplinary action should be taken against her.

7. All members of the Council should be notified of the outcome of the new investigation.

Please note that unless we must receive a full and detailed response to this letter by 4.00pm on 26th November we will seek further instructions to issue County Court proceedings without further recourse to either Ms Holt or the Council.

Yours faithfully
Lewis Solicitors.

Mediation agreed

The Council subsequently funded Ms Holt to take legal advice in a similar letter that was sent from Cllr Bailey to her directly. However, one month after the exchange of these letters both parties agreed to mediation. In addition to myself, Pauline Holt, Cllr Bailey and Gary Jones, Head of HR, attended the mediation.

In my private meetings with the parties prior to the joint opening session, I got a glimpse of what the day was likely to involve. When I met Cllr Bailey his first words to me were, "Where did they find you then?" Being used to hearing all kinds of similar remarks I remained deadpan and continued with the business of the day. I asked the Councillor how he would be approaching the mediation. He said that there were two things that he wanted. These were:

1. An apology from Pauline Holt
2. All the records relating to the investigation and any subsequent papers in relation to the alleged incident to be disposed of

We spoke for nearly an hour. Having not been put off or swayed by the Councillor's opening remarks seemed to gain me some credibility with him. As I prepared to leave the room he called me back and said that this case would not do well for his political ambitions. He asked me to keep the matter of his political aspirations confidential, but indicated that he would want to run for parliament in the near future. History had taught him that the route to Parliament was bumpy enough without the added component of encountering public conflict with colleagues who were also voters.

I went to see Pauline Holt next. She was a little more welcoming, informing me that she had breathed a sigh of relief when she had heard that the Council had appointed an external mediator. She was nonchalant about what had happened, saying that the Councillor had been aggressive for years and that no one had ever done anything about it. The episode had shaken her she said, but she was determined to do something about him, being as she was in her mid-fifties with only five years to go until retirement and therefore with nothing to lose against a man she said that she hated. She added that it wasn't just for herself that she was fighting but also her colleagues who had suffered in silence for so many years.

When I asked her what she wanted from the day, she replied that she wanted Cllr Bailey to:

1. Recognise the impact his behaviour had had upon her and her colleagues in public and how it disempowered her
2. Issue a written apology for the situation that had arisen and to ensure he did not treat her in a similar way in future
3. To agree to attend anger management training
4. To withdraw the legal action for defamation that he had commenced against her

I thanked her and asked if there was anything else she would like to say, to which she replied by stating that she was considering reporting the Councillor to the Standards Board if she didn't get what she wanted. The Standards Board being the body with the power to investigate elected councillors and, if necessary, suspend or terminate their election to public office. Pauline wanted me to keep this information confidential, to which I agreed.

My next visit was to the Head of HR, Gary Jones, who struck me as a pragmatic HR professional. He said that the ongoing conflict was not good for the Council and for the small ethnic minority charity that had been affected by the falling out. Gary hoped that the mediation would lead towards a speedy solution and wished me well.

The joint opening session followed. After my opening comments all three gave their remarks about their hopes and aspirations for the day, with Cllr Bailey and Pauline holding back from sharing the confidential information that they had both shared with me. I thanked all of them for engaging and said that I would be having a series of private meetings to explore areas for settlement, informing Gary that it was likely that most of my time would be spent with the Councillor and Pauline. It was now around 10.00am.

For the next four hours I shuttled between the rooms of the Councillor and Pauline, exploring options for resolution. Things seemed to be progressing well, although there was one issue still on my mind; Pauline's plan to report the Councillor to the Standards Board if she didn't get her way. This presented a problem for me as mediator. Ethically, to reach an agreement in full knowledge that the Councillor would probably be reported to the Standards Board at the end of it presented a problem. I wasn't sure how to deal with this quandary but continued to press ahead, hoping for a way out somewhere along the line.

By 2.00pm there was an outline agreement on the table. This included the following:

• Cllr Bailey would issue a written apology to Pauline
• The Councillor would attend anger management training
• Any further legal action in relation to defamation would be stopped

Another aspect had arisen during the mediation discussions however, namely the Councillor's wish for all records about the incident to be erased. Being powerless to act on behalf of the organisation I referred this point to Gary. He declined this proposal, stating that the Council could not delete records relating to an investigation.

He assured the Councillor that the information would be kept on his file and only shared with those with the appropriate authority to access such information. The Councillor wasn't enthralled about this but recognised that the organisation had no flexibility on this matter and that his further insistence would be a deal breaker.

Joint meeting

It was time to invite Pauline and the Councillor to meet for the second time, with the purpose of ironing out the detail of the agreement and in particular a form for the apology to take. The three of us met in the room that had been assigned for me and I first thanked them both for sticking with the process. I asked Pauline to outline what a written apology would need to say to appease her. We spent the next 20 minutes or so talking this through. The discussion was moving towards being cordial when, out of the blue, the Councillor asked Pauline if agreeing upon an apology and finalising the other areas under discussion would bring the whole matter to an end. Pauline paused and thought for a few seconds before looking at the Councillor and responding that no matter what agreement they reached, she would be reporting the Councillor to the Standards Board. It was a bombshell. The Councillor then knew what I myself had feared – that any further efforts would be futile. He slammed his pen on the desk, looked at me and said, *"Well, now we know that there is no point in us being here don't we?"* I asked Pauline in front of the Councillor whether anything could be done to change her mind. She replied that there wasn't before stating, *"Councillor, I hate you,"* and adding that she was acting on behalf of all her colleagues who were too afraid to speak up in fear of bringing harm to their careers. She even went one step further and criticised the Councillor for having married a black woman, saying he had brought shame to his community by deciding to marry outside of his race. This was the first clue either of us had that Pauline felt this way; we were both shocked. Cllr Bailey said he wouldn't let this rest, called Pauline a racist and said that he would continue with his legal proceedings against her.

I tried for another half an hour or so to establish whether the two might give any ground, but it was fruitless. Reluctantly I realised it was time to inform Gary of developments. I left Pauline and the Councillor in the room while I went to ask Gary to join us. It must have been very difficult for them to be in a confined space together for the few moments that I was away. I returned with Gary and updated him on the situation. He spent the next three quarters of an hour discussing the pros and cons of not settling the dispute with his colleagues, but neither of them moved their position.

We concluded the mediation at around 5.40pm with no settlement in place. The Councillor and Pauline left without even acknowledging each other, with the Councillor's last words to me being, *"Let's see where this goes."* Gary looked at me and then put his head in his hands in despair. He stated his wish that the matter could have been resolved today to allow him and his colleagues to deal with other matters that had not been able to get their attention of late. Based on the outcome of the mediation he said that he and his senior colleagues would have to spend continued time, energy and money in dealing with this protracted and increasingly difficult case.

Observations

My memories of this case remain vivid for a number of reasons. In particular I recall feeling a strange sense of freedom and liberation as I walked away from the local authority building. It was rather bizarre. I had just spent a full day attempting to help two people resolve a dispute that was making them enemies rather than colleagues and, despite my efforts, resolution had not been forthcoming. Mediation training includes advising trainees that ownership of any dispute must always remain that of the parties. It can be a difficult notion to get to grips with. As a mediator there is a natural tendency to want warring parties to get to a place where they can settle their dispute. I had expended my best efforts to help Cllr Bailey and Pauline resolve their dispute. The day had been long and had been full of twists and turns. It had not been easy dealing with either party. The information about the Standards Board and just how to deal with it had been particularly taxing. I felt as if I had done a good day's work and hadn't short changed the parties or the organisation in any way. In fact, the day had been highly valuable for all involved. On average 85% of mediated cases lead to settlement, but it was clear to see why this case belonged in the other 15%. I even managed to feel a spring in my step as I reflected on the events of the day and made my way home. There wasn't anything further that I could have done to help them. It was the first time that I had ever experienced this type of emotion and reaction following a mediation that hadn't settled and at first found it hard to equate why I felt this way.

As adults, we all face the challenge of taking ownership for our conflicts. Ultimately this dispute belonged to Cllr Bailey and Pauline Holt. Rescuers such as mediators can be parachuted in to help where parties have failed, but ultimately the responsibility to find an agreeable outcome rests with those who are in conflict. Mediators can therefore only do as much as the parties will allow them to do. In attempting to resolve our differences we each have to:

• Recognise the part we have played in the conflict
• Accept responsibility to do something about it
• Acknowledge the feelings of our opponent
• Realise that engaging in conflict wastes a precious amount of our lives
• Be willing to give something up in order to reach settlement
• Understand that no one wins in failing to resolve conflict situations
• Be adult enough to face our enemies
• Understand that while we may face our conflicts alone, we cannot solve them alone

Cllr Bailey and Pauline were involved in a tussle that neither was willing to let go of. The cost to both was great and perhaps continues to be. The Councillor ran the risk of bringing his political ambitions to an abrupt end whilst Pauline was paying the price of devoting her remaining working years to the conflict.

In another sense, she may have thought that she was doing her long-suffering colleagues a favour and considered her stance to be some form of public duty. Carrying so much hate against another person would have also meant that negative energy and harmful toxins will have impacted Pauline's health. Research indicates that constant conflict and the harbouring of ill feeling toward another saps us of energy, drive and desire (sexual and otherwise) and other related themes that are equally or more unpleasant. Unfortunately, Pauline and the Councillor failed to take the opportunity presented to them to lay their long running dispute behind them.

United by death

"One's philosophy is not best expressed in words; it is expressed in the choices one makes. In the long run, we shape our lives and we shape ourselves. The process never ends until we die. And the choices we make are ultimately our responsibility." – Eleanor Roosevelt

Bill and Margaret worked in the finance department of a local grammar school. Officially Bill reported to Margaret but a relationship breakdown from 18 months prior meant that both were now reporting to the Bursar, resulting in a mediation session being called by the Deputy Head. The background to the dispute stemmed from the fact that Bill didn't respect Margaret; he thought her lazy, overpaid and not very good at her job. Margaret had also taken a lot of sick leave over the years.

Bill's role included collecting money from schoolchildren. They would come to his office throughout the day and hand in money for lunch, school trips and workbooks. There were multiple occasions when Bill was on holiday and expected Margaret to step in and collect any monies on his behalf. On these occasions however Margaret often turned the children away and told them to come back when Bill had returned from holiday. Parents began complaining that their children were returning home with the money.

Bill and Margaret also used to share a small office together, and one occasion Margaret returned from a period of sick leave to find that Bill had erected a solid partition to create his own office, clearly unhappy at the prospect of continuing to share an office with her. Bill also talked about how Margaret's heavy smoking led to her taking constant breaks, stating his belief that her working week was probably cut by a third as a result of her smoking.

I heard about these and other examples of discord between the pair as I met with each of them in private sessions. I also heard Bill describe how he tired of always making the tea and coffee. He said that for much of the time they had worked together he was always willing to put the kettle on and make hot drinks but that Margaret rarely reciprocated and he had begun to resent being taken for granted.

It took a while for the conversation to start flowing during the opening joint mediation sessions. Although they were both willing to talk to me in private they were reluctant to talk to each other. As the day unravelled both began to open up to me a little more, but it took a couple of hours to get to this stage.

Earlier that morning, when I had arrived at the local authority site that was hosting the mediation, I picked up an in-house magazine and began to glance through it. I found it interesting to learn about what was happening in the local community the school was part of. One of the stories that caught my eye was about a young lady called Lesley Forbes who, unfortunately, had died suddenly in her sleep the previous month. She was only 37 years old. I read the article and was saddened to learn of her premature death. It was to prove fortuitous, as you will see later.

Bill and Margaret remained frosty with each other but were showing signs that their glacial exteriors were beginning to thaw. Late in the morning I did something that I had never done during mediation before and am sure was not advised to do during my training. In the midst of a joint meeting where Bill and Margaret were still requiring some prompting to engage in continual dialogue, I got up from my chair and said to them that I was just going to check that arrangements for lunch were in place. Both of them looked at me with a startled expression. They had realised that by doing so I would be leaving them in the room together. This was, in fact, the reason behind my temporary exit – a double-check would provide me with an excuse to leave the room and encourage them to converse. I had an assistant mediator with me, and she was horrified as I asked her to accompany me to check on the lunch arrangements. I explained that I had never done what I had just done but that it felt right and I was going along with my intuition. I had calculated that the risk of any harm coming to either of them would be low. This was different to the experience I described earlier in 'Women and computers'.

I returned 15 minutes or so later. Bill and Margaret had managed to refrain from strangling each other and were instead talking about Cyprus. By coincidence, they had both taken a holiday to Cyprus in the previous year. To build on the conversation that was flowing I asked them to think about what a successful mediation session would look like. The list comprised:

- Reporting arrangements to return to normal
- Margaret to help with collecting monies from students during Bill's absence
- Bursar to conduct performance reviews by the end of the financial year
- Cash to be taken to the bank on Thursdays unless funds do not necessitate the need. If so, all finance team members will be communicated about the

change of banking day
- School to investigate the possibility of introducing an electronic payment system by the end of the calendar year

Stories of death

Although both were being cordial, we had not yet made a real breakthrough. I decided to move to private sessions to explore how each was feeling. Margaret said that she was finding the proceedings stressful. Although she welcomed the opportunity to talk to Bill, she found the intensity of the session to be gruelling. I asked Margaret if she could outline any successes from the day so far. She replied that the fact that she and Bill had been able to be left alone together in the same room was a success in itself, and then began to outline how the past three to four years had been difficult for her. Since the death of her daughter she had never really been able to get back on her feet, and believed that this may have been partly attributable to her taking so many days of sick leave. I offered my condolences. Margaret said that the pain was unimaginable and that she compensated for it by pouring all her love and emotion in the direction of her one remaining child – a son.

I asked Margaret how her daughter died. One Saturday evening, Margaret said, her 17 year old daughter went out with four friends, two girls and two boys.

One of the boys had recently passed his driving test and, on the way home that evening, misjudged the distance of an upcoming roundabout, approaching it too quickly and sending the car into a skid before it overturned. Everyone in the car survived apart from her daughter whose head was smashed against the side window leading to instant death. The others escaped with severe cuts and bruises. Margaret said that when she heard a knock at the door at 11.45pm she knew what had happened before she even got out of bed to go downstairs. She still saw the parents of her daughter's friends from time to time and would often think just how unfair it was that their children survived and her child didn't. Being a parent myself I felt a deep sense of empathy for her. I wondered for a moment how I would feel to hear similar news about my son or daughter. I couldn't dwell on it for long. I had recently and regrettably become, for the first time, familiar with the death of a loved one. My father had passed away a few months before, whilst my wife's identical twin sister had also died two months before my father. She had been only 41 years old.

I left Margaret and went to speak to Bill. When I entered, Bill asked me if I thought we were making progress. I said that I thought we were and explained that I had just heard about the death of Margaret's daughter. Bill agreed that the death had been shocking. This was the first glimpse I had of Bill which suggested that he still held some sense of compassion for his colleague. Bill said that he didn't have any children but that he and his wife had experienced the death of their dog 12 months earlier. He said it had brought a huge sense of loss and had led to some time off work while he grieved for the passing of their beloved pet. I had a sense of what Bill must have experienced. In addition to the close family deaths mentioned earlier, I had had a pet chinchilla called Chuckie for seven years. Since her death I have not been able to bring myself to acquire another pet for fear of having to experience this type of pain and distress a second time. Bill had to pause as he told me the story of losing his dog. The mediation was now on a trajectory that I had not imagined it would move to.

I suggested that we break for lunch and that we reconvene in 30 minutes with a joint meeting to explore in further detail what the future might look like. Margaret didn't come back from lunch on time, with Bill quipping that she was probably outside having a cigarette. She returned a few moments later, apologising for being late but saying that she had needed a smoke. Bill gave a sardonic smile.

I asked if we could begin to look at the five bullet points that had been captured earlier, and began to go through each one. When we got to the point about electronic payments, Bill said that progress would probably be slow while a replacement for Lesley was found, which would probably take some time, to which Margaret responded by saying that she still couldn't believe that Lesley was gone. This was followed by a conversation about Lesley, how good she was, how long she had been at the school and, ultimately, her death. I listened keenly but couldn't work out who exactly this Lesley was. Margaret started to cry as she described their former colleague, and Bill also shed a tear. I asked when Lesley died, and Bill told me it had been only the previous month. Suddenly it hit me – they were talking about Lesley Forbes, the young lady I had read about in the in-house magazine while I waited at reception. It transpired that Lesley had worked at the school for ten years before being seconded to the local authority to run a project on helping schools get up and running with electronic payment systems. Bill said that one Friday afternoon Lesley complained about feeling unwell. She went home at 3.00pm and went to bed a few hours later. She never woke up.

By this stage, the mediation was no longer at a surface level. We were now absorbed in conversation of a profoundly deep nature. It seemed as if death had surrounded us.

I told Bill and Margaret that I had been gripped by the stories of death that I had heard over the last hour or so. I said that they had both shared in some traumatic and painful experiences. Margaret described how, about a week after

Lesley's death, a colleague whom she refused to name expressed an interest in taking over Lesley's position. The comment backfired badly. Everyone recognised that the expression was premature, ill-timed, inconsiderate and thoughtless. Bill too had heard about the incident. They both shook their heads in disbelief that someone would do such a thing. It created another talking point for them both to engage in.

This conversation over, I asked whether they recognised this shared interest and whether they viewed their dispute any differently after reflecting and reliving the stories involving loss of life. Bill said that he found it to be a useful if unplanned way of putting things into perspective. He acknowledged that they would always be united by death even when they stopped being colleagues. They then spoke with affection and reminisced about Lesley for a few moments more. It appeared to me that stumbling on the memory of a former colleague had been a catalyst to bringing Bill and Margaret closer together.

Looking ahead

Before long we had moved on to discussing the detail behind each bullet point. A way ahead was agreed by both of parties, including:

* Bill to revert to reporting back to Margaret after 30 days
* Margaret to collect fees in Bill's absence
* Both would meet once a week to talk about day to day issues
* They would move back in to the same office after 30 days
* Both would approach the Bursar for a performance review and to clarify department objectives

The proposed settlement represented a *'try it and see'* solution for both Bill and Margaret.

It was now time for all three of us to meet with the Deputy Head and the Bursar, with whom we had previously agreed to meet when we had reached this stage. We met in the Deputy Head's office and, whilst Bill and Margaret were not yet best buddies, they were at least talking to each other. The Deputy Head was about ten minutes late and, as he arrived, saw Bill and Margaret chatting to each other and sharing light humour. Judging by the expression on the Deputy Head's face, he was surprised to see them being so courteous to each other, exclaiming, *"It seems as if you have made some progress."* The Bursar then also joined us. With everyone together, I said that Bill and Margaret had worked hard on their differences in the morning and we had covered much ground. I asked for permission to provide a summary of where we had got to. I did so, without going into the detail of some of the more sensitive issues of the day. I thought that if Bill and Margaret wanted to do so they should be the ones to start that part of the conversation.

Both the Deputy Head and the Bursar were pleased that good progress had been made. I asked Bill and Margaret if they would like to add anything further to my comments or whether there were concerns that they would like to talk to the Deputy Head or Bursar about. Bill started by saying he had found the session useful but tough, adding that they might need further help clarifying their roles and for each to have an annual review to which Margaret agreed. The Bursar said that formal discussions on this matter were overdue, and said she would meet with both of them over the next week or so to put a date in the diary. Despite these assertions, I could sense that something wasn't right. As the Bursar spoke, the body language displayed by both Bill and Margaret suggested that they were doubtful that anything of this nature would happen. Recognising this I decided to push a bit harder. I thanked the Bursar for her willingness to move things forward but asked whether she would be willing to put a date in the diary for follow up discussions now, seeing as we were all together. She wriggled like a child confronted with a challenging parental discussion. The Deputy Head agreed that this was a good idea and asked the Bursar to get her diary so that a date could be scheduled. When the Bursar left the room the Deputy Head looked at me. I recognised the *'I'll explain later'* expression. The Bursar returned and a date was finally set for both Bill and Margaret. Bill began to set down what he wanted this next session with the Bursar to achieve, namely the opportunity to talk and to get clarity on his position. The Bursar gave short, curt answers, her responses suggesting that she wanted to move on to another topic. It soon became clear to me that the Bursar had been a major contributor to the conflict that engulfed Bill and Margaret. Her reluctance to have a full and frank discussion and deal with the difficult situation concerning her colleagues was acting like a multiplying effect on their woes.

With a date now fixed we were getting to the point where our joint meeting could come to a close. I wanted to do three things before the mediation concluded.

1. Have a quiet word with the Deputy Head about the Bursar
2. Have a conversation with the Bursar about the next steps
3. Have a document that captured the relevant points of the settlement that all would sign up to

Once we had achieved point number three I brought the joint session to a close. The Deputy Head thanked everyone for their contribution and wished Bill and Margaret well, signalling to me that he wanted a quick chat. When it was just the two of us he told me how much he appreciated what we had achieved, saying that he found it remarkable to see Bill and Margaret engaging in dialogue together again. He went on to state that he now realised that the Bursar might have been part of the problem but hadn't noticed quite how much until the session we had just experienced. He said that he had taken on some of the line management responsibilities of the Bursar as he knew how difficult she found them. It seemed to him now that this had been a mistake. Seeing the Bursar wriggle so much when faced with the prospective meetings had allowed him to see clearly why some of the problems with Bill and Margaret had escalated to the extent that they had.

Both seemed to recognise that clarity and firm leadership were necessary, but the Bursar was either unwilling or unable to provide this combination. The Deputy Head then asked me to ascertain the Bursar's thoughts on the day's progress, which I did directly.

The Bursar explained that she could see that Bill and Margaret had made good progress. She had not seen them talk to each other informally in that way for some time. I asked how she felt about the next stages, to which she replied that she sometimes hated managing people. There were eight in her team in total she said, and managing issues associated with conflict required up to three days a week in some cases. She wished that she could do the job without having any responsibility for people. Regarding Bill and Margaret's case, she knew that there were difficulties between them and it was likely that the dispute wouldn't have got so quite out of hand if she had stepped in sooner but she loathed dealing with conflict. She had only four years to go before she could apply for early retirement and she was desperate to "hide" for this period as she had done for many previously. I reflected that this life sounded sad, adding that four years was a long time to tread water until retirement came. I encouraged her to think about her job, career and life, but stopped short of talking to her about her life values. Although we were getting on well I didn't think that we had struck up a rich enough relationship in two hours to enter into such a meaningful and deep debate just yet.

The Bursar agreed to do her best to help move things on during the meetings that had been scheduled. I said that she shouldn't feel so down trodden and that many hundreds of other line managers felt the same way when it came to managing people. I then talked to her about how each of us appreciates guidance – a framework in which to operate. I then spent the next hour coaching her on how to plan for and conduct the upcoming meetings. At the end of our meeting she thanked me for listening. I wished her every success and reminded her to have a think about the areas I had mentioned.

The follow-up meeting

I went back for a pre-arranged follow-up meeting 60 days later, keen to hear about progress on all sides. Sometimes I call parties a few days or weeks following the mediation session, but on this occasion I decided to wait and hear first-hand how things had moved on. When I arrived at the school site I was welcomed by the Deputy Head, who suggested that all five of us meet together straight away. I usually prefer to meet each party individually to get their perspective on how things have developed and so, with some apprehension, I followed the Deputy Head to his room. One by one the others arrived, all smiles as they entered. My levels of anxiety lowered immediately.

With the group complete I asked them how things were. There was a general acknowledgement around the room that things were better. I looked in the direction of Bill and Margaret and asked them directly how they were getting on. Bill said that they had made good progress – the reporting line had been restored and they had moved back to sharing the same office. Margaret interrupted to say that they were even sharing the tea and coffee making throughout the day which raised a laugh. Bill also said that the meeting with the Bursar had been constructive and that there was now much more clarity around objectives and work requirements.

I was witnessing a totally transformed team. Something had happened on the day of the mediation that seemed to set in motion a programme of change which meant that the team that I was speaking with now was almost unrecognisable from the team I had engaged with two months earlier. I could see why the Deputy Head had been so enthusiastic to have a joint meeting. They had achieved a great deal and I congratulated them for it.

Observations

There are at least two main observations to note from this case. The first is that individual experiences that are shared can bring us closer together. As this mediation progressed, the stories of death were deep, revealing, profound, intense and full of meaning. There is more to each of us than what we see on the surface. Many of us interact and network with our colleagues every day, usually unaware of the history, pain, grief, remorse and stories that some may carry. We all have a story to tell. Some stories might form an in-depth novel and some less so, but the fact is that the more we know about a person's background and experiences the more likely we are to feel empathy and warmth towards them. In my book 'The Definitive Guide to Workplace Mediation' I refer to the concept of each worker holding a carrier bag or two as they cross the threshold of the organisation each day. These bags are likely to include, amongst much else:

- Family concerns
- Financial worries
- Concern about organisational change
- Concern about job security
- Worry about past or present performance
- Jealousy towards other colleagues
- Past hurts, failure and anger

I acknowledge that the picture I paint is one of bleakness and accept that it may not be the same for everyone. There are some who are delighted when Monday morning comes around as they can't wait to get to work and contribute towards exciting projects. They have no worries, no regrets from the past and no work opponents. They are full of optimism. They are also rare.

For those who are not in this category, which is most of us, carrying the bags of issues can get tiring. When someone listens to our hurtful experiences it can be as if we have taken one item out of the carrier bag and made the load a little lighter to carry. In doing so we build an invisible bridge with the listener who has taken precious time to hear what we have to say. The situation becomes even more powerful in situations where the listener has experienced something similar and can show compassion in a more genuine and authentic way.

In the UK, the three step statutory grievance process introduced in 2004 and later repealed in 2009 brought in a barrier for those who had a story to tell and wanted someone to listen. This is because many were, and still are, encouraged to lodge a grievance if they want their situation to be taken seriously. I recall having a pre-mediation meeting with a health consultant some time ago. The meeting lasted for one hour. His dispute had been rumbling along for eight years, and at the end of the meeting I thanked him for his contribution and outlined how the next steps would work. At this point he asked me, *"Is that it?"* I asked him what he meant. He said that no one had ever sat and listened to him talk about this situation before. It seemed that what he had been crying out for was a channel to vent his feelings. His cries had gone unheard and the organisation's rights based procedures had taken over when what he needed was so much simpler than that. For Bill and Margaret, sharing their stories of death allowed them to rise above the more material matters of tea and coffee making and put things into a more meaningful context.

The second observation from this story is that of the role of the line manager. When I think of the Bursar I think of the phrase *'Esse quam videri'* which means *'To be, rather than to appear'*. Research suggests that around two thirds of line managers would prefer to do something else rather than have a difficult conversation with a colleague at work. The majority of direct reports expect line managers to set boundaries and provide guidelines for what is expected of them. The best line managers hold tension between getting the job done and recognising the individual needs of their team.

The Bursar was not doing Bill or Margaret, or indeed herself, any favours by failing to address the apparent difficulties. Line managers are unlikely to be respected by their teams when they (the teams) do not feel challenged and when difficult issues do not get addressed repeatedly. It is a dilemma. There are very few senior positions that exist today that remain specialist enough to warrant that the role is undertaken without any people management responsibility. It is a prerequisite that as the ladder of seniority is climbed, with it comes the burden (or pleasure, to some) of managing people, an outlook purely based in the personality of the incumbent.

I would estimate that more than half of the cases that get to the stage of going to mediation could have been headed off by being *'nipped in the bud'* very early on through having one difficult conversation.

Trouble in church

"Do unto others as you would have them do unto you." – The Bible

Some time ago, I received a telephone call from the HR Manager of a well-established church body. She outlined a situation where a woman, Sheila Harvey, had been recently promoted to the role of Minister's Assistant. For the new appointee this was the final step in a long development path that would ultimately lead to her being assigned as Minister of her own church congregation. Sheila was delighted. She moved 50 miles with her supportive husband and two young children to take up the unpaid position. Her husband, who did not share her Christian faith, was a self-employed management consultant and could work from anywhere in the country. The house move went well, they found a good school for their children and they began to settle into the small village community, making many new friends. Sheila had put on hold her career as a practising barrister, specialising in family law, to do what the HR Manager described as *"answering God's call."*

The church Minister Sheila had been assigned to work with, Reverend Carnegie, was in his tenth year at the church. He had a good reputation and the church had experienced substantial numerical growth under his leadership, with current Sunday service attendances around 600. Reverend Carnegie had come from a line of many generations of Carnegies who had been Ministers in the church organisation to which he and Sheila belonged, and he had no plans to move. Sheila would be joining three other Minister's Assistants who were also in training to become future Ministers. She was to be the only female member of the leadership team.

Reverend Carnegie welcomed Sheila and invited her to participate in the leadership development meetings. He also gave her the specific task of arranging the church events for the next 12 months. Each of the leadership team was also scheduled to deliver the Sunday sermon up to four times per year. Reverend Carnegie advised Sheila that she should deliver her first sermon to the congregation within her first month so that this could form part of her induction. All was going well. Sheila was particularly popular with the women and younger people, while her husband had also started to attend church on some Sundays.

After about six months, problems set in. Reverend Carnegie and Sheila clashed. The Reverend was becoming uneasy with the pace at which Sheila wanted to introduce change. She had set up a series of coffee mornings for women, introduced a new after-school club, launched a singles networking club and made new connections with the local authority to access funding for current or new initiatives. Reverend Carnegie wasn't used to progress happening at such a fast pace. He had been used to doing things his own way for many years. Other members of the leadership team also tended to let things happen in the Reverend's own time.

The Reverend and Sheila agreed to meet over coffee to have a chat about how things were progressing. The meeting didn't go well. The Reverend wanted Sheila to slow down and reflect on the initiatives that she had put into place since her arrival. Sheila was surprised as she thought that she was making good progress and said as much to Reverend Carnegie.

They attempted to talk about adjustments that both might need to make, but neither gave up much ground. After this, Sheila continued working on existing projects but didn't introduce anything further. Things carried on between them as before, but they both knew the unspoken truth that their working relationship had been damaged. The public and private conversations with each other were now both cordial and frosty at the same time. Eventually, help came in the form of Reverend Carnegie's line manager, Bishop Thoroughgood, who had played a major role in the appointment of Sheila.

The Bishop had heard on the grapevine that all was not well between the pair and offered to meet with them to see if he could be of assistance. He did. It was a disaster. His interpersonal skills were good, but they didn't quite stretch to taking on what was now growing to be a significant falling out. Following this meeting, conversations between the two had to be relayed through third parties. Church members caught on that something wasn't quite right and the whole episode was becoming the main talking point at dinner parties, the school playground and at the local pub. It was at this stage that the church realised professional help would be required to help move things on. It was now a year since Sheila's appointment. Her husband had now stopped going to church.

I was called about three months after the meeting with the Regional Bishop had taken place. The mediation took place on a Saturday at the offices of one of the church members who ran his own business and involved myself, Reverend Carnegie, Bishop Thoroughgood and Sheila. In the joint discussions at the start of the day, both parties provided an outline that was similar to the one provided by the HR Manager. I then moved to private sessions.

Private time with Sheila

I went to spend some time with Sheila first and asked whether she wanted to add anything further. She referred to the many things that she had given up in order to pursue her vocation. She also talked about the strain that the dispute was putting on her family. Her husband was now refusing to have anything to do with the church, at a loss to understand how there could be such ongoing conflict and tension amongst two church leaders. He had said that whilst he didn't follow the Christian faith he had understood one of the key principles was that of forgiveness. It was all rather strange to him, and the journey that he had started in order to explore more about the Christian faith had been brought to an abrupt halt by what he had witnessed.

Sheila had also said that she was finding it difficult to continue working with Reverend Carnegie as she felt like he treated her as a child. She commented that she was an experienced barrister used to providing professional legal services to clients and wasn't used to being talked down to in that manner. Sheila felt that the Reverend talked a good talk but was reluctant to embrace change, particularly if it involved a woman leading it. She was beginning to wonder in fact if Reverend Carnegie was sexist, citing one example when the Reverend took her to one side after a service to which she had worn trousers and commented that as a member of the leadership team she should be very mindful of how she was attired. When she asked the Reverend to explain he said that others were looking on and she should set a good example. The only aspect of Sheila's dress she could make a correlation with was her trousers. This surprised her. It made her feel as if she had climbed into a time machine and turned the clock back 20 years.

The Reverend had also always been lukewarm to the development of the ladies group that Sheila had been nurturing. She knew that her experience, educational background and intellect could be intimidating but had always been mindful to respect the Minister's position. She didn't want this blip to dent her chances of assuming her own Ministerial position in the future and was willing to extend an olive branch to Reverend Carnegie and put their past troubles behind them.

I thanked Sheila for being so open and said that I would like to spend some private time with the Minister. She said that I should feel free to talk about any aspect of our conversation if it would be helpful to move the situation on.

Private time with Reverend Carnegie

Once with the Reverend I asked him for his thoughts on the opening session, to which he replied that he found it useful to find out how Sheila felt. I then asked him for his views on the prospects of resolution through mediation. He commented that he was open to Sheila's thoughts and ideas on how their relationship could be rebuilt, which represented a positive start. He acknowledged that Sheila's appointment had led to the church making great progress; attendances were up and there was a new sense of vibrancy amongst the congregation. He was unsure whether all sections of the congregation were on board with the developments, but the results were welcomed nonetheless. In particular, he mentioned that funding and sponsorship had increased for projects relating to social action. The weekly offertory had also increased significantly. When I asked the Reverend if he and other members of the leadership team liked Sheila he said he thought she was a nice, educated lady with good intentions, adding that other male colleagues agreed with these sentiments.

After half an hour with the Reverend I suggested that we meet together again to have a joint discussion that might put particular issues on the table, with Bishop Thoroughgood also in attendance. Reverend Carnegie agreed to this idea, as did Sheila.

Private time with Bishop Thoroughgood
I went to see Bishop Thoroughgood to obtain his thoughts before the joint meeting. As the official commissioner of the mediation I asked what an ideal settlement would look like for him. He said that he was very impressed with what Sheila had achieved and was mindful that she had given much up to take on the voluntary role. He believed that she had potential and this was a good test for both her and Reverend Carnegie. Sheila had been identified as a future leader in their church organisation and it was important that the appointment was a success. He was sure that the Reverend Carnegie and Sheila would be able to put their differences behind them.

The joint meeting
The four of us met together and I sat by a flipchart and explained that I would like to capture what each thought were the key issues that separated them.

The list comprised of:
- Slow the pace of change (suggested by Reverend Carnegie)
- Working with various groups (Reverend Carnegie)
- Freedom to get things done (Sheila)
- Be honest with each other (Sheila)
- Have monthly one to one progress meetings (Sheila)
- Agree a series of objectives and focus areas (Sheila)
- Leadership team to sign off new initiatives prior to implementation (Reverend Carnegie)

I asked the Bishop if he wanted to add anything. He said that he would like to have quarterly meetings with each following the mediation session to ensure that the final outcomes continued to be worked towards.

I asked the Reverend and Sheila to identify what would be required under each bullet point to fix the situation. Sheila began to outline her points. I noticed that Sheila was very quick intellectually, much more so than Reverend Carnegie, which wasn't really surprising given their respective backgrounds. She was also incredibly articulate, her legal training demonstrating her ability to be able to select words that summarised her position succinctly. As she continued to talk I noticed that Reverend Carnegie appeared to lose interest, frequently rolling his eyes and looking at his shoes. To re-engage him I asked him what he thought about what Sheila was saying. He replied by saying that he thought she had some good ideas, adding that the challenge for the church was to make sure that the pace of change was such that everyone, old and young, could embrace it. Sheila asked him if he had received feedback suggesting otherwise. As he was responding she asked him another question, then another. It was a side to Sheila that I had not seen – her cross examination side. I suspected that Reverend Carnegie may have felt this way too.

Bishop Thoroughgood, who seemed like an elder statesman in every sense, had also picked up on this and made a joke of it asking Sheila if she could slow down and give us all a chance to catch up. It was a remarkable interjection. He had spotted that there was potential that the touch paper could be ignited and he seemed keen to put it out before it did so. Sheila refrained from asking any more questions and allowed Reverend Carnegie to respond.

By now it was around 10.15am and we continued with this session for another two hours. Just before we broke for lunch the topic of discussion moved on and we were talking about a young woman who Sheila thought had potential. She said that perhaps at some stage the church could sponsor her for some training and development and maybe she could join the leadership team. Reverend Carnegie's response took us all by surprise. He said, *"We've already got one and that's tough enough. I'm not sure that we could cope with another. Before long every woman in the church will be wearing trousers on a Sunday."* As he finished I felt our impending lunch break disappear in a flash. The Bishop's concerns about the touch paper had now become a reality. The fire had started.

The choice
When faced with dilemmas such as these in mediation, all mediators have two choices. One is to defuse the situation by splitting the group up and continuing through private meetings. The other is to allow the parties to deal with the situation head on and face truths that may, as yet, have been unspoken. In less

than a split second I had decided to opt for the latter. I could see the Bishop looking at me out of the corner of his eye and I could sense some nervousness on his part about the trajectory of the discussion.

I broke the stunned silence by asking Sheila if she would like to comment on Reverend Carnegie's comments. Unsurprisingly she said that she would, and followed by saying that when she was a girl aged about ten she saw her father beat her mother. The day after the beating her father was admitted to hospital. He died three weeks later. She said that some of her early childhood memories were of her mother and father arguing and fighting, with her mother always coming off worse. Sometimes Sheila would be lying in bed at night and would hear the sound of her father hitting her mother. Despite this abuse her parents both went to church every Sunday.

The prompt for this final beating had been her mother's registration for an evening college course so that she could learn how to read. Her father, who had benefited from a good education, had objected. Sheila's mother never spoke to her about the arguments and the fighting but always told Sheila that she should do her best to get a good education and to make sure that a man never walked all over her. Her mother had died two years ago, Sheila said, and on her death bed she had congratulated Sheila on getting a good education, a good job and a good husband.

Throughout this story Sheila was emotional but remained coherent. When she stopped Bishop Thoroughgood asked if we should break for lunch, but I was sure that Sheila hadn't finished and said so. Everything about the situation was close, including the room itself, which only added to the atmosphere. Sheila continued by saying that she almost broke down at her mother's acknowledgement of her achievements, especially her appreciation of Martin, her husband, who, Sheila admitted, had had much to put up with as far as Sheila herself was concerned. She said how she had goaded and pushed him over the years to see whether he would retaliate and hit her just as her father had done with her mother. She had even struck him on more than one occasion and, although he defended himself, he had never retaliated. Martin was a noble man, husband and father Sheila said. He had started to attend church to find out more about the Christian faith, but when problems set in between her and Reverend Carnegie he had backed away, confused as to how two church leaders could be in dispute for such a long time but still preach sermons on a Sunday morning. Sheila said that she was deeply sorry, ashamed and embarrassed for how she had treated the man who had restored her faith in men.

Sheila then moved onto Reverand Carnegie who, she said, reminded her of her father, not in looks so much but in his voice and her perception that he wanted to dominate her. This brought back her childhood memories and made her want to rebel against him silently. It was partly the reason why she had pushed to achieve so much so quickly at the church. She had noticed soon after her arrival that the Reverend didn't seem to regard women and men as equals.

The fact that she was the first female member of the leadership team gave her the first inkling, but it was his comment about her clothes that confirmed in her mind that the Reverend had a sexist trait. She hadn't given up a corporate career where she'd had to fight for equal footing day after day to encounter the same battles in the church.

For 20 minutes or so Sheila had delivered faultless oratory outlining some very sensitive issues in her life, whilst providing the Minister with some feedback on how she felt about him. It was first class. When she finished her composure remained impressively intact. I could see that both the gentlemen in the room had been touched by what they had heard.

I considered the next step and decided that it would be best for Sheila to have lunch in her own room while the Bishop and the Reverend remained in the room we were using. I withdrew to the small room that had been assigned for me, but found that my hunger had left me though. I was gripped by Sheila's words. I went straight back to see Reverend Carnegie and Bishop Thoroughgood. The mood in the room was still sombre as I entered. The Bishop spoke first, stating that they should do something for Sheila. She had an incredible story, he went on to say, adding that he had spoken to Reverend Carnegie, but didn't get a chance to finish his sentence; the Reverend interrupted, stating that he could speak for himself, which he then proceeded to do.

Sheila's arrival had evidently been tough for Reverend Carnegie. He said that he had been brought up in a church that had been dominated by men, but now the role of women was beginning to become much more influential. Initially he had tried to work with Sheila on the modernisation as best he could, but it had been difficult on a number of levels. Her story had moved him however and had profoundly changed his view of her. I asked if he would be willing to share his thoughts with Sheila, to which he assented. Bishop Thoroughgood interjected by asking the Reverend if he was happy to continue working with a woman in leadership. Reverend Carnegie replied in the affirmative, stating that he was getting used to it. Bishop Thoroughgood gave me a look however that indicated to me that he wasn't totally convinced.

I went to see Sheila and asked how she was feeling. She said that whilst she was glad that she had revealed what she had, she felt that she was now vulnerable and that her story could be used against her at some stage in the future. I said that her two colleagues had appreciated her honesty and wanted to talk with her about the way ahead. I suggested that a further joint meeting could take place, but this time it should be in her room. She welcomed the idea.

When we met together again, Reverend Carnegie started the conversation by saying to Sheila how much he appreciated her honesty, adding that he was mindful that she had shared some deeply personal information and that she had also been frank and blunt in her feedback about him. He finished by saying that he wanted to work with her to rebuild their relationship and was open to suggestions about how to do this. Over the next couple of hours we worked on a plan that would help the pair of them move forward constructively.

They agreed that:
- They would have a bi-weekly private meeting
- Sheila was to hold off introducing new initiatives
- Bishop Thoroughgood would meet both for quarterly reviews
- Sheila would be kept up to date with plans for her to assume leadership of her own congregation at some point in the future
- They would keep Sheila's personal story a private matter

We had been together a number of hours but agreed that it had been a fruitful day and much ground had been covered. We agreed to conclude the day and scheduled to meet again in three months. I was keen to see how Reverend Carnegie and Sheila would say goodbye to each other. In the event, Sheila approached the Reverend and gave him a hug. Reverend Carnegie seemed somewhat surprised by this but responded in kind.

I thanked everyone for their contributions and said that I looked forward to seeing them again in three months time.

What happened next
Two months later my phone rang. It was Bishop Thoroughgood, asking whether I might be free to visit him and have a chat. We set a date and time for the following week. When we met, the Bishop informed me that events had taken a strange twist following the mediation. The Bishop confirmed my suspicions that he had been concerned about Reverend Carnegie's willingness to forgive and move on. He believed that Sheila had given most during the mediation session, something Reverend Carnegie confirmed when we met with him later on the same day. He went on to say that the mediation had prompted him to think about his

ministerial career, concluding with the notion that it was time for him to step down. He wanted to explore whether he could devote time instead to teaching and training younger people who were at Bible School.

This was clearly news to Bishop Thoroughgood, who asked the Reverend what it was that had prompted him to reach this decision. The Reverend said that Sheila's story had troubled him and that he hadn't realised the impact he was having on someone who had so clearly given up so much to answer the call of God, revealing that the incident had been another link in a chain that had indicated to him that the time may be right for him to move on. He then added that in fact much had been decided between the mediation and now, including the selection of his replacement, which had happened thus.

Once Reverend Carnegie had informed his congregation of the news that he was stepping down, he had then invited them to take part in the selection of the new Minister. A range of delegates had been put forward, but one name omitted was Sheila's. This had been noticed by some members of the church congregation who said that they would like Sheila's name to be added to the list.

Reverend Carnegie hadn't thought for a moment that Sheila might be a contender for the position as the plan had always been for her to begin her ministerial career in a small congregation, but the indication from some of the congregation was that she would be an ideal candidate. Bishop Thoroughgood then admitted that this was an unusual step, but he didn't see too much of a problem with it. He also added to me that he had heard that another church organisation had approached Sheila and had indicated that they were willing to offer her a Ministerial position within 12 months if she was interested. The selection process for the Reverend's position then took place with Sheila coming out as the clear front runner. The continued absence of Sheila's husband Martin from church life had raised some eyebrows, but not enough to put her promotion in jeopardy. The transition from Reverend Carnegie to Sheila would therefore go ahead in six months time.

To me this had been a remarkable turnaround of events. Bishop Thoroughgood added that he had known about the congregation's desire for Sheila to eventually replace Reverend Carnegie and that the Reverend had been gracious about this. If the mediation session hadn't have taken place, the Bishop continued, then the situation would have probably run on for years. He was very grateful for the breakthroughs that had been made that Saturday two months ago. He had also suggested to Sheila that she share her story more widely as it may help others, but Sheila still wasn't sure about this.

Following her appointment, Sheila met with the leadership team and proposed that Reverend Carnegie provide ongoing mentoring and coaching for current and aspiring leaders. The team agreed. Reverend Carnegie was surprised and humbled at her suggestion. He hadn't expected Sheila to do anything like that for him. It provided a good next stop for the Reverend's career, allowing him to eventually bow out with some dignity.

Observations

There is an elephant in the room waiting to be tackled amongst many faith groups. For those who may be unfamiliar with the phrase, 'elephant in the room' is an English idiom for an obvious truth that is being ignored or goes unaddressed. The expression also applies to an obvious problem that no one wants to discuss.

The elephant is conflict and dysfunctional relationships in churches and other places of worship. One of the fastest growing areas in the field of mediation and conflict resolution is faith groups, both same faith and different faith. Despite numerous scriptures and texts advising how to coexist harmoniously, many faith groups struggle to keep positive relationships intact. Arguably, faith groups have the largest group of volunteers of any organisation throughout the world, and a person in a conflict situation can very easily give up their voluntary position.

There is another dimension too. The psychological contract is getting harder for faith groups and churches in particular to win. Being mainly made up of volunteers, if one church fails to meet an individual's needs then those needs may be satisfied by another congregation. Part of the reason that some people attend church is because of the collegiality that relationships can bring. Church can be a great place to meet people. However, churchgoers find it much easier now than, say, 20 years ago to leave one church for another. On some occasions this is down to unresolved conflict.

There are even a good number of churches existing today that came into being as a result of a breakdown in relationships amongst leadership in a previous church.

Managing conflict and keeping positive relationships intact in faith groups and church organisations is a leadership issue. Unfortunately for most churches, conflict management doesn't form part of the curriculum for ministerial training. This was what one might call 'on the job' training for Sheila. Every church is likely to face situations of conflict and tension at some stage. This could be about money, positions, titles, tenure or church doctrine. Conflict management skills should be a fundamental aspect of a church leader's toolkit. In the UK there are examples of churches going to an Employment Tribunal to attempt to resolve differences with ministers or colleagues. Based on my admittedly limited understanding of the values promoted by faith groups, this seems rather bizarre.

It was interesting that Sheila decided to leave her legal career for such a different path. In line with the focus on this case study, in Ken Cloke's book 'Conflict Revolution – Mediating Evil, War, Injustice and Terrorism', he says that the law largely ignores the human, emotional, relational, social, economic and political elements that underlie the facts and merely transforms specific behaviours into crimes, for the most part regardless of the context in which they took place. It does so through legal language including syntax, definitions, and consequences. It does so by focussing on the facts and being preoccupied with the past, unaware of the present and unable to imagine the future, by means of pomp, liturgical recitation, and dismal formality.

Cloke then refers to a scripture from the Bible, saying that the law preaches and moralises to others without applying the same lessons to itself in ways that remind us of the condemnation recited in the Gospel according to St. Luke (11:46, 52):

"Woe unto you, also, ye lawyers! For ye have laden men with burdens grievous to be borne, and ye yourselves touch not the burdens with one of your fingers... Woe unto you, lawyers! For ye have taken away the key of knowledge: ye entered not in yourselves and them that were entering ye hindered!"

I have no idea whether Sheila had an awareness that this verse from the Bible even exists and whether her conviction to enter the ministry was prompted in any way by her legal career. The influential social theorist Niklas Luhmann argued:

"Law does not serve to avoid conflicts; compared with the repression of conflict in societies....it leads to immensely greater opportunities for conflict. It merely seeks to avoid the violent resolution of conflicts to make suitable forms of communication available for every conflict. As soon as someone appeals to the law, communicative material is sorted. Texts become relevant, other cases are consulted, the opinions of specific authorities become important. Law must fulfil the function of an immune system, and it is given the freedom to do this. But it is not permitted to wander outside the problems that can be expected."

At the very minimum, church leaders should attend an introductory programme on managing conflict and understanding mediation. It is likely to be a skill that they will need to draw on many times throughout their career and may help save someone's ministry. It might even turn out to be a key ingredient to help their church to grow and flourish.

Chapter 5
Stories of transformation and failure

"To be free is not merely to cast off one's chains, but to live in a way that respects and enhances the freedom of others." – Nelson Mandela

As we have seen, not all mediation sessions end on a happy note. A mediator can do his best to bring a hard day's slog to a satisfying conclusion, but sometimes two parties just aren't willing to concede ground on any issue. A mediation session that ends with a resolution, regardless of who are the *'winners'* and who are the *'losers'*, is judged a success by a mediator whose sole aim is to bring the two parties to a conclusion and end their dispute one way or another. A failed mediation is one that ends with a continuance of the status quo which will see the parties returning to their lives no further on than they were beforehand with all the stresses and strains still intact and having passed up the opportunity to put these issues behind them and make a fresh start. Between these black and white lines there are of course shades of grey with both huge successes and huge failures just as possible as minor successes and minor failures. As we will see with the stories to follow, when the extremes of these two ends of the spectrum are reached the effects can, unsurprisingly, be life changing.

In the title of this section, the word *'transformation'* refers to a positive alteration of an individual as a result of the mediation process. It is common for a mediation to be life changing in a positive way, but frequently this refers to the acknowledgement at the end of a long running battle and the personal relief that comes with that, as we have seen in previous areas of this book. Less common an outcome is the gaining of a professional or personal advantage such as a promotion, the acquisition of a new contract or a new friend, but these rare and often totally unforeseeable ends show that mediation is far more a progressive means of conflict resolution than a tribunal or a court case. In these instances each incident is often as different as the next so it is hard to find a common denominator to touch on, but in professional terms a promotion or the acquisition of new business can be instigated by both sides; more often the retention of a current or previous position, or even a promotion, forms part of a negotiation package on behalf of the company as opposed to the employee (to use a standard conflict), but occasionally the employee can demand promotion as part of a settlement. A demand of promotion is much less common than the reinstatement of an existing or previous role, but it is not unknown.

In cases such as these however the position itself, or the application for a promotion, are often the cause of the dispute itself and so are expected to feature somewhere in the final agreement. Sometimes however an offer of promotion or a potentially more lucrative transfer to a different department or location can be seen as an ideal resolution – one that benefits everybody and would possibly not have been considered had mediation not been requested. Incidents such as these can demonstrate a lack of creative problem solving by those in management and reiterate once again the fact that conflicts do not happen overnight – there are dozens of steps on the way to the request of mediation, each one of which could have been flagged up and dealt with at the time but weren't.

In circumstances where a lucrative relocation or a promotion is offered, not only have the two parties patched up their differences to the point where the company clearly demonstrates their willingness to retain the services of the individual, but the individual themselves has come out of the mediation session from a position of consternation and conflict to one of joy and excitement at an entirely unanticipated result of such greater value than they could have imagined. As we've alluded to, the overriding emotion from a successful mediation is often relief, but sometimes an individual's luck can be in and they can receive much more than they bargained for.

On the opposite end of the scale, some mediation sessions can end in relative disaster. The success of a mediation session is based around the end result – if a day of arguing ends with an agreement of terms then it can be judged a success, whereas a cordial mediation that ends with stalemate cannot be defined so. The success or failure of a mediation session is the sole responsibility of the feuding parties and not the mediator. This will be discussed later in this section, but essentially a mediator can employ various skills in order to try and edge conflicting parties toward a resolution, but, as a famous saying has it, 'you can lead a horse to water but you can't make it drink'. Never was a sentiment so prescient as when dealing with mediation! Mediation failure is much more complex than success. It can be the fault of either one or both parties and can leave all concerned with more negative feelings than they had when they went into the mediation.

Two of the most common reasons for mediation failure were actually touched on in the story 'I hate you' in chapter four, the first of which is the issue of a distorted conflict story. A distorted conflict story is one where, as we discussed at the beginning of the book, the original conflict story, like Chinese whispers, has grown out of all proportion with constant retelling and additions from other affected parties such as equally disgruntled colleagues to the point where, in the mind of the individual, the resolution and compensation has to reflect what the story has now become. This is where getting to the core story is vital in order to forge the way ahead, as failure to strip away these puffed up layers will inevitably lead to a chasm of difference in the opening compensation offers from both sides. If the real story and real sources of conflict can be extracted and the additional layers cast aside then a positive outcome is much more likely. In the case of '*I hate you*', Pauline had taken not just her own issues into the mediation session but also those of her colleagues who all disliked the Councillor.

Pauline took it upon herself to fight their battle, a fight which undermined everything the mediation session had set out to achieve between the two individuals alone. Through adding the woes of her colleagues to those of her own she artificially inflated her grievance so that she not only wanted closure for herself but she also wanted to make an example of the Councillor to quench her colleagues' thirst. Mediation cannot and never will act as a platform for this kind of single-minded retribution – it is for the resolution of conflict through realistic, sensible means and not as an opportunity to start a witch hunt. Those with a sense of inflated conflict and a determination to hang their aggressor out to dry do not make good candidates for mediation and will therefore probably leave the mediation session with the stresses and anguish that events have so far cost them still firmly intact, or more probably enhanced through a day of discussing it.

The second most common reason for mediation failure is based largely on the personality of the individual(s) involved. The brick wall that meets many mediators when opening one-to-one discussions is sometimes purely a front put up by the party in question in order to try and protect themselves, a wall that is eventually broken down and the core story revealed. Some individuals however are so resolute in their innocence and determination to get their way that they refuse to move an inch in the direction of compromise, even though it would spell the end of the weeks, months or years of conflict. This resolve can sometimes be the result of previously ill-conceived attempts by the other side to appease the individual or it may have been instilled from the very moment the individual decided to press ahead with the grievance procedure. Dealing with such bullish individuals can be very taxing and will ultimately lead to them being the only one who loses out. This stubbornness was evident in '*I hate you*' and is also evident in one of the following stories where an individual retracts their apology less than 12 hours after agreeing to it in the mediation session. This just shows that a day's hard work that had previously been considered a success can, with the obstinacy of one person, turn into an instant failure. This type of failure is the most galling for the mediator but, thankfully, the rarest.

As well as the professional aspect of success and failure in mediation, personal relations can also be renewed, lost or even gained as a result of the process. Being in the same room or building for an entire day often magnifies emotions, leading to much more extreme reactions than would normally be experienced in a modern workplace; two friends who have suffered a falling out for example may end up either wondering what they were fighting about or swearing never to see each other again! It is rare that relations are the same at the end of the day as they are at the start, but, like the individuals themselves, these relations too can result in dramatic transformation or failure.

Mediators can use all the tools in their arsenal to try and convince an individual that even the slightest compromise will be to their advantage, but they must also remember that the conflict must remain with the parties themselves and if one or both is not interested in resolution then that is their decision. They cannot force their hand, nor should they try, even if it means the inevitability of a failed mediation session. The individuals have to live with their decisions and, if they feel so inclined, take it to a higher level. This is their risk, their story and, as long as the mediator has done everything in his/her power to try and convince them to take even a small step towards a resolution, the mediator can walk away with head held high whilst the affected parties have to go home and prepare for the next taxing stage of battle.

Trading sex for power

"The man who first flung a word of abuse at his enemy instead of a spear was the founder of civilisation." – Sigmund Freud

Seagrove Consulting is a large telecoms company, listed in the FTSE 350, who specialise in supplying high speed IT networks. They are based in the UK but around 55% of their business comes from overseas. Jenny Pitman, a confident, outgoing and gregarious woman, was appointed to the role of global Sales Director about a year before this story starts. Jenny was forty-nine years old, but people regularly guessed her age as being about 6-10 years younger. Jenny was delighted to have got the job, especially as she was the only female Executive Director at the time. Married with two children at university, she had moved back from Australia for the role where she had been performing a similar function for a smaller company.

Charles Manning had been working for Seagrove Consulting for three years. He was 36 years old and married with two small children, one three years old and the other six months. A member of the sales team, Charles was quiet, thoughtful and reflective. His line manager was Gary Hubbard, the Regional Director for Europe and Africa who reported to Jenny. Charles, a fibre optics technology expert, originally heralded from New Zealand. Governments around the world were and still are promoting the utilisation of fibre optics technology, given its increased internet speed and bandwidth using technology with a smaller footprint, highly important with the increasing amounts of data being placed on the World Wide Web daily. Charles was on the organisation's list of employees who must be retained. Although not officially part of the senior operational team, he was regularly invited to advise the team on issues relating to fibre optics technology. The board had targeted 25% of its revenue to come from fibre optics technology within the next five years. At that time the figure was 11%.

Charles spent about 40% of his time travelling across Europe and Africa on business development. He was well remunerated, sometimes earning more than his line manager because of commission payments. A recent breakdown in the relationship between Charles and Jenny had evolved, but it was not clear why.

The mediation commissioning

One afternoon I received a phone call from Seagrove's Chief Executive, Bill Ramsey, who I knew well. He said that a difficult situation had arisen for which he would like my help, asking whether I might be free to meet for an early morning breakfast the next day before he travelled to Russia. I agreed.

We met in London the following morning, and he explained that Jenny and Charles had fallen out a few months ago but he wasn't sure why. Although it was business as usual, the difficulties with their relationship were beginning to have an impact on revenue. I asked Bill if he could think of any reason why this could have happened. He said he couldn't.

He then explained that although Charles worked directly with Jenny on some fibre optics initiatives he didn't report directly to her, continuing that Seagrove was developing country level relationships in key markets such as Brazil, Russia, India and China and although these countries were outside Charles' region he was critical to market penetration. Seagrove had also identified a series of emerging economies from across the globe, commonly referred to as 'next 11'.

Bill was anxious that Jenny and Charles might be putting their jobs at risk if their difficulty couldn't be resolved. The board had identified the need to bring in a senior director for these emerging markets, but it would be at least ten months before a person they had identified could start. Bill had spoken to both of them individually about engaging with a mediator some months ago, an approach they had both initially dismissed, but he had now managed to persuade them to have a preliminary discussion with a mediator. He gave me permission to make contact with both of them as well as Charles' line manager, Gary.

Pre-meeting discussions

I called Bill and Jenny and made an appointment to meet with each of them separately. Both had heavy travel schedules, which meant that a preliminary discussion on the phone would be the best way ahead. I spoke with Jenny first. She was initially frosty and sceptical, but business-like. She said that her job was to grow global revenue and that Charles was an important player, but not irreplaceable. I asked if she could pinpoint the beginning of their difficulties. She said it probably had something to do with a clash of personalities but that as colleagues they were getting the job done. I sensed that Jenny was being rather guarded, but thought it best not to push her for more detail at this point. I explained how the process would work and discussed the time and location for the scheduled joint mediation session.

Charles appeared to be a little less defensive during our chat, but his story was more or less the same – their breakdown was not affecting their business together. I asked Charles if he could recognise the commencement of their difficulties. He offered the opinion that Jenny might feel threatened by him or that she might be having difficulty settling in England. When I asked Charles if he had an ideal solution in mind he said he didn't know and would see what the mediation brought up.

My next call was with Gary Hubbard, Charles' line manager. Gary said that he was at a loss to explain what might have caused the difficulty with Charles and Jenny, adding that they had seemed to be getting along fine up until quite recently when their previously warm, friendly and courteous relationship had suddenly deteriorated. They even seemed less keen to travel together, which they were required to do a lot. I asked Gary if he had any thoughts on what a settlement might look like. He replied that repairing Charles and Jenny's relationship was crucial to the business, but that because he was the person who officially reported to Jenny the business could function quite adequately on that basis.

The mediation session

The day of the joint mediation session arrived. We had arranged to meet off-site at a London hotel. I asked Bill and Gary if they could be on hand to join us at the mediation session later if necessary as I wanted to spend some time with Jenny and Charles first. I gave the opening comments in the joint mediation session before inviting Jenny and Charles to add their own comments. Jenny went first. She said that she and Charles had always got on well and that she was sure that the blip in their relationship could be ironed out quickly. She said this in the same business-like manner and added nothing else. Charles said that he just wanted to continue doing a good job and be recognised for it. He said that he had no issues with Jenny and that things had been fine up until recently. I asked both whether, since we were all together, they thought they might be able to identify potential areas to move towards settlement. Both said that they would like time to think about it.

Removing the blockage

I got the feeling that the mediation session wasn't moving forward. Since the start of the discussions with Charles and particularly Jenny, I had developed a suspicion that there was something that was being hidden from me, although I couldn't put my finger on just what it was.

For the next hour I went to and from Jenny and Charles' separate rooms trying to find out more information. I decided to take a different approach with Charles and talked to him about his life, his family and why he decided to come to the

UK from New Zealand. His face lit up as he talked about New Zealand and being brought up there. He had come to the UK on a short term secondment and met an English woman. They had fallen in love, got married and had started a family together. We then moved onto the topic of Rugby – a great passion of mine, as it was for Charles. I asked Charles what he thought the secret of the All Blacks' success was. He replied that for as long as he could remember, rugby had been part of the culture and ethos of the New Zealand sports education system and that coaches instilled success on the rugby field from a young age. We talked about the team I support and traded stories about the standard of the game, the size of the players and rugby as a professional sport.

Charles and I were now getting on well. We were both talking freely and had discovered a shared area of interest during our half hour chat. Building rapport with parties is a key part of the mediator's role, and backing away from discussing the dispute itself can often be a good way to make progress. With Charles, I had been fortunate to touch on an area that we had a joint interest in. It could have been cars, films, art or any number of other subjects, but it allowed us for a moment to suspend the real reason for being together and talk about matters that were considered easier and more fun.

When we have such conversations with others we subconsciously begin to open the doors of our heart and mind. The synergy that develops between people as they discover shared interests can mean that guards and barriers come down and a new desire to open up and talk, share knowledge, information and wishes emerges. It is the reason why there are jokes about business deals taking place on the golf course.

Being on the golf course is a form of relaxation where other people who like golf will meet. As they meet, play and talk, other areas of interest will surface, possibly including business opportunities. The same happens in churches, gyms, pubs, bars and a whole host of other public areas.

I now asked Charles about his family. He spoke about his wife and about their two young children, which opened up another shared interest. I spoke of my experiences, including adjusting to life with children compared to life without as my wife and I had waited ten years to start a family. Charles said that he was still getting used to coming second to the children and that working long hours filled the void that had been developing since the children had come along. The mood in the room changed at that point. Charles began to open up further and said that he wouldn't trade his wife and children for anything in the world, but that life was certainly different now. His six month old wasn't sleeping through the nights and any time Charles could get to travel meant that he could get a good night's sleep. Then he gave me what I needed.

The story

The reason for things developing as they had done with Jenny, Charles said, had probably stemmed from this change in his family life. Fearing the risk of appearing too eager to hear the rest of the story I said nothing, hoping that Charles would tell all. Happily, the silence prompted him to go on. He said that he and Jenny had been working on a project together in South Africa, a project that required them to work in Cape Town for days, sometimes weeks, at a time. One day, they had had a particularly good meeting with a customer. It led to a significant sale. They had been working on the deal for about a year.

That evening they went out for a meal to celebrate the sale. This wasn't unusual as they ate together most evenings, the only difference on this occasion being that they weren't entertaining a client. Although Charles didn't report to Jenny, she viewed him as a direct report because of his knowledge of the product, experience in the industry and gravitas which helped him command authority with clients. She and many others considered him more senior than his grade suggested.

After the meal they went on to a nightclub which they left at about 1.30am and took the short walk to their hotel. On the way back however they took a wrong turn and ended up on a dark, unlit street. As they turned to go back, three young men approached them and asked Jenny for her bag. Jenny refused and they continued walking. One of the young men reached for her bag and, in the ensuing scuffle, knocked her to the ground. Charles attempted to fight off the men, and, although he had some success, he picked up a bruised eye and cut lip. The young men ran off without Jenny's bag. Jenny herself was shaken but not injured.

They made their way back to the hotel. Jenny was concerned about Charles' injuries and told him to come up to her room so that she could treat them. Charles did so and Jenny tended to Charles' cuts and bruises, despite still being shaken herself. They discussed reporting the incident to the police but decided not to as Jenny's bag wasn't stolen. When Jenny had finished cleaning Charles' cuts they talked some more. At this point Charles told me that it was as if their success from the meeting with the client, followed by their shared experience of the attack, had formed some kind of chemistry between them.

Although Jenny was never unpleasant to her colleagues she had an edge that typified her role as a commercial senior director. Seeing her care for and tend to him in the way she had was strange for Charles. Charles asked how Jenny was feeling and whether she would be okay getting to sleep. She said that she might have difficulty sleeping but she should be fine. They talked some more, before Charles said that he should be going to bed. He then hugged Jenny and thanked her for cleaning him up. The hug lasted for more than a few seconds. He then kissed her on the cheek and hugged her again. Sensing that Jenny wasn't put off by his close proximity, Charles then kissed Jenny again – this time on the lips. Jenny didn't flinch. The kiss became more prolonged and developed into a long, deep, passionate and intimate embrace. He touched and stroked her hair and, as he took things further, Jenny reciprocated. Things continued to develop and before long they had made themselves more comfortable on the bed. Charles said that as he took it further and further Jenny responded in kind, telling me then he was surprised at how "hot" she was. He then said Jenny had an incredible body and that soon he got to the point where holding back from going further, if Jenny allowed it, would be difficult. They eventually had sex, with Charles saying that he thoroughly enjoyed every moment of the experience. He spent the night, the pair of them having sex again in the morning, then again and again.

Charles then resisted from telling me more about this night of lust, admitting that he had probably said more than he should have already and requesting that the information be kept confidential. I said that the conversation would remain between the two of us. Charles admitted that he felt better having shared a secret that brought with it constant reminders. He added that at the stage of the tryst he and his wife hadn't resumed a normal sex life since having their second child and he was at a low point. Jenny had filled a big void in his life.

The morning after their night together, Jenny was due to fly to Germany and Charles to England. Jenny was flustered however, and neither she nor Charles knew what to say. Despite this initial awkwardness their evening together sparked the start of a six month affair. They continued to see each other when they could, and both made a good job of keeping the relationship a secret. When they were both in the London office they would disappear for a few hours over lunchtime if possible and check in to a nearby hotel. He said that their relationship was passionate, fervent and in many ways loving.

While they were together one afternoon, Jenny mentioned to Charles that the company were looking to bring in a senior person who would take global responsibility for growing the fibre optics market. The role would report to her. Whilst she didn't say so explicitly, she implied that the job would be Charles' if he wanted it. He was excited by the possibility. A few weeks later however, Charles was beginning to feel uneasy about the potential to secure the bigger role. He had heard that the company was starting to see people about the role, but that he hadn't been included in the process. He also said that he usually deleted voicemails and texts sent by Jenny, but after a few months he started to keep them. I asked why this was and he admitted that he would consider using them if he didn't get the promotion to the senior role.

Jenny and Charles' sexual relationship fizzled out after around six months, when Jenny began to change towards Charles. She became cold and was doing anything possible to prevent them travelling alone together on visits. He hadn't told anyone in the organisation about their relationship and suspected that Jenny hadn't either.

We had been together for over an hour. I thanked Charles for his openness and asked him how much I was allowed to share with Jenny. He told me I could share everything, but as I was leaving he added that in fact he wanted to keep the saved texts and voicemails aspect private. He also said that he would like Jenny to know that he would continue to be adult and professional about their relationship.

Jenny's denial

I went to see Jenny, apologising for keeping her waiting for so long. She asked what Charles had been speaking to me about for all that time. I said that we had a good discussion but I would like to hear from her first before I put across Charles' views. Jenny said that she had nothing further to add to her opening speech. As far as she was concerned, she and Charles had a working relationship and that she could continue in the same way. I asked if there was anything else she wanted to add. She said there wasn't and asked if I was referring to anything in particular. By this stage it seemed as if Jenny was wondering if Charles had mentioned their relationship, but I got the impression that she wasn't about to say anything just in case I didn't know. She seemed fidgety. I told her that Charles had told me about their relationship. Jenny dismissed the notion instantly. I told more of Charles' story, but still she denied any involvement. I informed her that his last words to me on leaving the room had been that he would continue to be adult and professional about their relationship, that he hadn't discussed the relationship with anyone else and had no plans to change that. Jenny didn't respond directly but asked if Charles had given any indication of what he wanted from the session. I said that Charles had made mention of the new global role supporting the development of fibre optics and that he was very interested in securing the role. Almost before I could finish, Jenny asked if Charles was planning to use his fabricated story as blackmail. I said that I didn't think so and asked if she would like to have a chat with him. She declined.

Our deliberation continued for the rest of the morning, with Jenny's denial continuing and Charles sticking to his story. I suggested to both independently that I call Bill, as the mediation commissioner, to update him on the progress.

Charles was fine about this, but Jenny was more reticent. She paused and questioned whether Bill's presence was necessary. I said that my hand had been somewhat forced by the deadlock. She mentioned that a progress report would include sharing Charles' story with him and she didn't consider it appropriate to include the Chief Executive in such nonsense. I could tell that Jenny was somewhat edgy, but in the absence of agreement on the story I couldn't think of an alternative solution. Eventually however, she agreed.

I made the call to Bill. He arrived about 20 minutes later and I briefed him on how the day had developed. I took time to outline the story Charles had relayed to me. Bill was shocked. I said that Jenny had denied it and that we had hit a blockage. He asked for my advice on what to do next. I suggested that we go and see both of them independently which we did, first visiting Jenny. She continued to hold her position that the story of a sexual relationship was a lie. We spent about half an hour together and Jenny didn't shift from her position one iota. We then went to see Charles who retold his story, sparing Bill the detail that had been revealed to me. At the end of his comments he repeated that he had both texts and voicemails that would prove his story but would rather save Jenny the embarrassment of disclosing them. This time, he said that we could share that information if it seemed necessary.

Bill left the room shaking his head and rubbing his hands in his hair, wondering how all this could have happened right under his nose. He added that Jenny and Charles were two of his best people and that he couldn't afford to lose either of them. We went back in to see Jenny to ask her one more time if there was any truth in Charles' story. Again she said no. I asked if I could see Bill outside for a moment. He obliged. When we were alone I said that I wanted to share the information about the texts and voicemails with Jenny but that this should be done privately as it would probably be less daunting for Jenny. Bill agreed.

The breakthrough

I went back through to see Jenny once again, this time stating that I had requested to speak to her without Bill's presence. I then revealed that Charles had indicated that he was in possession of texts and voicemails from her that would corroborate his story. I could see that Jenny wanted to respond but I quickly continued by saying that I had the impression that Charles cared for her and would therefore continue the mediation in a professional and adult manner. Jenny went silent. She finally broke the silence by saying simply, *"okay."* I pressed her for the meaning of her reply. She admitted that she and Charles had had a relationship but that it hadn't affected their work in any way. Realising the potential enormity of what she had admitted to, Jenny began to cry. She kept saying repeatedly, *"What have I done? What have I done?"* I passed her a tissue and sat and waited for about ten minutes for her to regain her composure. I asked what she wanted to do next. It seemed as if her confession, followed by her tears, had helped her regain energy and focus. The drive that must have helped her secure such a senior position had returned. She said that she would like to go and see Bill and explain the situation to him. I checked with Bill who said that he would be delighted to hear Jenny's version of events.

Jenny, Bill and I met in Bill's room. Jenny led the way and explained to Bill that she had made a huge error of judgement. She explained that a six month affair had started between her and Charles in South Africa just over six months ago. She acknowledged that it was a mistake and that apart from her closest friend she hadn't told anyone of the affair, including her husband. She continued by saying that one of the errors of her judgement had been to talk down Charles' readiness for taking on the new fibre optics role and that she had done so to avoid the potentially increased exposure to each other the role would bring and any ramifications that may follow. She went on to inform Bill that Charles had mentioned during the mediation session that he still wanted to be considered for the role. Bill was struggling to keep up with all the new information that he was receiving. He asked Jenny to give him some time so that he could think things through.

Charles had been alone for some time and needed to be updated too. Bill asked me to appraise Charles of developments and indicate that he was considering the next steps. Charles was surprised that things had moved so quickly, but was relieved that things were now out in the open and we would now be able to move forward. I went back through to see Bill. He said that he would need to speak with his HR Director and probably his Chairman about the situation. I asked if he would be willing to speak with Charles and Jenny first. He agreed, but only if they were together. The mediation session was now going in a direction that would have been difficult to predict at the start of the day. Both agreed, albeit reluctantly.

As Charles and Jenny entered the room, the embarrassment could be felt. They sat opposite each other as if they wanted to send a message that their relationship was well and truly over. Bill said that he was surprised and shocked at how the day had turned out and he would need to seek some advice from higher authorities on the way forward but he would be interested in hearing from Jenny and Charles first. Jenny repeated what she had said to him in their previous session. She knew her judgement was questionable but said that their liaison hadn't affected her job. Charles went one stage further by saying that the moments they had shared were special, albeit inappropriate, and he would always treasure them. He then said that he had now moved on and as part of moving on wanted Bill to know that he wanted to be appointed to the new role.

Bill was taken aback by the maturity displayed by both, although he was disappointed that Jenny had denied the truth for so long. He said that he was not at all sure about what to do and asked to be excused while he spoke to the Chairman and HR Director, asking me to join him. It was now 5.55pm.

The HR Director joined us at the venue whilst the Chairman joined on the phone from Paris. The telephone meeting lasted for two hours and ended with no decision. They suggested that all would benefit from some sleep and should re-engage with the discussion the next day.

The following day at 8.00am I met again with Bill, the HR Director and the Chairman via telephone. Bill said that he thought the organisation should deal with the situation in the same adult way that Charles and Jenny appeared to be dealing with it, adding that losing either of them would be a problem and losing both would be a disaster. His proposal was to offer Charles the bigger fibre optics role and move Jenny to a Regional Head role with responsibility for all products within the 'next 11' markets that had been identified. Charles would continue to report to Gary, who would be promoted to the global Sales Director role, and a replacement would be found for Gary in due course. Jenny meanwhile would continue to report to Bill. The Chairman thought this a pragmatic solution, but the HR Director disagreed and spoke about the organisation's requirement to go through the disciplinary process to demonstrate that they had dealt with the matter fairly. Bill snapped at the HR Director, saying that now wasn't the time for HR to hold up the process. He considered this a commercial matter that required a speedy solution to ensure business continuity. He said that he would like Jenny to continue in the Sales Director's role but had thought of too many potential difficulties. He said that the 'next 11' role could be positioned as a sideways, equivalent and strategic move. He did acknowledge however that a conversation should be had with both about their actions. The Chairman asked what would happen to the candidate that had been earmarked for the role. Bill said that he would handle that discussion. The trio then agreed to implement Bill's plan. It was now 9.00am and Charles and Jenny arrived as planned. Both went to their separate rooms with no idea of the agreement put forward.

Bill decided to move quickly and have separate conversations with Jenny and Charles. Jenny could not be persuaded that the proposed move would be the right solution. Bill told her that he was not inclined to tread the disciplinary route and was proposing what he considered to be a pragmatic solution. He said he would leave Jenny to think it through while he went to see Charles.

Charles was delighted with the news brought by Bill and thanked him for the opportunity. Almost immediately he asked what would be happening to Jenny.

Bill merely informed him that Jenny was considering a proposal that he had put to her. As Bill and I were about to leave the room, Charles called me back to stress that he hadn't intentionally traded sex for power, but that he was nevertheless aggrieved that he had been overlooked for the bigger role.

Jenny asked to see Bill again. She was wondering whether his proposal had any flexibility, to which Bill replied that if flexibility meant remaining in her current role, then no. Jenny asked for a day or so to think things through. Bill stressed again that he didn't want to lose her. The next day, Jenny called Bill and made an appointment to meet with both of us. At the meeting she said that she had reflected on the events of the last few days and had decided to accept the alternative role, admitting that she would pay for her error of judgement for some time to come. She confessed that she had still not felt able to discuss the situation with her husband, and leaving the company would have prompted too many questions that she would have found difficult to answer. Bill said he acknowledged how difficult this experience must have been for Jenny but he thought that this was a situation that they could both make work. He said that the positive esteem in which he held her abilities hadn't altered, but the events that had unfolded during the mediation had compromised her position. Jenny thanked him and then asked if she could talk to him in more detail about the transition, desiring the company to do everything possible to put a positive spin on the moves. Jenny also requested a few weeks off before starting her new role.

Jenny then left, leaving Bill and I alone. He said that he would never have guessed for a moment that his call to me a few weeks ago would be the stone that caused such a ripple effect. He was grateful for the mediation intervention, particularly for the honesty that it had brought. He had some work to do on managing the change he said, but at least for the time being he hadn't lost any of his key players.

Observations
Getting people to talk:

Getting discussions started given the sensitive nature of this dispute unsurprisingly proved difficult; Jenny and Charles had formed an unspoken pact to keep their affair a secret. There were a few factors that prompted Charles' blockage removal in this case. These included:

- Use of silence
- The pressure of the mediation process
- Appropriate timing
- An interest in being set free from the bondage of the secret relationship
- Speaking to a person who might understand Charles' position (in this case a male mediator)
- Trust in the mediator
- The realisation that sharing the story might strengthen Charles' position
- Rapport with the mediator

It is not unusual for truth, anxiety, angst, fretfulness, worry and history to be expressed during mediated discussions. Like many of us, Charles longed for the opportunity to be heard. His motive for securing promotion, and trading sex for power, seemed to factor as a subset for the greater priority of getting his surreptitious tale off his chest. As soon as the moment presented itself, Charles seized the opportunity. In this case I was the chosen recipient of such vital information.

Getting people to talk during the conflict resolution process is half the battle. However, the mediator becomes required to operate at a more advanced level in circumstances where parties are economical with the truth or reticent to talk. In this case it was Jenny who thought that she had too much to lose to make talking worthwhile. As the pressure increased and the realisation dawned that she may lose her job, Jenny then began to speak. The temptation for mediators can be to want to jump in too early and not allow the parties to keep unambiguous ownership for resolving the dispute. Once parties start dialogue, it is quite normal for them to continue until their story has been completely articulated. In effect, once started, it becomes difficult to stop.

The role of the mediation commissioner:

The person who commissions mediation is often, although not always, the person who has the authority to settle a dispute. The mediator himself is powerless when it comes to agreeing what the organisation may or may not be willing to do to bring about a solution. This is particularly true in cases where a financial settlement or some organisational change, reform or restructure may be required. In many organisational mediation sessions, there comes a time when the mediator has to take a judgement about the best time to call the commissioner or person with authority to settle. In this case, Bill was the only person who could have acted to commit the organisation to a series of actions; his clout in dealing with Jenny and Charles allowed the process to move on swiftly. The mediator's role then becomes one of facilitator and sounding board to the organisational decision maker. If the commissioner is not also the person with authority to settle, this will hopefully have been established at the commencement of the mediation process.

The role of Human Resources professionals in mediation:
In the last 20 years or so, the role of the Human Resources professional has changed beyond recognition. The cultural shift has included moving from being referred to as *'Personnel'* where an inference was sometimes taken to associate the function with welfare, tea and tissues. HR buzzwords and phrases now include titles such as *'HR Business Partner'*. One of the other enormous changes has been the requirement for HR practitioners to come to terms with huge swathes of employment legislation changes. Some time ago, I remember facilitating a workshop on *'Managing Difficult Conversations, the Equality Act and Preventing Bullying and Harassment'*, supported as I was by an in-house trainer. During the workshop the group had healthy banter on aspects such as policies and the grievance and disciplinary procedure. I proposed that in many cases common sense and a *'nip it in the bud'* discussion might be all that is required to put a stop to a problem and prevent it from escalating, whilst my co-facilitator extolled the virtues of the company policy and procedure on such matters.

The group had a long discussion about which option they would chose depending on the circumstance that they were in. After the training session, my co-facilitator and I shared good humour about the difference in our perspectives. He was, of course, doing his job.

Tension can build in an organisation when the *'HR process'* gets in the way. Bill's reaction to his HR Director was an example of an executive wanting to take a practical, sensible and no-nonsense decision quickly with business continuity at its heart. The HR function faces an ongoing challenge to ensure that the organisation is protected by properly dispensing correct employment law and advice and at the same time knowing when a light, idealistic and down-to-earth touch is the right thing to do.

A case of mistaken identity

"You can accomplish anything in life, provided that you do not mind who gets the credit." – Harry S. Truman

Chargrove Health Services provides healthcare for more than 735,000 people. The previous year 350,000 men, women and children were cared for as inpatients (stayed at least one night) and almost 400,000 attended outpatient clinics. The accident and emergency departments had also cared for about 150,000 people. The hospital is recognised as being amongst the top performing hospitals in the US.

At the time of this story the pathology department had a team of six consultants – three men and three women of various ethnic origins. A year ago the Team Manager and Clinical Director, Dr Walsh, moved on, citing bullying by some members of the team. She had raised the issue with HR, but despite intervention nothing changed. Dr Walsh had by now moved to a neighbouring hospital, fulfilling a similar role there. Before she left she was subjected to a year long investigation due to some of her direct reports alleging that she had falsified figures in order to meet healthcare targets. The investigation found this not to be the case, although they reported that there was room for increased accuracy. Dr Walsh felt that she could no longer trust any of her colleagues and thought that the best option would be to move on. The strain had taken its toll however. She had been seeing a doctor for treatment for stress and sleepless nights and had also developed a permanent squint over the course of the previous year. She believed that there was a correlation between the tension with her colleagues and her deteriorating health.

Chargrove advertised the Team Manager vacancy but few people came forward, with feedback suggesting that Dr Walsh's story had got out amongst prospective candidates and that they had become concerned that they might experience the same fate if they took the job. Unexpectedly, one of the pathology consultants from Chargrove, Dr Walker, broke ranks and applied for the Team Manager and Clinical Director role. She was successful in her application, much to the surprise of her colleagues who thought that although she was a competent specialist she would make a poor line manager. There were also a few eyebrows raised on the basis that, in the view of some, Dr Walker had made a noteworthy contribution to Dr Walsh's downfall. Soon after her appointment, Dr Walker attempted to put some team principles into place including setting objectives, clarifying roles, agreeing overtime and on-call arrangements and confirming the criteria for the consultants to take on private paid work. For the first six months or so everything seemed fine.

One Monday morning one of the consultants, Dr Arnold, walked into Dr Walker's office to ask her a question. This was not unusual, but Dr Arnold was taken aback when Dr Walker snapped and told him to get out and either knock and wait or make an appointment to come and see her. Dr Arnold was a greatly experienced doctor from Sri Lanka who was perceived as being highly competent at his job, having previously worked in England, Canada, India and Germany. He was highly offended at Dr Walker's attitude and could not work out why she had reacted in such a manner. He decided not to go back to her office again, making sure that he told his fellow consultants what had happened.

The next day Dr Walker came to Dr Arnold's office and asked him what he had wanted of her the day before. Dr Arnold responded by saying that the issue had passed and she wasn't to worry. Dr Arnold was still secretly angry about their previous exchange and couldn't bring himself to have a conversation with her. This feeling of outrage lasted for several days, right up until a team meeting a week or so later. Dr Arnold said very little during the meeting, after which Dr Walker asked him to stay behind whereupon she told him she could sense some tension between them and asked him what had caused it. Dr Arnold reminded her of her rant of the previous week. Dr Walker said that she had been on the phone to the Chief Executive at the time and that it hadn't been convenient for Dr Arnold to wait around. When Dr Arnold started to talk about how he had felt as a result of the incident, Dr Walker told him to *"put a sock in it and get over it"*. Dr Arnold didn't respond, but again told his consultant colleagues of his experiences later on. They took his side and also began to give Dr Walker the cold shoulder treatment.

By now, Dr Arnold had started to take on an increasing amount of private work. Part of the difficulty in the relationship between him and Dr Walker was that she regularly accused him of doing more paid private work than he was actually doing. Dr Arnold was a principled man and to him the implication was that he wasn't working enough for the salary he drew, a charge he strenuously denied.

Part of Dr Arnold's duties was to read a number of image films each month to keep patient records up to date. The target for him was 1,000 films per month but his monthly output was currently down to about 550, a statistic Dr Walker used to strengthen her argument.

The crisis

One Thursday morning Dr Walker barged into Dr Arnold's office. He was on the phone. She stood over him, impatiently waiting for him to finish his call. When he had finished Dr Walker could hardly speak for nervous tension. She eventually spluttered out that the Chief Executive had just called her and during the conversation he had asked her about a deceased Mr Lichfield. Dr Walker didn't know anything about the patient and said so. It transpired that the previous week Mr Lichfield's family had been given an incorrect cause of his death. Dr Arnold had got the labels mixed up on two bodies during a post mortem and Mr Lichfield's family had spent a whole day at the hospital trying to get the matter sorted out. Dr Walker had just returned from three weeks holiday and no-one in the team had informed her of the tragedy. The Chief Executive's call had been to inform Dr Walker that the story had been leaked to the media and the local newspaper had called the hospital for comment.

Dr Walker was livid. She couldn't understand how something so serious hadn't been brought to her attention, even if she had been on holiday. Dr Arnold said that it had been a genuine mistake and that he had apologised to and placated the family. Dr Walker said that she would deal with Dr Arnold later, and went off to deal with the PR crisis. The local newspaper ran a story about the incident the following day and it also featured on the regional TV news bulletin. It was a disaster for the hospital. Dr Arnold and his colleagues were asked to meet with HR the following day. An investigation into the mistaken identity was launched but Dr Arnold was suspended while the investigation took place.

A few weeks later the decision was given, resulting in verbal warnings for all the staff for failing to follow the required process in such cases. The relationship with Dr Walker and her team had now hit an all-time low. They were barely on speaking terms. Nevertheless, Dr Walker attempted to tackle the working schedule arrangements. The timing couldn't have been worse.

Mediation

It was at this stage that the HR Director suggested mediation for the team, and the arrangements were made. Dr Walker, her team, the Chief Executive and the HR Director all attended. On the day of the mediation, as part of the joint opening session, I invited Dr Walker to provide her version of events. She was articulate, professional and almost robotic in her manner. She explained the background of Dr Walsh's departure and her promotion to the post of Clinical Director, revealing that Dr Walsh had referred to the problems she had experienced with the consultants in the handover. One particular problem centred around a lead consultant who did not channel his work through the department in the normal manner. An example being that he would send written requests for items with no or little justification for the request. Dr Walker said that the situation had grown steadily worse and had begun to make her ill. She said that she had had many sleepless nights, encountered stress and worry, suffered from psychosomatic symptoms such as headaches, migraines and depression, all of which were then putting her relationships under strain.

Annual leave and collective grievances

Dr Walker said that she noticed that some consultants were taking holiday at the same time, leaving the service vulnerable. Over the Easter period of one particular year, two consultants took annual leave successively over a five week period with no arrangements made to cover the workload. Instead, the workload of the absent consultant was allowed to accumulate and a holding report was sent out to clinicians in the fictitious name of 'Dr Etha'. This resulted in reporting delays, forcing the work to be outsourced to a private company.

Difficulties with annual leave continued, Dr Walker said, despite meetings between managers and consultants to organise leave better and reduce reporting delays. Eventually, Isobel Griffiths, then General Manager for Support Services, wrote to all the consultants underlining the principles of leave arrangements for the whole department and the need to obtain leave authorisation from the Clinical Director. This meant that no two consultants could take annual leave together. A few of the consultants raised objections to these arrangements. They approached the Director of HR and Chief Executive to revoke this decision and requested further meetings to discuss the situation. Dr Walker continued by saying that things escalated about six months later when, once again, two consultants requested annual leave together. The request was turned down and the consultants put in a collective grievance. A meeting took place and a compromise was suggested whereby during the summer and Christmas breaks, two consultants would be allowed to take leave simultaneously, provided only a week overlapped. However, this compromise, one that Dr Walker felt was reasonable, was not accepted by the consultants. Meanwhile, one of the consultants took two weeks annual leave without seeking permission. Dr Walker reminded the staff that unauthorised leave was a disciplinary offence and she decided to raise a grievance. No disciplinary action was taken against the consultant however, and the ad hoc leave arrangements continued.

Once Dr Walker had concluded this part of the story she asked for a short break as she needed to visit the bathroom.

Appraisal

Dr Walker returned and continued. During her tenure, she said, the consultants refused to have their appraisals conducted by her. Collectively they wrote to the Chief Executive requesting that on the grounds of incompatibility it would not be appropriate for Dr Walker to carry out their appraisal. The Chief Executive consented and located a Clinical Director from a nearby hospital to carry out the appraisals.

The new contract job plan arrangements

During their time in power, the previous government had introduced new contract working arrangements for consultants, arrangements that were being phased in over a number of years. This created another area for dispute. Issues were raised about private practice work, coroners, post mortems, time scheduling and a range of other matters. Dr Walker said that she sought help from some of her senior colleagues at the hospital on the matter and an agreement was finally reached with some of the consultants. The others remained on their current terms and conditions but raised individual grievances while they did so. This included requests for years of back pay to recognise previous work.

Dr Walker again asked for a short break as she needed to go to the bathroom again.

Mistaken identity

When she had returned, Dr Walker said that the case of mistaken identity that had drawn media interest to the hospital had been unforgivable. She stopped and recomposed herself at this point as she was close to tears. I sensed that she did not want her tears to be seen by her colleagues who were still with us as part of the joint session. Dr Walker then alleged that a culture of secrecy and underhand behaviour was prevalent in the department, again almost breaking down as she talked about her feeling of isolation, despite her best efforts to carry out her role and work with her colleagues in the department.

Dr Walker had now been talking for nearly an hour in total. When she stopped again, I suggested we take a short break before asking the team of consultants to respond. I then asked Dr Walker in private if she was okay, given her frequent breaks. She explained that the process had been making her sick. She was feeling very anxious about the day and it was directly affecting her health. I remember being surprised at witnessing how conflict was having such a profound effect on a medical professional.

After the break I asked the consultants if they would like to say something about the ongoing dispute. They had nominated a spokesperson, the aforementioned Dr Arnold. Dr Arnold said that listening to Dr Walker for almost an hour was farcical, that the department was in a mess and that a number of consultants had left and others were considering leaving as a result of Dr Walker's management style. He said that Dr Walker didn't listen, was not visible and had elevated herself from the rest of the team as soon as her promotion had been confirmed.

He said that discussions about a change of management hours, annual leave and private working arrangements had been handled badly by her. The situation had been going on for years and despite the efforts of the team to try and rectify the situation, Dr Walker had hidden her head in the sand. Dr Arnold also took the opportunity to clarify his position about working in private practice. He restated that Dr Walker had misunderstood his working arrangements. He explained them all over again, concluding with his opinion that the mediation process would not be complete for him until he had received a written apology concerning Dr Walker's treatment of him and the misunderstanding of his private practice work. At this stage, other consultant colleagues stepped in to offer words of support for Dr Arnold. One in particular spoke of Dr Walker's error of judgment in applying for the Clinical Director role, saying that it had not been appropriate considering the contribution Dr Walker had made to Dr Walsh's downfall.

A mini war broke out as Dr Walker refuted these allegations. She remained composed, but kept on talking even though her colleagues and I were trying to speak to her at the same time. It was as if a robotic programme within her prompted her to keep going until she had come to the end of a preloaded script. Finally, I was able to ask both sides a question. I asked if having considered everything they had been through they could envisage a way in which they could work together in the future. The Chief Executive stepped in and encouraged his colleagues to work out a plan to work together for the sake of the patients they served.

We continued in group dialogue for the next few hours before the group felt ready to start scoping a plan which they could sign up to. With some reluctance, both sides said that they would give the continued working relationship a try. Dr Walker and Dr Arnold were still not engaging in eye contact with each other however. The team drafted a plan which had action points such as:

- Dr Walker to visit departments within the service to gain a better understanding of the people and the way in which the service is provided
- Review information on activity and staffing levels benchmarked against comparable services. Dr Walker will share the data with the consultants and the consultants will respond

- All consultants will engage in discussions about how the service should look in the future
- HR to provide ongoing support for Dr Walker
- The team will meet and communicate verbally on a bi-weekly basis to sort out issues and problems
- Everyone to finalise new working arrangements and sign new contracts within four weeks
- All consultants to have an appraisal in the next two months
- Dr Arnold to receive a written apology and acknowledge the inaccuracy in figures relating to private practice from Dr Walker within 48 hours

It was now 5.45pm and we had been together for the whole day. I congratulated the group on their achievement of sticking with the mediation for so long. The group said goodbye to each other and made their way home. I did notice however that, despite working together on thrashing out a settlement agreement, Dr Walker and Dr Arnold still appeared to have some way to go to reach forgiveness and reconciliation. They didn't say goodbye to each other and avoided eye contact. I hoped that on reflection of the events of the day, an overnight transformation would be experienced by each. This mediation session took place on Monday.

The apology
Although the action points above were documented and signed by all who were present, the detailed written apology by Dr Walker to Dr Arnold was due to follow within 48 hours. To this end, at 1.57pm on Wednesday afternoon an email arrived in my inbox. The sender was Dr Walker and in the subject box was the word 'apology'. I got excited. I thought that my hopes for transformation had come true. I didn't have time to read the email at that moment, but opened it on my return after a meeting some two hours or so later. The attached letter read as follows:

Dear Dr Arnold,

In the mediation session on Monday I agreed to write to you with an apology for how things have been between us and for misunderstanding the arrangements you have in place for working in private practice.

Since the marathon of Monday, I have had two nights to reflect on this. I don't think I owe you an apology at all. In fact, you should be apologising to me! How dare you accuse me of not understanding your work arrangements and berate me in front of the Chief Executive and HR Director. You are out of order. The situation has always been that I have worked hard to get the department in the best shape to service the needs of the community. You have done nothing but attempt to get in my way since I started my new role. You have done the best you can to make things difficult for me. Congratulations. You have succeeded. There is no way that I can write an apology to you. I suggest you be more honest and acknowledge the areas of shortfall that I continue to point out to you.

I would be happy to discuss the way forward with you, but suggest that this would be best done with a witness from HR or some other support function.

Yours,
Dr Walker.

My heart sank. I phoned Dr Walker immediately. I thanked her for copying me in on the email and said that it didn't appear to be in the spirit of what we had agreed. She said that the more she thought about it, the more she thought that she was right and was the one who deserved the apology. While I was on the phone with Dr Walker, a message was passed to me asking me to phone the HR Director of the hospital. I did so as soon as my call with Dr Walker finished. The HR Director said that Dr Walker's letter was the last straw for the organisation and that he was just about to send Dr Walker an invitation for an audience with the Chief Executive. I was to find out later that Dr Walker was stripped of her management responsibilities and asked to work on other initiatives within the hospital. I was saddened that Dr Walker decided to run away from the opportunity for settlement at the last minute. The mediation therefore had met with limited success. Whilst it provided an opportunity for the team to speak and thrash out issues, Dr Arnold and Dr Walker were unable to forgive each other for the past.

Observations

This case raises at least two issues. The first is that success was celebrated prematurely. The mediation session finished on Monday evening with a false sense of achievement that resolution would be forthcoming. I had some doubts, but remained optimistic that Dr Walker, Dr Arnold and the other consultants would seize the opportunity to move on from their troubled past. In finding resolution to any conflict situation there are a number of levels that conflict resolution specialists may experience. These can include:

- Instant forgiveness and long lasting reconciliation
- Gradual restoration as trust is rebuilt over time
- Surface level settlement as parties agree to work together but underlying mistrust continues
- Deceitful settlement as parties sign up to a settlement agreement whilst continuing to ignore, snub or pay no attention to their opponent

This mediation might have brought a more positive result if a second day had been scheduled, but patient demands had prevented this. A second day could have been used to invite Dr Arnold and Dr Walker to work together to iron out the apology. Any matters of concern would have been flushed out during the process and would have prevented the catastrophe of Dr Walker sending the 'apology' in the form that she did. As the mediator, I have to accept some of the responsibility for not pressing hard enough to help the parties to recognise the risk of not fully completing the process.

The second issue about this case is the ill health experienced by Dr Walker. Some time ago I became interested in the correlation between conflict and health. I have become particularly fascinated with this theme in relation to health professionals. It is easy to forget that those who do such a great job of looking after us when we get ill are themselves prone to illness too. I have observed countless cases of conflict within the Health Service and its impact on its victims. This theme has also been recognised and picked up by others.

Many doctors find it difficult to admit that their work is stressful or that they need help in dealing with issues of conflict when they arise. The combined forces of stigma, shame and secrecy may make it particularly difficult for doctors to grapple with. A 2008 Department of Health report entitled 'Mental Health and Ill Health in Doctors' documents that medicine is a stressful profession. Stress and fatigue rates are high, especially in female and junior doctors. Sources of stress may include:

- Work pressure, workload, inadequacy of resources and poor support
- Nature of work – high demand and low control
- Poor relationships with colleagues – particularly poor team working
- Service pressures, investigations, complaints and court cases
- Lack of opportunity to delegate work
- Isolation
- Excessive working hours

Tackling conflict at work is seen as a priority for some organisations, but not all. The third bullet point helps to indicate the risk organisations face when mechanisms are not put into place to deal with difficult situations as they arise. In the health profession, the risk is arguably higher than many other sectors. A stressed doctor may:

- Misdiagnose illness
- Incorrectly label a dead or living patient
- Make an error of judgment during an operation
- Miscalculate the formula for a prescription

Firth-Cozens says that doctors are a committed and conscientious group. Personality traits such as perfectionism, self-criticism, and dependency are reportedly common in medical students. In some, such traits may influence their perceptions of work, making it more stressful. Employers should work hard to ensure that there is prompt resolution to stressful situations and that there is transparency across all fact finding processes.

Medical schools can contribute to improving the ability within the Health Service to deal with relationship breakdowns. For example, medical school trainers can incorporate learning on this area within the undergraduate curriculum. This will help to strengthen the message that the impact of conflict has many clinical and scientific similarities to the diagnosis of ill health for other reasons.

All boxed in

"The test of first-rate intelligence is the ability to hold two opposed ideas in the mind at the same time, and still retain the ability to function. One should, for example, be able to see that things are hopeless and yet be determined to make them otherwise." – F. Scott Fitzgerald

Viapack is an AIM listed packaging supplier employing 3,000 people and generating revenues of £375m. It is a specialist fulfilment business which has experienced double digit growth over the last few years, largely down to the recent increase in online and mail order purchasing. Although Viapack employ their own staff they also outsource the delivery of parcels to a number of other companies.

Viapack had appointed John Smith as their Chief Executive about two years before this story starts. John worked in retail for about 20 years before this post and therefore understood the industry well. He was highly regarded in the industry. 18 months before the start of this tale, Viapack outsourced the contract to deliver boxes for a major general merchandise retailer, Harbucks, who have around 200 sites across the UK and are a major player in their field. This contract was outsourced to Box Express, with John instrumental in the awarding of the contract. Box Express were to deliver around 5,000 units of Harbucks products each month on behalf of Viapack.

Box Express was run by Matthew Boorman, and both he and John were 49. They went to the same independent school and then later attended the same university. John was delighted that his old schoolmate would have the opportunity to take on the work, although it must be stressed that Viapack undertook an open and transparent procurement process and that Box Express were the clear winners.

The background
John was in New York on business when he received a call from his Finance Director, Martin, back in the UK. Martin had just returned from a meeting with Harbucks, and informed John that there was a problem. Harbucks had recently been running a nationwide internet-only offer of £44.99 for a product that usually sold for £99.99. Harbucks had got the advertising just right and as a result sales of the product were phenomenal, generating 500,000 orders after just one peak time television advert. Harbucks had forecast sales of 75,000 products during

that time slot. Fortunately Harbucks had enough stock to satisfy the increase in orders, although it did mean bringing in an emergency shipment from China.

The stock was delivered to Viapack, who in turn sent it on to Box Express to deliver to customers. About two weeks after the spectacular sales following the TV advert, Harbucks started to receive phone calls and emails from disgruntled customers, many of whom hadn't received the item and of those who had, some had received them damaged. The number of complaints soon ran into thousands, to the point where BBC consumer affairs programme Watchdog had shown an interest in taking up the case following an unprecedented number of calls to their researchers. Harbucks were understandably concerned about damage to their brand and reputation, and the board wanted an explanation of what had happened.

With John still in the US, it was left to Martin to meet with Box Express owner Matthew to explain what had happened. Matthew explained that they'd had difficulty getting enough staff to fulfil the orders, to which Martin responded by saying that Viapack should have been informed of any problems. Harbucks would probably demand some form of compensation, he said, as they were seeking to protect their brand and were focused on damage limitation. Martin asked Matthew to speak to John as a matter of urgency. Matthew did so. It wasn't a pleasant call. John had clearly put their history to one side as he tore into Matthew, stating that they would talk further when he returned to the UK.

Following this setback, Box Express pulled out all the stops and worked hard to get customers' products delivered. Fortunately for all concerned, Watchdog decided to drop the investigation in favour of something "more juicy." This represented a near miss for Harbucks who were now demanding urgent reassurances from Viapack that they could keep up with the demand from their customers.

Two weeks after the initial backlog of orders had been cleared, Harbucks summoned Viapack to attend a board meeting. John attended the one hour meeting with two senior members of his team, the upshot of which was retention of the contract but with a reduced margin. On balance, due to the mass volume of work generated by Harbucks, John and his colleagues considered it a price worth paying. Viapack then arranged a similar meeting with Box Express. John allowed Matthew to continue working on their behalf, but when Box Express began paying their invoices late John decided to find backup suppliers.

In the meantime, John had sought legal advice on actions Viapack could take against Box Express. The legal teams had taken over what was once face to face or telephone dialogue between the two companies. With a number of years remaining on the contract however, Viapack would have problems switching suppliers. There would also be expensive penalties in the event of premature termination of the contract. Thirdly, the tender process had indicated that Box Express were one of a limited number of businesses of its kind that could deliver on a national scale in this way. Nevertheless, Viapack began to redirect the Harbucks orders to another supplier but, upon discovering this via a tip off from a former employee, Box Express asked their legal team to write to Viapack reminding them of the clause in the commercial contract that prohibited another supplier delivering product for Harbucks. No response was received.

Mediation considered

A mediation session was eventually arranged but the route to mediation was somewhat out of the ordinary. One Tuesday morning, John attended a business breakfast session. The speaker was a highly respected businessman and government advisor, and the topic was 'industrial relations in the 21st century.' The session was attended by around 100 business leaders.

During the session, the speaker talked about the changing nature of business across the world, touching on what he described as new thinking with regard to industrial relations and new ways for organisations to gain and retain competitive advantage.

He described how conflict was running the risk of ruining some businesses and draining them of precious resources. He gave a story concerning the rebuilding of Wembley Stadium where contractors had fallen out. Costs had run way over budget and there was a danger that the FA Cup final, scheduled to be played there in a few months time, would need to find an alternative venue. The multi-party dispute went to mediation and Lord Carter of Coles was appointed as the mediator. The mediation was successful and millions of pounds of ongoing costs were saved. There was also the small matter that there would be no further potential disruption to the FA Cup Final. John had heard of the concept of mediation before, but wasn't aware that it could be used in this way.

He left the breakfast briefing session and decided to find out more on the topic. In order to do so he attended a half-day briefing session led by a leading mediation providing organisation which proved both useful and informative, especially when he considered the ongoing dispute between Viapack and Box Express which was costing more in legal fees every month. Only that morning he had signed off another invoice for legal advice relating to the dispute.

One of the principles that had been discussed during the briefing session was the importance of dialogue. The other aspect that John was also mindful of was that Box Express was run by his old school and university friend, Matthew, to whom he hadn't spoken for the best part of a year now. John mulled over his options for a few weeks, and then made a bold decision. He decided to phone Matthew and invite him for lunch. It took him a while to pluck up the courage to dial Matthew's number, but eventually he did so. Matthew was understandably shocked at the call. John said he wanted to explore whether their dispute could be discussed and wanted to invite Matthew for lunch. Matthew agreed and a date was set for the following week. John revealed that he wouldn't be telling his legal advisors about the lunch. Matthew quickly got the point and said that he wouldn't either.

The lunch

The two men met for their lunch date. It was a frosty start. They discussed families and sport and deliberated on other surface matters. When they had both finished their main course Matthew made the first attempt to get into the purpose of the conversation and the discussion slowly got underway. Matthew apologised for the problems with delivering the Harbucks orders. He explained that the spike in product sales had caught them unawares and they hadn't responded fast enough, adding that he was ashamed and embarrassed that the customer complaints had reached Harbucks and the media. Matthew reached for his bag and pulled out spreadsheets that showed how units were now being delivered on time or ahead of schedule for 100% of orders. He had prepared well for the meeting and was obviously keen to salvage what he could from the business relationship.

When Matthew had finished, John responded by saying how disappointed and angry he was. He said that although he had been detached from the procurement process that had led to Box Express winning the contract, he was obviously pleased to hear that Matthew had made his business a successful one and so felt personally let down when the news broke. He then spent time talking through the sequence of the events as he had understood them. He also spoke about the pressure Harbucks had placed upon Viapack to be assured that such a slip up wouldn't happen again.

This included:

- Viapack taking a reduced margin
- Weekly meetings between Viapack and Harbucks detailing delivery reports
- Viapack drafting a letter of apology to customers who had been let down

John said he was concerned about the damage to the brand and reputation of Viapack and that although they had retained the Harbucks contract, the relationship had been severely strained. Viapack had no choice but to seek legal advice on the options it should consider. He then touched on some of the aspects that were part of the legal argument, including Matthew's accusation that Viapack had breached the commercial contract by retaining another delivery company to deliver Harbucks' products. John informed Matthew that his board, wanting to mitigate and spread the risk, had made that particular decision for him and he'd had to go along with it.

The two men continued talking, each one setting out what had happened and why they had taken the action that they had, with both acknowledging the strengths and weaknesses of their actions. They also acknowledged a joint willingness to try and get things sorted out. Both businesses had by now run up huge legal bills.

The main points from their lunch conversation were that:
* They thought they could continue working together
* Viapack would want compensation as a result of what had happened
* Box Express would want to become the sole supplier once more
* Neither business wanted to spend more money on legal fees

Once these points had been decided upon, John then proposed mediation to agree the way ahead. He told Matthew of his recent experiences attending the business breakfast session and then the mediation briefing session, adding that mediation might be an avenue to help them get back on track. John commented further that as the dispute was so large that it now affected more than just the two of them, the solution should be a joint effort. Nearly three hours after the men had arrived at the restaurant for lunch, they ended their self-mediated meeting with John saying that his office would be in contact with Matthew's to put the next steps into motion.

The mediation session
John called me the following morning. He briefed me on the background and said that he wanted to arrange a mediation session as soon as possible to attempt to get the situation resolved. Three weeks later I met with both sides for that mediation session. Present for each company were:

Viapack:
John Smith – Chief Executive
Martin King – Finance Director
Lance Croft – Supply Chain Director
Judith Morgan – Lawyer

Box Express:
Matthew Boorman – Chief Executive

Kirsty Rosenberg – Finance Director
Gareth Wright – Lawyer

I initially met with each side separately to make sure that I understood both accounts accurately. More importantly, I wanted to get a good idea of what each side was looking for in order to achieve settlement. Within an hour, I had completed the private exploratory meetings.

In the joint opening, both sides were frank and candid about the background to the dispute and what they were looking for on the day. Although they both had their legal advisors with them, it was interesting to note that John and Matthew were leading the discussions. After about forty-five minutes or so of being together, I was able to summarise the key points and write these up on a flipchart for both sides to see. The sticking points appeared to be coming from two areas – the first regarding potential levels of compensation and the second relating to Box Express continuing to be the sole supplier for the Harbucks contract. Although Box Express had ironed out their initial difficulties and were now performing well, Viapack still seemed to be reluctant to put all their eggs in one basket by relying on one supplier again. The dialogue relating to these two points took up the next three hours. I shuttled from room to room having discussions with all parties from both sides, asking to spend some time with Judith and Gareth, then John and Matthew, then John, Matthew, Martin, Kirsty and Lance. I worked hard to guide the parties to deal with each aspect separately which seemed to have some success. After lunch we had a breakthrough in agreeing the level of compensation Box Express should pay Viapack for the initial Harbucks fiasco, which was one point dealt with.

The second point about sole supplier arrangement was much more difficult. The Viapack board thought that it was their duty as a board to mitigate and prevent any further risk and as a result they were unwilling to allow Box Express to be the sole supplier for the Harbucks contract. This point proved problematic as it was stipulated in the contract that Box Express should be just that. This was where the mediation became really taxing. The parties worked on exploring a solution until late in the afternoon with neither side giving ground.

I had just spent some time with Box Express and wanted to go back to Viapack to see where we might go next. As I knocked on their door, John asked whether I would be kind enough to wait outside for a moment. Naturally I obliged, although I had no idea what was going on. The moment lasted for ten minutes, then 20 and then 30. I was getting concerned and was hoping that the mediation session wasn't about to collapse.

I updated Box Express to let them know I was waiting on Viapack. After waiting some 40minutes, John finally came to see me and invited me into the room. He apologised for keeping me waiting and said that they had been discussing a new proposal to put on the table for Box Express to consider. He continued that Viapack had just secured a contract to be the sole outsourced fulfilment company to a global online stationary and publishing business. The contract would be worth around US$100m per year. It was significant. The negotiations and contract had only been finalised 48 hours before, but they still needed a smaller supplier to work with to fulfil the contract.

John said that his board were still not willing to give ground on the Harbucks contract, but they could see the efforts that Box Express had gone through in order to rectify the damage from the episode. If Box Express were willing to relax the sole supplier clause relating to the Harbucks contract, Viapack would be willing to enter into dialogue with them about the new contract they had just won. It was an extraordinary turn of events. I asked John a few questions about the new contract, wanting to know whether this was a genuine opportunity. To prove it, Martin showed me a copy of the signed contract. I told John and his colleagues that this information was likely to change the course of our discussions and asked whether Viapack would be willing to talk to Box Express directly about it. They consented.

I went swiftly back to Box Express and told Matthew and his colleagues that Viapack would like to update them on a recent development. They seemed surprised and a little bewildered and pressed me to give them an idea of what it was about. I asked them to work with me and trust my judgement that this would be the right way to handle the next interaction between them.

Matthew and his colleagues joined me in the Viapack room. I invited John to tell Matthew and his colleagues what he had recently told me. He obliged and outlined in detail the scope of the proposal. It was the tipping point. Matthew and his colleagues couldn't believe what they were hearing. They had come to a mediation session to try and settle a dispute and it was turning into a business development opportunity. The issue about sole supplier status relating to Harbucks was instantly pushed to one side. Matthew knew immediately that Box Express' revenue would increase substantially as a result of this deal.

We then spent until 9.30pm ironing out the Heads of Agreement in relation to the new contract and closing out the final points of detail on the original dispute. The final settlement position was that:

- Box Express would pay compensation to Viapack for the Harbucks incident
- Box Express would agree to amend the clause in the commercial contract relating to sole supplier status
- Each side would bear their own legal fees
- Viapack would appoint Box Express to be one of three suppliers they would work with to deliver the new contract
- All contracts would include a clause stipulating that in the event of any dispute, mediation would be considered prior to litigation

As a side note, both companies decided that they would also introduce the final point into all existing and any new contracts.

It was a remarkable end to a lengthy day. As the parties were getting ready to leave and wishing each other goodbye, I overheard John and Matthew wishing each other and their families well, with John inviting Matthew to get in touch with him to arrange a drink in a rather more informal setting, before also inviting him to a rugby match in a few weeks time. Their business and personal relationship seemed to be back on track.

Observations
Mediation as a commercial tool

Most of the stories in this book focus on how the tool of mediation can be used to help restore interpersonal or group communication breakdowns. As I have already mentioned, mediation is sometimes accused of being a soft non-commercial option. This story demonstrates however that mediation can in fact be used as a value-add tool by organisations that are facing commercial difficulties. It would have been improbable that had John and Matthew pursued litigation to resolve their dispute, the case would have resulted in such a win-win resolution. Using mediation presented them with opportunities that would not have otherwise come along as well as giving John and Matthew the opportunity to rebuild their broken relationship. On this second point, the relationship wasn't simply rebuilt between John and Matthew but also between Viapack and Box Express, thus meaning personal and commercial success.

The inclination for organisations to use mediation in this way is currently at a low level. Over time, at least two things will need to happen to promote and encourage the use of mediation in this way. Firstly, more case studies of this type will need to be promoted and shared. Secondly, more Chief Executives and non-HR business leaders will need to be convinced about the merits that mediation can bring.

There are very few processes that can potentially be used to save money and deliver commercial success in this way. One of the downsides of mediation is of course that success brings the elimination of ongoing difficulties. People can quickly forget some of the problems that they had to encounter while the skirmish was live, thereby neglecting to remember just how much mediation has saved them from.

Mediating yourself - by having honest conversations
We all have the ability to mediate disputes ourselves in the way that John and Matthew began to do so over their lunch appointment. Earlier in this book I mentioned that more than half of all cases that go to mediation needn't have got that far. Striking up dialogue with an opponent, however initially unappetising it may seem, is all that is normally required to iron out wrinkles that may have developed as part of a personal or business relationship. There are some easy steps one can follow to achieve this:

1. Prepare - This is critical. Make notes about what you want to say. Make sure you think about specific examples. Ideally, these should not be based on something that happened five years ago. The more recent, the better.
2. Set the time - Make sure that enough time is put aside. Matthew and John lunched for three hours. Also agree on an appropriate and neutral venue where you won't be interrupted.
3. Have the discussion - Make it factual and stick with it. Be careful not to clam up and opt out at the last moment. Also, make sure that you allow the other person to have a say too.
4. Don't flinch - Giving a tough message and having an honest conversation isn't easy. Your message will be diluted if you 'dilly dally' when giving it. Keep eye contact and speak confidently.
5. Don't worry about switching between positive and negative feedback throughout the conversation. Research shows that human beings are more likely to remember bad news over good. For example, we might have six successes throughout the morning, received some bad news at 2.00pm and then experience another run of success in the afternoon. It is however more than likely that the bad news is what will occupy the space in our mind. There is therefore no need to be too concerned about sandwiching good news or praise in the middle.
6. Get back to business - Don't let an honest conversation get in the way of your ongoing relationship, where possible.

It is possible to teach others how to become more skilled in problem solving and communication. This involves equipping leaders with the tools they need to do this for themselves and helping them learn how to use them.

Novelist Roberston Davies once said:

"To instruct calls for energy, and to remain almost silent but watchful and helpful, while students instruct themselves, calls for even greater energy. To see someone fall (which will teach him not to fall again) when a word from you would keep him on his feet but ignorant of an important danger, is one of the tasks of the teacher that calls for special energy, because holding in is more demanding than crying out."

Insert mediation clauses into contracts

In 'The Definitive Guide to Workplace Mediation', I mention the notion of including mediation clauses within contracts of employment, policies or employee handbooks. It takes time for the notion of mediation to become embedded within the culture of an organisation. One way of helping cultural change is to prompt discussion by including mediation clauses into both employment and commercial documentation. An organisation can then include discussions about the role mediation plays in the organisation as part of the recruitment, selection, induction and supplier appointment processes. Over time, the organisation should experience a cultural shift where all stakeholders will recognise the benefit of attempting mediation in preference of litigation as the first dispute resolution option.

Ultimately, any company seeking to incorporate a mediation framework within its contractual and policy procedures will need to ensure that senior managers are brought in to the process. An organisation can help build the business case for mediation by setting a range of objectives that will determine long term cost savings. These might include:

- The number of tribunals or grievance and disciplinary cases prior to introducing a mediation scheme set against the number after a mediation scheme has been introduced
- Stress related sickness absence days before and after introduction
- Employee turnover before and after introduction
- Project delivery success before and after introduction
- Employee productivity levels before and after introduction

Here are some example model mediation clauses
Policy statement for corporate organisations

We recognise that for many disputes there is a more cost effective method than litigation. Mediation procedures involve collaborative techniques which can often be embraced for a fraction of the high costs associated with going to litigation. In recognition of this we subscribe to the following statement of principle on behalf of our company:

In the event of an internal dispute, or a business dispute between our company and another company, we are prepared to explore resolution of the dispute through mediation prior to pursuing litigation. If either party believes that the dispute is not suitable for mediation, or that mediation will not produce satisfactory results, either party may proceed with litigation or statutory procedures.

Contract clause

The company promotes the prompt resolution of disputes. In the event of any dispute arising out of or related to this agreement, or any subsequent agreement between the parties ("dispute"), and if the dispute cannot be resolved through normal line management channels, the parties agree to submit the dispute to mediation by a mediator selected in conjunction with the Globis Mediation Model. Your statutory rights are not affected through the mediation process.

The mediation shall take place within 30 days of the date on which the party gives written notice of its desire to mediate the dispute. The duties to mediate shall extend to any other employee, officer or associate of the company.

Clause relating to collective bargaining agreements

The company promotes the prompt resolution of disputes. In the event of any dispute arising out of or related to this collective bargaining agreement, or any subsequent agreement between the parties ("dispute"), and if the dispute cannot be resolved through normal line management channels, the parties agree to submit the dispute to mediation by a mediator selected in conjunction with the Globis Mediation Model. Your statutory rights are not affected through the mediation process. The mediation shall take place within thirty (30) days of the date on which the party gives written notice of its desire to mediate the dispute. The duties to mediate shall extend to any other employee, officer or associate of the company.

The company will work with _____ (the recognised union) within the terms of the Globis (or in-house) Model Mediation Guide as outlined in section ___ of the employee contract [and/or] employee handbook.

Clause relating to the grievance and disciplinary process

The company promotes the prompt resolution of disputes. In the event that a dispute arises relating to the grievance and disciplinary process between parties ("dispute"), and if the dispute cannot be resolved through normal line management channels, the parties agree to submit the dispute to mediation by a mediator selected in conjunction with the Globis Mediation Model. Your statutory rights are not affected through the mediation process.

The mediation shall take place within thirty (30) days of the date on which the party gives written notice of its desire to mediate the dispute. The duties to mediate shall extend to any other employee or associate of the company.

If mediation fails, you retain your statutory entitlement to pursue the grievance and disciplinary procedures.

Clause relating to equality/fairness at work

The company promotes the prompt resolution of disputes. A line manager and employee should attempt to solve any dispute in the first instance. Where this is not possible, the parties agree to submit the dispute to mediation by a mediator selected in conjunction with the Globis Mediation Model. Your statutory rights are not affected through the mediation process. Dispute resolution should be attempted at the earliest opportunity to prevent further escalation.

The mediation shall take place within thirty (30) days of the date on which the party gives written notice of its desire to mediate the dispute. The duties to mediate shall extend to any other employee or associate of the company.

Note:

When drafting appropriate mediation clauses it is important to consider:
- The culture of the organisation
- Whether there is union recognition
- Buy-in from key stakeholders
- Wording that reflects the flexibility of the mediation process
- Inclusion in the company induction documentation

Any wording should be ratified by your in-house or external legal team. If your organisation has union recognition, the union should be consulted and advised on the company's intention to incorporate mediation clauses within the employment framework. This framework then becomes the reference point for any dispute or point of difference.

Chapter 6
Mediation and dispute resolution

"The people who I have trouble dealing with… are people who tend to not give full information. They purposefully leave out certain parts of the story – they distort facts." – Shelley Lazarus

The historical context
Throughout the previous stories I have referred to the concept of mediation and the role it can play in helping to solve disputes. This chapter will provide a little more background information about mediation and how it works.

There is a mood swing across organisations in the UK relating to how conflict and its related elements are managed. This has been developing for a number of years but can be particularly attributed to some notable happenings such as:

* More data about the costs associated with conflict
* Staff, line managers and HR professionals feeling increasingly stressed
* Companies' increasing accountability to shareholders
* The spread of success stories relating to alternative dispute resolution
* A waning desire for people's willingness to give a significant portion of their lives to conflict situations
* A revised ACAS Code of Practice
* Rising legal fees
* Government encouragement

The uptake of mediation and conflict resolution practices in the UK has been slow, although to date the public sector has picked it up much more quickly than the private sector. One of the possible reasons for this is, arguably, the willingness of some sections of the private sector to throw money at problems to make them go away through things such as compromise agreements. Whilst this provides a temporary reprieve, it is unlikely to unearth and provide a solution for what might be ingrained cultural issues within an organisation. Therefore, the organisation enters a cycle of throwing financial resources at problems for a quick fix, but this means the infection is likely to remain untreated as the root has not received the relevant attention. There is also a high likelihood of another injury, possibly worse than before, being sustained at some future stage. This method encourages the rewarding of poor management and systems, and in the most extreme cases leads to problems such as those faced by Enron in 2002. Documents show that at Enron, simply talking about what was going on was off-limits. Organisations that fail to support open communications are doomed to fail. With the emergence of more and more data on the costs of conflict and the increased government focus on this area, organisations are likely to embrace conflict resolution strategies more swiftly over the next few years.

Few of us want to be in conflict or involved in some form of litigation procedure. Mediation is not intended to be positioned as the be all and end all of dispute resolution tools. It is one of a number of Alternative Dispute Resolution (ADR) options.

It is however probably the most flexible. ADR as a range of formal techniques emerged firstly in the US in the 1970s and the UK followed around 20 years later. The three main areas in which mediation first became established were commercial, family and community. Other ADR choices include arbitration (where an arbitrator or panel of arbitrators will hear a case and then make a binding judgement), collaborative law (in which two sets of lawyers attempt to resolve a case and agree to stand aside to allow other lawyers to try and reach agreement in the event that discussions break down) and negotiation.

Until recently, it has been the legal profession that has done the most to raise the profile and extol the virtues of mediation. In a commercial context, the use of mediation has grown phenomenally due to the pressure being put on established courts to adopt it as part of the reforms recommended some years ago by Lord Woolfe. These reforms mean that in many cases parties are being compelled to attempt mediation prior to going to trial. Something similar for the UK Employment Tribunal system is long overdue. The uptake of employment and workplace mediation will only become mainstream when this happens.

Alternative Dispute Resolution
Mediation is a derivative of the term 'Alternative Dispute Resolution' (ADR) which has its origins in the USA. ADR was introduced as an alternative to the legal system of dealing with disputes which was seen to be costly, adversarial, damaging to relationships and limited to rights based remedies compared to creative problem solving. Since its emergence in the late 1970s, ADR has found a sympathetic audience amongst litigators and litigation users in many countries. The acceptance of the term ADR grew as the preferred term in the business and civil litigation worlds.

Despite many lawyers training to become commercial mediators there is varied acceptance in the legal profession to the concept of ADR – specifically mediation. With the emergence of workplace mediation, the primary embracers of the model are employment lawyers and HR professionals. The strength of mediation lies in its flexibility of practise, where it has helped to introduce new ways of thinking and float options available to parties engaged in a dispute or potential dispute. Mediation has introduced new thinking when it comes to moving from conflict to resolution. Of the many forms of ADR, mediation has proved to be the most flexible and user-friendly approach. Some countries, such as Australia and New Zealand, have been practising a form of mediation for many years.

ADR began in earnest in the UK in 1990, but recognition of the need for mediation in the workplace now spans the country. Few organisations are without problems in their established ways of working. The increase in the type and complexity of employment legislation since the early 90's has had a major impact on HR professionals and line managers in how they manage people and introduce change. Today, employees generally have less loyalty to organisations, are well informed of both their statutory and human rights and are more willing to invoke them at the earliest opportunity.

Mediation is one of the solutions available to organisations. It is a voluntary, non binding and "without prejudice" process in which a specially trained third party intervenes in a dispute and attempts to bring the parties together and agree a settlement.

If the mediation succeeds, then it ends with a binding agreement. If anyone is dissatisfied with the process, either party or the mediator may terminate the mediation at any time. The aggrieved individual may then proceed to assert their legal rights through the tribunal or court system if they wish.

The legal framework
Over the last 20 to 30 years, numerous pieces of employment legislation have been imposed on UK organisations. These included changes such as:

- Maternity and paternity provisions
- Age discrimination
- Equal pay monitoring
- Protection for part-time workers
- Sexual orientation legislation
- Religious belief legislation
- Harassment and bullying discrimination legislation

In the 'Stories of difference' section I wrote about the Equality Act. The Equalities Office is estimating that its implementation is likely to cost somewhere in the region of £310 million, mainly as a result of extra tribunal and court cases.

Perhaps the other piece of employment legislation that has had the most day to day impact on organisations is the statutory grievance and disciplinary procedures introduced in October 2004 as part of the Employment Act 2002 (Dispute Resolution Regulations 2004). Until 1st October of that year, every employer, whether they operated a formal grievance procedure or not, had to include in every statement of particulars of employment a note of the person to whom an employee could apply for the purpose of seeking redress for any grievance relating to his employment, and the manner in which any such application should be made. If they had a formal grievance procedure and had 20 or more employees they were also obliged to include details of the procedure in the written particulars of employment. All employers also became obliged to operate minimum statutory grievance procedures and the small employer exemption to provide details was abolished. Employees and employers would suffer a severe penalty in the event that they failed to use the statutory grievance procedure process. The time limits for making applications to an Employment Tribunal were also extended to allow time for proper discussion between employer and employee in implementing the grievance procedure.

Unfortunately, the introduction of this legislation didn't have the desired effect. What was intended as an opportunity to increase transparency and help both employees and employers alike went horribly wrong. As a result, the number of grievance cases lodged with employment panels rose by a third after the new rules were introduced when the government had intended a sizeable fall in cases. According to research by the CIPD, 29% of employers felt that disputes were less likely to be resolved informally following the introduction of the statutory dispute resolution procedures in 2004.

In December 2006, the DTI launched a root and branch review of government support for resolving disputes in the workplace. Michael Gibbons was asked to review the options for simplifying and improving all aspects of employment dispute resolution in order to make the system work better for employers and employees. The review involved business representatives, unions and other interested parties considering the options for change. The review looked at all aspects of the system, including the current legal requirements, how Employment Tribunals worked and the scope for new initiatives to help resolve disputes at an earlier stage.

The effect of legislative changes brought in between the 1990s and 2009 were colossal. HR professionals and line managers spent large amounts of time ensuring that correct procedures were being followed when any indication of grievance or disciplinary measures were encountered. As a result, the number of grievance cases lodged with employment panels rose by a third during 2005/6 after claims initially fell by one quarter after the 2004 dispute resolution rules came in.

In its document 'The Government of Britain', the government's draft legislative programme plans were announced to simplify the employment regime through the 2008/9 Employment Act. The main purpose of the Employment Act was to, "Simplify, clarify and build a stronger enforcement regime for key aspects of employment law." The Confederation of British Industry (CBI) regularly lobbies government on the cost of 'bureaucracy' being introduced to the UK. Latest estimates suggest this cost is as high as £40 billion per annum.

A few days before the publisher's deadline for this book, the coalition government announced the 'Employers' Charter', a series of reforms aimed at cutting red tape and boosting the economy. Amongst the changes announced were an extension from one year to two in the period during which new employees were barred from resorting to an Employment Tribunal. Those who do claim for unfair dismissal will have to lodge a fee before they can submit their claim, the idea being to deter nuisance litigation. Claims for discrimination however would still be permitted after any term of employment.

Revised ACAS Code of Practice
The statutory procedures for handling discipline and grievance issues introduced in October 2004 were widely criticised for creating high administrative burdens, for leading to the formalisation of disputes and for allowing lawyers to become involved at an early stage. Although the provisions were only in force for less than five years, the statutory dispute resolution procedures were repealed when the provisions of the Employment Act 2008 were implemented.

The new ACAS code came into force on April 6th 2009 as part of the Employment Act 2008. This code is designed to help employers, employees and their representatives deal with disciplinary and grievance situations in the workplace more effectively. In the code, the concept of mediation was introduced for the first time.

I always encourage employers and employees to 'nip things in the bud' where possible. Many potential disciplinary or grievance issues can be resolved informally, with a quiet word. Where this is not possible, employers and employees are increasingly using an independent third party to help resolve the problem. The third party need not come from outside the organisation – for example an internal mediator could perform the role, as long as they are not involved in the disciplinary or grievance issue. In some cases, an external mediator might be more appropriate.

The concept of mediation

Mediation is a process used for resolving disputes in which a third person helps the parties negotiate a settlement. It is future focused and less concerned with who is right or wrong, concentrating instead on solving problems so that they don't occur again. The parties retain responsibility for achieving a solution. At another level, mediation can be described as an invisible bridge that connects one person to the other or as a path by which each warring faction can be guided to find a new beginning. This type of description should not be translated as a process for wimps. It certainly isn't. In mediation the parties are put under pressure to find a resolution to a settlement to their dispute. The mediator, as a third party, manages or facilitates a process to help the parties get to a point where they can reach settlement. The mediator, however, does not impose any settlements.

The strength of mediation lies in its flexibility of practice, where it has helped to introduce new ways of thinking and tabling options for parties engaged in a dispute to consider. If the mediation succeeds, then it ends with a binding agreement. Mediation is voluntary in the sense that it takes place as a result of the parties agreeing to enter the mediation process. It cannot happen if one or more of the parties refuse to participate, although it is quite possible that parties who initially refuse may agree to mediation at a later stage. Recently, some non-voluntary mediations have taken place. These happen in commercial disputes when parties are required by a court or contract to mediate before or instead of arbitration or litigation.

Mediation is non-binding unless and until an agreement is reached. Until this point, parties may walk away from the mediation at any time, as entering the process itself does not bind any party to settlement. There is however an important distinction to be made. In employment mediation cases, any settlement that is underpinned by a compromise agreement becomes legally binding. For example, if an organisation agrees to make a payment within 21 days, it will have breached the terms of the agreement if it fails to do so. Legal action could be taken in such scenarios. In workplace mediation cases any settlement reached is binding in as much that the agreement should form a psychological contract between the parties. The mediation process does not take away any party's statutory or human rights. This means that in the event of an agreement breaking down and the relationship becoming strained once more, two options apply – to attempt mediation again or invoke (or re-invoke) the organisation's grievance procedures. The difference between employment and workplace mediation is explained in a little more detail later on. The mediator is a neutral person who is there to assist the parties in their negotiations. The mediator provides a clear head, impartiality, process management, encouragement, optimism and, above all, brings hope to situations that may seem hopeless, whilst always leaving the problem and the decision to rest in the hands of the parties. A skilled mediator doesn't necessarily need to be an expert or specialist in the field to which the dispute is linked. The mediator also operates by a principle called 'omni partiality', which means being on both sides at the same time. This is because in a professional capacity we become used to giving advice or stating an opinion. It can feel quite alien to hear about a situation and have a personal view about the balance of probabilities and yet refrain from expressing it. This is not an easy skill to develop, but is built over time with experience.

Mediators often feel responsible for ensuring that the parties find a solution. It is tempting to suggest one that seems obvious, logical or expedient. Mediators however should remember that their role is to guide the parties to their own solution. Not only would a mediator's solution, if adopted, probably be less suitable than one the parties create themselves, it would also deprive the parties of the right and responsibility to determine their own future. Also, if the mediator's solution should fail, the parties could blame the mediator rather than take responsibility themselves. Experience has also shown me that people have a higher commitment to a decision that they have generated for themselves. As long as the parties are progressing well on their own, the mediator should not intervene. The mediator can and should be prepared to intervene however if the parties become stuck and appear to have run out of ideas.

Mediation is private, conducted without prejudice and with total confidentiality. This means that in the event that the parties are unable to settle their dispute and they go to tribunal or some other recognised legal process, the content of the mediation cannot be discussed. The mediator, however, will agree with the parties how information from the mediation session will be shared with the organisation.

Why mediation works

Mediation works because, unlike other dispute resolution processes, it fully addresses emotional needs. You can see this illustrated in the 'A question of advice' story. Whilst the opportunity might be given to discuss aspects such as injury to feelings in the litigation or grievance process, the opportunity is rarely given for the disputing parties to discuss emotional issues in detail with each other. I have yet to hear of a case where a tribunal judge pulls up a chair next to a claimant or defendant and asks, "How did you feel as a result of what happened to you?" In an Employment Tribunal, for example, where the employee wins the tribunal claim, although a judgement may take account of the emotional effect that the dispute has had on someone, it is unlikely to result in full closure for the 'winner'. Issues probably still exist between them and their former employer about how they felt as a result of the way they were treated. It is amazing the power that a simple 'sorry' has.

There are typically three ways to attempt to resolve a dispute. The first is to use POWER. To take an extreme example, in a work context, this could mean a manager saying to their direct report, "I'm the boss, you're not. Do what I have asked you to do." This intimates that the line manager wants to use their position in the hierarchy to get something done.

I acknowledge that in day-to-day working life there may be circumstances in which using a direct style might be necessary, for example in a medical situation where a patient might be at risk or where the failure to take swift action may result in losing a customer. In a broader sense we might also see power being used to resolve country to country conflict. A country might use its size and ability to employ weapons to overthrow a smaller country that has less human, financial and armoury resources.

The second way is to use RIGHTS. The last few decades has seen a plethora of legislation being introduced to bolster each of our rights as human beings. It is possible for us to use this enhanced level of protection as a bargaining tool to get what we want. For example, a person might use their race or gender as a reason to state that their rights have either been violated or not considered. Using this platform could even disempower the "I'm the boss" manager.

The main learning point from using either of these methods to resolve disputes is that they both result in a winner and loser, or perhaps two losers. Let me explain a little about the 'two losers' theory. An Employment Tribunal winner may soon find that their celebrations are cut short. Why? Here are some examples of what they might have experienced along the road to 'success':

- Lost a huge amount of their life preparing for the case
- Suffered damage to their reputation
- Suffered poor health
- A legal bill to pay
- Reduced their chances of re-employment within the same industry
- Still failed to resolve emotional issues with their former employer

As you can see, in winner/loser cases even the winner can feel deflated afterwards to say the least.

The third option is INTERESTS. Using interests to find out what someone wants and, more importantly, why they want it, is the only method that is likely to result with the emergence of two winners. This might require taking an extra 30 seconds to consider an appropriate response to a situation that looks like it could escalate into something more menacing. Interests help discover not merely what people want but why they want it. Interest based processes require consensus and they are less likely to result in entrenched positions, abuse of power or resistance to implementation. It is this third option on which mediation is based. It uses the combination of getting parties together (physical), providing each with the opportunity to hear the point of difference in their dispute (mental) and gives them the chance to express what needs to be addressed in order to be able to move on (emotional).

There are a number of advantages to mediating a dispute rather than resorting to litigating.

• It's quick
People do not like being in conflict. It is worrying, time consuming and a drain on both financial and management resources. Mediation sessions can be set up very quickly – within days if necessary.

• Mediation does not affect statutory or human rights
The mediation process can take place while any statutory organisational processes are suspended. As it is without prejudice, mediation poses little or no risk to parties who engage in the process.

- **It saves money**
Issues can be settled quickly and can avoid direct/indirect costs.

- **It gets people talking**
People in conflict tend to take up rigid positions and will avoid communicating with the party with which they are in conflict, or will communicate with them through an intermediary. The face to face meeting which occurs at the joint session allows open communication directly between the parties again. This can help ensure that methods of prevention of future conflicts are addressed within the process.

This is probably a good point at which to outline some of the things that mediation is not:

- **It is not an easy way out**
Organisations are entitled to invoke and enforce organisational processes such as the grievance and disciplinary procedure, instead of conflict resolution principles such as mediation. Where an employee may be in dispute with the employer, the employer may feel that it has acted properly in every sense and that an Employment Tribunal should decide who may have been right or wrong. This may be an appropriate course of action where the organisation wants to send a message to its employees about its willingness to defend itself. Even if an organisation wins its legal process, it must of course weigh up the costs of such action and consider whether this is the best use of its resources.

- **It doesn't stop you litigating**
Mediation does not preclude the use of other methods of dispute resolution. In some cases legal action may have commenced before mediation is adopted. Proceedings may or may not be stayed pending the outcome of the mediation. Parties may also want to begin litigation to demonstrate seriousness and engage with mediation to obtain a more secure, viable and speedy result.

- **It is not a waste of time and money if it fails**
If settlement is not reached in mediation it is often reached soon afterwards. This is mainly because it has raised the issues on which the dispute has been based. Parties then have better clarification of these issues and on reflection may choose to move to settle issues of difference.

- **It is not soft and fluffy**
The value of using mediation as a conflict resolution tool can be financially proven. In an environment where a return on investment is critical for business leaders, mediation is a justifiable investment. Mediation helps to reduce

unproductive management time and enhances the skills of line managers and the HR function. It is a period of concentrated negotiation that requires focus, persistence, agility of thought, flexibility and imagination. It is hard work for everyone involved in intellectual, physical and emotional ways.

- **It is not counselling**

The mediator and counsellor share a number of core skills. Both mediation and counselling can take various forms but, in general, the mediator preserves a neutral relationship with the parties, whereas the counsellor develops what can sometimes be described as an intense relationship with the client. The mediator uses problem solving techniques and acknowledges feelings, whereas the counsellor explores emotions and applies psychological analysis.

The mediation process

Mediators often speak reverently about 'trusting the process'. There are many examples of mediations where parties begin the process bitter and entrenched, but by mid-morning the same parties become engaged in productive, sometimes friendly discussions. A broad framework for the mediation process has been defined over time. Mediation is a flexible process and, with experience, a mediator can use that flexibility to their advantage.

Prior to any mediation taking place, the mediator should make preliminary contact with the parties. The principle reasons for this contact is to:

- Confirm agreement to the mediation
- Understand the nature of the conflict
- Agree terms for the mediation including dates, times, location, duration and documentation
- Outline how the mediation process works

If the mediator is external to the organisation, issues such as mediation costs should be discussed with the stakeholder who is authorising the process to take place. The core of the mediation session is then made up of a number of elements.

These include:
- Opening statements – Outlining the process and the role of the mediator
- Uninterrupted time – Giving each party an opportunity to express the key points about the conflict
- The exchange – Held either as joint meetings or private and confidential meetings (called caucuses) between the mediator and each party separately
- Exploring the options – Attempting to shift the discussion into the future e.g. What would you like to see happen? What would prevent this situation from happening again?
- Constructing the agreement – Beginning to document ideas for solutions and testing thoughts with each party
- Writing the agreement – When parties agree to settle, it is the responsibility of the mediator to draft an agreement that is a true reflection of settlement points
- Closing the mediation – Thanking the parties for their engagement in the process

The mediator's role

The mediator fulfils several important roles. The mediator is:

- A manager of the process, providing firm but sensitive control, conveying confidence that the process is yielding fruit and maintaining momentum and a sense of progress
- A facilitator, helping the parties to overcome deadlock and to find a way of working co-operatively towards a settlement that is mutually acceptable
- An information gatherer, absorbing and organising data and identifying common ground
- A reality tester, helping the parties to take a private realistic view, rather than public open scrutiny
- A problem solver, bringing a clear and creative mind to help the parties construct an outcome that best meets their needs
- A sponge that soaks up all the frustrations, emotions and uncertainties of the parties and helps them channel their energy in more positive ways
- A scribe who writes or helps write the terms of any settlement agreement ensuring the points are clear
- A settlement prompter who, if no agreement is reached at the mediation, will help parties to keep the momentum towards settlement

It is important that the mediator gains the trust of the parties so that they have faith that they are competent enough to fulfil the required role. When parties have this trust of the mediator they are much more likely to disclose information relevant to the settlement of the dispute.

Impartiality and neutrality are clearly fundamental to the role of the mediator, who must always remain impartial in relation to content, process and outcome of the mediation. This is particularly important for workplace mediations. For example, if trust is broken by an in-house mediator during a workplace mediation session, any organisation and its employees henceforth will struggle to have faith in the process.

The phases of the mediation

I developed the LAETR mediation cycle model based on my experiences within mediation. Using the LAETR™ Mediation Cycle during workplace mediation training courses helps delegates understand the process for helping to resolve differences in the workplace. This model has been used in many workplace mediations with notable success.

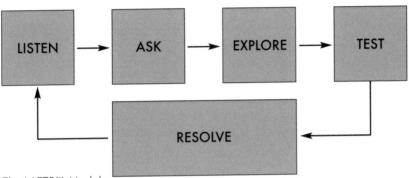

The LAETR™ Model

Listen: Listen within another person's frame of reference to fully understand the issues that have led to the dispute

Ask: Ask appropriate and relevant questions that help clarify understanding of the background to the dispute

Explore: Explore options for resolution that will help the parties focus on the future rather than on the past

Test: Test and reality check that any potential solutions have been thought through and are workable for the parties

Resolve: Resolve the dispute by summarising the parties' position and bringing the mediation to an appropriate close

Workplace or employment mediation?

Often two terms are used interchangeably for mediating disputes at work. The two terms, however, have different meanings:

- Workplace mediation refers to a dispute where, at the commencement of the mediation, there is an ongoing working relationship between the parties
- Employment mediation refers to a dispute where, at the commencement of the mediation, the working relationship between the parties is in the past

It is important to note however that a workplace mediation could also turn into an employment mediation midway through the process. This would happen as a result of one or more parties indicating a desire to sever the working relationship and seeking to negotiate mutually agreeable terms for settlement.

The difference is important to note as there are some issues a mediator will experience when conducting an employment mediation that they may not experience when undertaking a workplace or internal mediation. Three examples of this are interaction with lawyers or other representatives, issues about legal costs and arrangements for a party leaving an organisation as part of a settlement. In employment mediation cases, the mediation commissioner is much more likely to be an employment lawyer.

The mediation is often more commercially focused and leans more towards negotiation. The mediator will have to work with both the parties and their legal representatives, and will have to understand issues around potential compensation. When reality checking, the mediator may also refer to case law. Arrangements for compromise agreements to be drafted and signed off will also have to be made.

In workplace mediation there is much more of a requirement to work with people's emotions and consider potential cultural issues for the organisation. Mediators will often have to display large amounts of patience when dealing with the parties and will also have to think about potential flaws in the organisational structure that may have led or contributed to the dispute in the first place. In this sense, the mediator can also become a trusted advisor to the organisation.

Internal or external mediator?

There are a number of considerations for the organisation when deciding whether to appoint an internal or external mediator, such as:

Internal or External Mediator?	
Internal	**External**
+ Knows and understands the organisational culture + Potentially requires less briefing + Little or no cost − May not be perceived as impartial − May have historical baggage − Experience level may be low	+ Comes with little or no knowledge of the organisation or parties in dispute + May be a more experienced mediator with the ability to pick up issues quickly + Likely to gain trust of parties more readily + Able to provide the organisation with a fresh view of possible cultural or organisational issues − Charges for services

Leaving the competency of the mediator aside, it is ultimately the choice of the organisation to decide which option will work best, based on the merits of each case.

How the mediation process works

There can be a number of trigger points that will indicate the necessity of mediation being required. For example, it could be related to a race or sex discriminatory issue, a performance management issue, a stand off, a breakdown of trust or a clash of values. Once an agreement has been reached to engage in mediation, there are a number of steps the workplace mediator should follow. These include:

- Understanding the brief from the mediation commissioner
- Having pre-mediation discussions with the parties
- Choosing the location
- The phases of the mediation
- Advising the organisation on issues for future prevention

If you are considering engaging a mediator there is a seven step guide at the back of this book that you should find useful. If you are a mediator or are considering training to become one, the following is a best practice guide on getting the mediation process started.

Understanding the brief from the mediation commissioner

The mediation commissioner is the person who takes the responsibility of recognising that something needs to be done to sort out a situation. This person will typically have the power or authority to take action to commission the mediation intervention. This could be the line manager/someone from the HR function. It is important that the mediator spends sufficient time engaging with this person to understand the issues of the case. It is advisable to have a face to face meeting for this purpose but it is not always necessary, especially for more experienced mediators. This discussion should cover areas such as:

- The background to the dispute
- The length of time that the situation has been developing
- The current situation
- Whether the dispute is an isolated occurrence
- Whether the parties have agreed to mediation
- The terms for the mediation including dates, times, location, duration and documentation
- Explaining how the mediation process works

As mediator, it is important to get an understanding of the facts from the commissioner's perspective. Issues such as hearsay, gossip and rumour may come up, but the mediator should concentrate on the facts. The mediator would also use this session to discuss the contract for the mediation. If the dispute relates to a former employee, issues such as legal fees also might form part of the discussion.

Pre-mediation discussions with the parties

Following discussion with the mediation commissioner, the mediator should have separate preliminary talks with the parties. The principle reasons for this are to:

- Allow the mediator to introduce themselves to each party
- Confirm agreement to the mediation
- Understand the nature of the conflict from the perspective of each party
- Begin to build rapport with the parties
- Explain how the mediation process works
- Establish whether each party is ready for a joint meeting
- Determine the best way to approach the next steps
- Discuss arrival times (schedule around 20 minute gaps between the arrival of each party)

Choosing the location

It is usually best to conduct a mediation session away from the parties' normal place of work where possible. The best facility will be a neutral location with comfortable rooms and appropriate furniture. Each party should have a similar room that can be used as their private base and which the mediator can use for caucus meetings. Each room should have a supply of refreshments.

The mediator should also have their own room, which should be used for joint sessions as it will be perceived to be neutral space by both parties. Where rooms are next to each other be careful to check for thin walls as parties may be able to overhear confidential information.

The room layout

It is also advisable to arrange the furniture in a formal way with desks arranged in the traditional U shape. Newly trained mediators might be tempted to have more informal furniture set up. This might, for example, include creating an open space with chairs but no tables. Informal settings usually fail for two reasons.

Firstly, parties who attend mediation may not have seen or spoken to their opponent for some time. They are highly likely to be entrenched and harbouring strong feelings of anger and resentment. Bringing the parties into an open space in close proximity of each other is likely to have the negative effect of increasing anxiety levels. Secondly, parties usually want to make a lot of notes on what they are hearing. Informal settings aren't always adequate for this. On some occasions it might be appropriate to move to a more informal setting at a later stage during the mediation.

The phases of the mediation
Usually the mediation will follow a regular process:
- The mediation agreement
- Opening phase
- Joint session
- Private sessions (caucuses)
- Negotiation phase
- Constructing the settlement
- Writing the settlement agreement
- Closing the mediation
- The follow up

The mediation agreement
It is important that any mediation is documented and summarised by a mediation agreement. It is the responsibility of the mediator to ensure this happens. Mediation is voluntary and without prejudice, so the content of any mediation cannot be discussed at any future tribunal or court hearing. Failure of the mediator to conduct a mediation underpinned by the appropriate documentation could bring unwelcome consequences.

An organisation can choose the wording of their own mediation agreement, but it is advised that some key points are included in any agreement.

The key points of an agreement would be that:
- The mediation is without prejudice
- The mediation is non-binding up until the point of agreement
- The mediation is voluntary
- The mediator is named
- The parties are entitled to seek independent legal advice prior to the mediation
- The mediation is confidential
- The mediator cannot be called as a witness

Opening phase
Before the parties arrive:
- Arrange the rooms: chairs, tables, lighting, room temperature, privacy, flipcharts etc.
- Carry out a final review of any pre-mediation notes, memorise names and job titles
- Check the venue for all facilities and conveniences
- Double check that coffee, tea, water, juice, snacks and lunch arrangements have been taken care of

When the parties arrive:
* Meet each party at the reception point of the venue. Use the 20 minute gap to settle the first arriving party and go over the stages of the mediation process
* Ensure that the mediation agreement has been signed and check for any questions the party may have since the last contact
* Give both parties the time to be settled before calling them to the first joint session. One of the ways in which the mediator can encourage and enhance the informal approach is by setting up the room for the opening joint session
* Be willing to maintain firm management over the proceedings – the parties will look to you to exercise control and will respect you for doing it

I recall doing an employment mediation some time ago. One of the employment lawyers seemed determined to upstage me as the mediator by making alternative suggestions to decisions I had made. This included comments on the room layout, timings for lunch and which party should come into the main room first. After realising that I would stick to the decisions I had made, the lawyer eventually stopped making such suggestions and began to work collaboratively with me. Maintaining firm control over the process in this case was crucial for me as mediator to establish credibility.

* Use your intuition. Even though there is a scripted process for mediations, situations may sometimes arise which require creative thinking.
* Keep note taking to a minimum. Note the essential points and make more detailed notes during breaks between meetings. Mediation is different to an employee investigation or the disciplinary and grievance process. In mediation, the aim is to focus on the key points of the dispute rather than making sure that who said what and when is fully documented.

Mediator's opening
The mediator's opening has four main purposes:
* To set the tone of the mediation
* To establish the mediator's authority as manager of the process
* To inform the parties about the mediation process
* To establish ground rules for the mediation

The mediator's opening is important as it should be used to help establish an environment that will be conducive for discussion and resolution. A poor opening could sufficiently harm the credibility of the mediator enough to impede the process.

Welcome the parties individually. Keep in mind that the parties are likely to be tense, wary and sceptical. Whilst the mediator is well versed in the mediation process, this is likely to be the first time that the parties have participated in such a process.

The mediator should use the opening to clarify neutrality and explain the mediator's role. The mediator's role is to facilitate a process that will highlight issues of the conflict and ideally lead to a resolution of those issues. The mediator's role is not to impose a solution. It is the parties' problem and therefore needs to be their solution too.

It is important that during the mediator's opening comments that he/she restates to the parties that they will have the opportunity to outline their case uninterrupted. This opening session of the mediation enables:

1. The mediator to set the ground rules
2. The parties to state their side of the story

Confidentiality

Maintaining confidentiality is a crucial factor for the mediation process to work. As mediator, it is wise to be explicit in the opening about what can and cannot be repeated during the mediation. Confidentiality works on two levels:

- The entire mediation is confidential to those taking part, unless there is an explicit agreement to publicise any resolution
- Information given to the mediator in private caucus is confidential between the mediator and the party. This is crucial. If this aspect is broken, it will be impossible to regain it and the mediation may have to be deferred and a different mediator appointed. The mediator should always check confidentiality at the end of each private session. This can be done by asking the parties if there is anything that has been discussed that they would like to be kept confidential

Another tip on confidentiality is that you, as mediator, should also keep any notes concealed. Remember that some people can even read well upside down!

Finally, the mediator should check for any final questions and obtain assent from each party that they are ready to proceed.

Joint session
Parties' opening comments

The parties' opening comments give everyone at the table the chance to hear each others' case. The mediator will get an overview of the mood whilst also learning a little bit more about the personalities present. Equally as important, each party, perhaps for the first time, has the opportunity to hear the others' view of the conflict. It has been known for mediations to resolve issues at this stage of the process as parties are often unaware of the details or severity of the conflict. Once the specifics are heard it can cause some parties to offer an apology and the hand of reconciliation.

You might recall the story I mentioned earlier in the book of the shortest mediation I ever conducted lasting all of around 30 minutes. This was the length of time it took to get to the parties' opening comments. When one party heard for the first time what the impact of her behaviour had been on her colleague an apology swiftly followed, and my role as mediator was done.

The joint session which follows the caucus session should be used to continue exploring issues or to move to resolution. The mediator would have been sharing information from the caucus sessions through 'shuttle diplomacy' between the parties. Sometimes the information that has been raised during the caucus sessions may cause a party to push for a joint session to discuss 'new' understandings.

There is no rule on whether the mediator should use caucus or joint sessions; it is a matter of what is appropriate at the time. The main disadvantage of a joint session is that parties are less likely to give sensitive or confidential information to the mediator in the presence of the other party. In mediations where an ongoing working relationship is being explored, it is likely that joint meetings offer more opportunity to make progress. The skill applied by the mediator during the joint meeting stage often closely resembles the skills associated with the facilitation process. The two processes complement each other.

The advantages of a joint session are that:

- It allows parties to talk directly to each other to outline their positions
- It allows parties to negotiate directly
- It can boost the momentum of the mediation
- It can break deadlock by allowing parties to give explanations on specific issues

The speakers

The person who is most aggrieved, or has been instrumental in requesting the mediation, should speak first. In commercial mediations, this would be *'the claimant'*. The mediator should inform the party who will be required to speak first during the pre-mediation meetings so it isn't a surprise when both parties are together.

There may be occasions when it becomes difficult for the listening party to contain themselves from commenting. If this happens, firmly remind the interrupting party that they will have their turn to speak as soon as the other party has finished. Once both parties have spoken it is the judgment of the mediator to decide whether dialogue should continue as a joint session. This can be helpful to continue exposing any issues that arise during the opening comments. If ill-judged however it can be fatal to the mediation. Experienced mediators will develop an instinct for the appropriateness of such a continuation.

Private sessions (Caucuses)

Caucus sessions usually follow the joint opening session and allow the mediator to explore issues further and discuss thoughts following the joint session. The mediator should remember during these sessions to check for information that parties would like kept confidential. The caucus sessions are also the forum for reality checking. Reality checking allows the mediator to help parties think through potential ramifications of failing to resolve a dispute or going to litigation. Reality checking can be extremely helpful in moving towards resolution, but the mediator walks a tightrope when doing so. If you push too hard the party may feel that you are not taking them seriously or that you are taking sides with the other party. Any suspicion of this can damage the credibility of the mediator. If the mediator fails to reality check appropriately, they do a disservice to the party and the mediation may never reach its objective of resolving, rather than settling, the conflict.

Moving towards resolution

The resolution of a workplace related dispute may vary depending on whether there is the intention for an ongoing relationship. For example, an appropriate conclusion to a dispute may be that one or both parties (if the conflict is between two people) leave the organisation. In this case the mediator may move to discussions about terms on which any termination may take place.

The ideal situation in any mediation is to secure a *'win-win'* solution. Any win-win agreement is likely to involve the requirement for either or both parties to *'give something up'*. It is useful for the mediator to summarise issues as discussion progresses. Where there are numerous issues, it is often helpful to *'cluster'* them to make it easier to work through. Where it becomes clear that the interests for each party are becoming aligned, the mediator should begin to document them for the party/ies to see. This will help put issues where there appears to be agreement to one side, thus allowing the mediator to begin working on other areas. Depending on the number of issues being discussed, the mediator follows this process until there is clarity that all issues have been highlighted, discussed and resolved.

As mediator, you sometimes need to work actively to help parties recognise that settlement is in their best interests. Parties can have difficulty moving from entrenched positions to a more flexible and open view about options for resolution. The mediator's understanding of negotiation and negotiating strategies will be very important during this stage. During private meetings in the negotiation phase the mediator may help in:

- Prioritising parties' concerns and aspirations
- Being a sounding board and allowing parties to vent their feelings and test out their positions
- Shaping proposals that meet the other party's needs
- Exploring interests
- Deciding when and how to share parties' interests

During the negotiation phase, the mediator also seeks to uncover all the things that are of interest to each party. For example, this could be a list of financial and non-financial needs. It is quite normal for parties to be open and up front about their non-financial needs, but less so for financial interests. This is because most people will attempt to get as much as they can financially. A key point to remember as mediator is that only you will know exactly what is happening at any point in time within the mediation.

As mediator, it is your choice to decide what information is shared and when. For example, during caucus Party A might give you a list of five concessions for Party B to consider. During your caucus with Party B, you might decide to withhold two of the concession points and negotiate on three (instead of five) points. As the negotiation continues you can introduce the two omitted concession points. This will give the impression to Party B that Party A have moved, when in reality they haven't. If you decide to attempt this strategy, you will need to always remember to be one step ahead of Party A. I make this point because as you shuttle from room to room, parties will always want an update on the current position.

Therefore, continuing with the current example, the mediator may say to Party A that they have relayed some of the concessions but are waiting for a response, or they may thank Party A for the list of five concessions and promise to inform them when they have feedback, before asking about the other areas of consideration that were raised. This approach keeps the mediator in control of the process and prevents the mediator from being on the back foot.

If you are mediating with an assistant, it is crucial that your assistant is clear that you are in the driving seat. I recall mediating a dispute similar to the example above. When speaking with Party B about a list of concessions Party A was willing to make, I said that there were three points that I had permission to relay to them. I then proceeded to outline what the three points were. My enthusiastic assistant mediator then said, "Clive, what about the other points they discussed?" I can have a chuckle about this now, but believe me, it wasn't funny at the time. Thankfully the mediation still settled, and I had a productive feedback session with my assistant mediator after the mediation.

The parties in dispute will normally be clear about their interest points. As mediator, it is important to understand the significance that each party places on an interest. For example, you might negotiate a financial settlement only to find out later that because a reference can't be agreed the whole negotiation falls apart.

In cases where an ongoing working relationship is being negotiated, it is normally better to carry out the negotiation in joint sessions. In employment mediation cases (where an ongoing working relationship is not being considered), the negotiation is likely to make more progress when carried out in private sessions. This is because, as mediator, you are acting as an emotional sponge and sieve, which will allow the negotiation to move forward based on the pertinent points. The mediator may have to push the parties during this stage, reminding them that this is their opportunity to reach settlement. The mediator might use phrases such as:

- This is your opportunity to wake up tomorrow morning without having to think about this ongoing conflict
- It is now 3.00pm, and although we hadn't scheduled an end time I wasn't planning to be here at midnight
- I'm going to leave you to have a think about your current position and when I return in 30 minutes, please tell me where you want to go next

Reality testing within the negotiation phase
The mediator has a key role as reality tester during the negotiation stage. Soon after completing my mediation training, I remember assisting one of the UK's most experienced mediators. In the late stages of the afternoon she decided to use a caucus session to reality check the position of one of the parties. The party reacted badly, suggesting to the mediator that she was taking the side of the other party. When we left the room, the mediator commented to me that she thought she might have overdone it and blown her credibility. We revisited the same party

around 30 minutes later.

A miraculous transformation had taken place; the party had thought about some of the tough questions that the mediator had put to him and, on reflection, decided to climb down on some of the demands that he had been making.

This was a perfect example of a mediator taking a party to the edge to help remove blockage that was preventing progress. A mediator may also choose to use employment case law when reality testing. This can be very powerful. This is also applicable for HR professionals or line managers who are non-lawyers. I recall mediating a complex race discrimination case. During the negotiation phase, when the employee was pressing for a high financial compensatory award, an opportunity came up to reality test. I referred them to the 'Vento' case.

The Vento case relates to a civil servant who complained to her employer that she had encountered sex and race discrimination following actions of colleagues in the workplace. Her complaints were investigated. The report from the investigation said there was no evidence of discrimination, but there were some "management issues" which needed consideration. Advice was sought on likely prospects of success with a tribunal application on the grounds of sex and race discrimination and the likely level of compensation in the event of a successful claim. The Court of Appeal in the case of Vento vs. Chief Constable of West Yorkshire Police eventually gave guidance on the assessment of damages in discrimination cases. The judges stated that damages for injury to feelings can be divided into three bands:

A) The top band should normally be between £18,000 and £30,000 and that sums in this range should be awarded in the most serious cases, such as where there has been a lengthy campaign of discriminatory harassment.
B) The middle band of between £6,000 and £18,000 should be used for serious cases which do not merit an award in the highest band.
C) Awards of between £500 and £6,000 are appropriate for less serious cases, such as where the act of discrimination is an isolated or one-off occurrence.

Providing a verbal outline of the summary of this case provided an excellent sense-check for the employee. She had been thinking in line with band A, but quickly realised that band C was more applicable to her. She quickly realised that adjusting her position on any financial expectations would be in her best interest. As there was a significant gap between what the employee was demanding and the organisation would be willing to pay, this information provided a timely intervention to smooth the wheels of negotiation.

Getting stuck

The main reason parties come to mediation is because they need help to overcome a blocked route that would otherwise lead to resolution. There is always the potential for deadlock in any negotiation, sometimes deliberate and sometimes inevitable. Parties can get into deadlock for some of the following reasons:

- Emotional baggage. All negotiations carry some element of emotion. Parties have their own pressures, such as a reputation to maintain, career to preserve, ambition or matters of principle they want adhered to
- Parties become entrenched in their positions, digging in, conceding nothing more
- One party has reached their bottom line and have nowhere else to go
- Holding things up. Enforcing a delay prolongs the waiting and can put pressure on the other party to soften and concede more
- Self preservation. As a mediator, it is important to be sensitive to this and ensure that the need for saving face is met during the mediation process. This is likely to help you to help the parties move toward settlement

Becoming unstuck

Settlement rarely comes easily, and having patience and stamina as a mediator will greatly improve your success rate. Deadlock may have arisen because of animosity or other ill-feeling between individuals on opposite sides. A mediator can help break situations of deadlock by:

- Taking a break – Allowing emotions to cool and giving time to reassess positions will help the process. It could also be helpful to put particular issues of difficulty to one side and revisit them later on to allow progress to be made in other areas
- Introducing wit and humour – If natural and appropriate, consider telling a funny story or saying something light hearted. This will momentarily allow the parties' minds to come away from the dispute and give respite for relaxation. For example, in a past mediation a member of one party incorrectly called me Carl Lewis (instead of Clive Lewis). I laughed and said that Carl was my brother. This comment broke the apprehension in the room and brought a brief period of respite to the parties in what was an intense and highly complex dispute
- Changing strategy – If you are taking an approach that isn't working, then try something else
- Find a concession that is low cost but high value. Not all issues in negotiations are of equal value to each party
- Introduce a deadline – This is helpful as it focuses the minds of the parties to work to an imposed timescale. This can of course be moved if need be

- Highlight progress made so far. This will help the move towards problem solving
- Introduce new information or reframe the issues that have been causing the blockage so that they carry different weight or perspective
- Intervention by more senior executives. Sometimes a more senior person might be needed to impose or approve next steps

Breaking deadlock can often be a problem because neither side wants to 'go first'. There will always be difficulties, but the mediator carries the responsibility of thinking about creative solutions that will help free up a process that has stalled.

Getting to settlement

Mediation is a great tool for pursuing win-win solutions and producing a solution that leaves both parties satisfied. However, the mediation process often brings pain as both parties may need to 'give something up' in order to reach an agreed settlement. In general, to help move towards settlement, a mediator should:

Avoid bottom lines

Despite attempting to build a relationship with the parties to get them to trust you, any bottom line figure that you are told is likely to move as the day progresses. So be careful about how you choose to use 'bottom line' figures.

Leave the figures until later in the day

It can be tempting for parties to go straight to the figures and begin a negotiated settlement as quickly as possible. This usually fails. Parties want the opportunity to express themselves and talk about what has led them to get to the point at which mediation is necessary. Moving to discuss figures too quickly is likely to mean that you lose precious ground and may have to go back to a previous stage of the process.

Think about conveying offers

As mediator, you are in total control of the process. As you get to the stage where offers are being put on the table, you might feel delighted that this stage has started, and begin to relay these offers between the parties. The mediator can use various strategies at this stage including:

- Reserving judgment on when to disclose an interest even if authorised to do so
- Judging carefully whether any offer for settlement would be seen as derisory by the other party
- Working out a strategy to close the gap between the parties as the mediation progresses

Don't impose settlement options

It is of utmost importance that any settlement is the parties' own, and not suggested or recommended by the mediator. If the mediator suggests a settlement, the parties may accept this and then recoil at a later stage because they don't own it. It might take time for the parties to get to a position that, as mediator, you feel they should arrive at, but it is much more likely to stick if the parties suggest it themselves.

Point of despair

Most mediation sessions will hit a low point. At this stage you will be wondering whether you, as mediator, will be able to settle the dispute and will perhaps even question your own competence. The important thing to do here is keep optimistic and keep your mind on settlement. Perseverance and determination will help you keep moving towards settlement.

The settlement agreement

As terms for settlement become clear, the mediator should work with the parties to begin documenting the outcomes. A tip is to write settlement terms up on a flipchart and ask each party to confirm their understanding of the terms for the settlement. If this is being done via caucus meetings, ensure that this has been done prior to sharing the information with the other side. Another tip is to refrain from displaying a flipchart with proposed settlement terms before talking it through with the party. This is because if you decide to show the flipchart prior to talking through the proposed settlement terms, it is unlikely that the party will be listening to you as you do so.

For some parties, formalising the conclusion of a mediation session can feel incredibly formal. If there is unwillingness at this point, it may suggest that resolution has not quite been reached. The settlement agreement will provide a point of reference for the parties, the mediation commissioner and the mediator. It is good practice for mediators of workplace disputes to include a provision in any settlement agreement that there will be a check on how well the process has worked one to three months after the mediation.

The settlement agreement should provide a record of the closing position of the mediation. It is important to capture this and ensure that it is agreed by both parties. If it is an employment mediation session and lawyers are present, you should allow them to write any settlement agreement. As mediator, you still have the responsibility to make sure that the agreement accurately reflects the agreed settlement position of both parties. This stage of the process can be difficult, as everyone is tired and nerves may still be frayed. An agreement covering a range of complex issues can take a couple of hours, so the mediator's job is far from over. This part of the process needs the same attention as the mediation discussion.

The key points of any settlement agreement should cover areas such as:
* Identification of the parties
* Terms of settlement
* Timelines
* Confidentiality
* Announcements/press
* Signatures

If settlement isn't reached, remember that, as mediator, the problem doesn't then become yours. The parties are always responsible. You should, however, attempt to make arrangements to keep dialogue going.

Some mediation sessions can settle the day after the session itself as parties realise after a night's sleep that the main issues have resolved and therefore continuing stand-off would be futile. I would recommend that you ask permission to maintain contact with the parties, meet the parties separately and agree a programme of action for the next steps.

A workplace mediation settlement agreement may include aspects such as:
* Fred agrees to use face to face, two-way conversation rather than e-mail for work updates
* Jane agrees to keep all conversations with Fred on a business and appropriate level
* Fred agrees to draft a departmental organisation chart by 23rd February
* Jane agrees that the agenda for team meetings will be circulated at least 48 hours ahead of any meeting

An employment mediation settlement agreement may include aspects such as:
* The organisation agrees to pay Bill £25,000 in lieu of notice
* It is deemed that the above payment can be made on a tax-free basis
* The organisation agrees to provide a reference as worded in annex 'a'
* The parties agree that a company announcement will be made in line with annex 'b'
* The organisation agrees to continue providing private medical care for the next three months after the date of the mediated settlement agreement
* The organisation agrees to pay Bill's legal costs in relation to the dispute up to the value of £15,000. These will be paid directly to Jam and Jam Solicitors, upon receipt of their invoice

The point of any agreement is that it is symbolic of closure and resolution. It should capture the main points of the workplace dispute and provide a document that can be used by the parties in any ongoing review. It is imperative that the agreement reflects an accurate summary of the conclusion of the mediated discussion.

Without wanting to cause alarm, I mentioned earlier that failure of the mediator to conduct a mediation underpinned by the appropriate documentation or process could bring unwelcome consequences. In the case of Farm Assist (FAL) v DEFRA, a mediation session was held in June 2003 which led to a settlement. About four years later, FAL, having since gone into liquidation, asserted through its liquidator that the mediated settlement agreement had been procured by DEFRA through "economic duress" and should therefore be set aside. DEFRA, concerned both by the allegation and by the delay in making it, sought disclosure of all documents in FAL's possession which impinged upon the advice given by lawyers and experts which had led to their decision to settle with DEFRA at the mediation.

This included the legal advice given to FAL and its officers on the interpretation of a key contract; the advice given on the merits of claims on offers to be made to DEFRA and responses to be made to counter-offers made by DEFRA; and advice given during and after the mediation, whether or not the mediator was present. FAL objected to disclosure of the advice tendered by their lawyers and insolvency advisers on the ground that legal professional privilege protected it from disclosure. DEFRA argued that FAL had effectively waived their right to assert such privilege by bringing proceedings against them in a way which made material the state of mind of the directing powers of FAL before and at the mediation.

Mr Justice Ramsey held that such advice was not disclosable by FAL to DEFRA by virtue of legal professional privilege, but he refused to strike out the claim for economic duress and hence the question arose of proving by other means what happened at the mediation. The mediator could well be a material witness as to the nature of any alleged pressure brought to bear by DEFRA on FAL by way of economic duress. He will have chaired joint meetings at which significant remarks will have been made and also carried both those and any further arguments and the proposed terms of settlement between the parties. At the time of writing however there has been no reported case in the UK of a mediator actually having to give evidence, despite some close-run occasions.

DEFRA and FAL's written and signed mediation agreement of 2003 provided for confidentiality as to the fact that the mediation took place and as to all information arising in relation to it including settlement terms, specific "without prejudice" privilege, and for the mediator not to be called "as a witness, consultant, arbitrator or expert in any litigation or arbitration in relation to the Dispute, and the Mediator will not act voluntarily in any such capacity without the written agreement of all the parties."

In the end, the matter was settled without the mediator having to give evidence to Justice Ramsey about matters relating to the mediation. However, it was a huge signal to mediators about the importance of robust processes and the importance of a signed mediation agreement being in place.

Mediation – a distressed purchase

I started my career in the retail industry selling brown and white goods. In our sales training we were taught the phrase *'distressed purchase'*. To explain, the phrase was applied to a consumer who was in desperate need to purchase a particular product quickly. For example, a working man wants to do the family's laundry on a Saturday morning but, upon attempting to use it, finds that the machine is faulty. The machine, being out of warranty and beyond repair, needs to be replaced before the weekend is out. The man in question would likely take a trip to his local electrical store and explain to the sales assistant that he was in need of a replacement washing machine and that it had to be delivered and installed on the same day, as well as being a reliable and quality machine. His voice and body language, combined with his reason for being there, indicate his distress – hence the term *'distressed purchase'*. Recently I have made a correlation between a distressed consumer seeking an essential product purchase and commissioning mediation.

Two of the reasons why people buy are to be happy and to avoid pain. Both of these would apply to the washing machine shopper. He would have been happy to have a replacement machine to do the washing and wanted to avoid the pain of going through another week without a washing machine, going to a launderette or having to buy a new set of clothes for the whole family.

When people are in conflict and showing no signs of reconciliation the effects can be significant. The line manager or Human Resources professional with a close link to those involved are likely to feel powerless, weary, exhausted, drained and worn out as they look on. It is often these feelings of helplessness that prompt for a mediator to be commissioned.

The distress purchase in mediation is derived from the dysfunctional relationship that is preventing essential work to be carried out. In the call to try and get the matter resolved the organisation will seek to find a competent mediator to help the parties get their relationship back on track. They are also likely to want this person to be engaged quickly. I recall one of my colleagues taking a call from an organisation recently who were seeking to appoint a mediator. The caller came close to tears as she outlined the conflict situation to my colleague, talking of the abhorrence and revulsion the colleagues concerned felt towards each other and how their hate was being played out day after day. Her distress had caused her to call for a rescuer who would be able to help the individuals face up to their differences and try to focus on a future where they could work collaboratively again. The caller simply wanted her colleagues to get on with each other again and put a stop to the pain of seeing them at war but being powerless to do anything about it, whilst also spending hours on the administration that accompanies such situations.

Difficult people in mediation

Some years ago I developed an interest in the topic of difficult behaviours and spent some time finding out a little more information about some of the traits that drive individuals who may be labelled as difficult. I have previously mentioned that somewhere in the region of 85% of the disputes that go to mediation settle.

Those that don't may have one or more of the following factors in common:

- An external problem such as the organisation structure
- More time might be required to work through the issues of the past
- Irreconcilable differences
- A terminal clash of personalities
- A desire by one or both parties to remain engaged in the conflict
- A failure to imagine what a future without conflict might look like
- Engrained difficult behaviours

On this last point, people can display a range of difficult behaviours. For a minority of people, continual engagement in conflict may present some satisfaction.

Four of the main difficult behaviour types are:

- Borderline
- Narcissist
- Antisocial
- Histrionic

Below is a summary of each. From time to time, we can all be guilty of displaying difficult behaviours. These short summaries are intended to be a guide only and are not my attempt to become a clinical psychologist.

Borderline Personality (BP)
People displaying traits associated with BP are often in fear of being abandoned. To prevent themselves feeling abandoned they attempt to control and manipulate, or become aggressive with those they believe have abandoned them. Borderlines have frequent mood swings and can easily switch between positive feelings to anger and hate. They can often put people into two extreme categories: extremely

wonderful and extremely terrible.

However, until you get to know this person or observe a BP in a crisis situation, on the surface they often appear normal, even appealing. Problems can frequently occur in intimate relationships and there may be a split between their frequently angry private behaviour and their friendly public image.

Borderlines may remain absorbed for years in trying to get a loved one back or to get revenge for abandonment. As a colleague or professional advisor they may comment on how special and competent you are. Be careful though – it can change. I speak from experience. They can become demanding and enraged in an effort to make the relationship fit a perceived fantasy. The praise unpredictably turns to blame and criticism. Often, just when you think it safe to settle back into the relationship, you will receive a new blast of anger at some perceived failure or abandonment.

To the bewilderment of many, Borderlines do not often understand why their actions get negative responses. Although they may be intelligent, there can be gaps in their perceptions and a lack of common sense.

Borderline personalities - a summary:
- They normally have a big fear of abandonment
- They often have frequent anger and mood swings
- Their behaviour can be controlling, clinging and manipulative
- They may have a tendency to lodge a grievance or go to tribunal

Tips when working with someone displaying Borderline symptoms:
- Try and be matter-of-fact
- Show that you are listening
- Don't ignore them
- Set undisputable SMART objectives

Narcissistic Personality (NP)
Those with Narcissistic Personality (NP) traits are often high risk takers who do not care much about others and are generally oblivious to the consequences of their own actions. They often feel like victims, when in fact their own behaviour usually causes the events that upset them. When challenged, they are likely to become highly defensive.

Narcissists often have an over-inflated sense of their achievements. This is not to be confused with successful people who are confident in their success, such as Simon Cowell.

Narcissists can be very charismatic and outgoing. On a side note, it's interesting that in Jim Collins' research in Good to Great, the average Level 5 leader was not charismatic, outgoing or gregarious. Narcissists regularly feel hurt from events in life. We all have to overcome setbacks from time to time, including being turned down for a job with a new company or not getting a desired promotion. Usually there is no-one to blame, but the Narcissist will find someone to blame because it must be somebody's fault. It cannot be theirs. This approach can lead to the beginning of long running battles for them.

In the workplace, disputes may arise because the Narcissist cannot accept being treated as an ordinary person, and therefore receiving potentially negative feedback. It is more likely too that this type of person will become the subject of a grievance or harassment claim because they are oblivious to the impact of their insensitive remarks and demands towards their colleagues. Mediators who work with Narcissists may struggle to achieve settlement as the individual will expect the outcome of the mediation to include more benefits to them than the other party.

In order to feel superior, the Narcissist gets comfort from putting other people down. Yet because of their frequent charm it is easy to become drawn in by them. Narcissists can though be equally irritating because of their constant boasts about their success and prowess. They may display behaviours such as impatience, lack of eye contact, lack of listening skills and constant discussion of themselves. However, they may also become prone to depressive episodes because of the gap between their high expectations and the crunch of reality.

Because of their lack of empathy, NPs are often caught by surprise when their opponent becomes resentful and angry. This is because Narcissists incorrectly assume that everyone else sees them as special and superior and will therefore tolerate their exploitative behaviour in the relationship. They simply retaliate in an angry manner themselves, or feel devastated and completely victimised, which they believe justifies their odd actions.

Divorce and strained business relationships are common with Narcisissts, for obvious reasons. They may also regularly lash out in relatively unprovoked verbal or physical attacks on those closest to them.

Narcissist personalities - a summary:
* NPs feel they are superior
* They may constantly demand attention

- They are likely to react negatively to criticism
- They can be oblivious to the needs and feelings of others

Tips when working with someone displaying Narcissist traits:
- Listen deeply and with empathy
- Share decision making
- Outline consequences, but do it carefully
- Don't ignore them

Antisocial Personalities (ASP)

Compared to the last two categories the chances are that most readers are less likely to encounter someone with an antisocial personality (ASP) in a work setting, unless you work in the health or criminal justice sectors.

People with ASP may attempt to win you over with charm and what on the surface appears to be incredibly good deeds. They work hard to keep their true intentions and bad acts hidden. When working with ASPs, you may sense danger or deceit around them, but they work hard to convince you to doubt yourself and to develop more confidence in their point of view. They can sometimes be referred to as 'con artists'.

ASPs try to dominate and control others because of their fear of being dominated themselves. Some may even be willing to cause hurt, harm and pain to others in order to get what they want. Bigamists are often identified as having this personality trait. Interestingly, research shows that up to 50% of the prison population are identified as ASPs. You may not therefore be surprised to hear that constant lying and manipulation are key characteristics of the ASP.

A personal experience

I am regularly engaged in charity work. Sometimes this involves working with ex-offenders or young males who have been identified as 'at risk'. I remember having a conversation with someone in this latter category some time ago. I had wanted to see him for a long time and had bumped into him unexpectedly on a Saturday afternoon. We agreed to meet later that day at 6.00pm. He gave me his word. I am still waiting. He was, and still is, incredibly convincing. Unfortunately, family, friends and colleagues often get hurt as ASPs make every effort to get what they want and then discard the giver.

By way of background, people in this category may have experienced difficulties in their childhood. This could stem from divorce through to witnessing domestic violence. Child abuse may also be a major factor. For mediators, an encounter with a person displaying ASP traits can take you into deep waters. An advanced level of skill is required for these types of cases. You may also want to choose to be assisted by a mediator with a background in psychology or similar discipline.

It will probably be of no surprise that ASPs struggle to build valuable relationships apart from those that are based on deception and dishonesty. In addition they may have difficulty in maintaining employment and frequently get into trouble for not paying debts and fulfilling normal financial obligations. One can imagine how working for such a person could be laced with difficulties.

Antisocial personalities - a summary:
- Fear of being dominated is a driving force
- Displays aggressive charm and deceit
- Drive to dominate others
- Likely to have a lack of remorse and empathy

Tips and techniques for dealing with antisocial personality disorder:
- Avoid being swayed by charm
- Avoid doing favours
- Do not expect to change or save them from themselves
- Be prepared to impose and enforce consequences
- Pay attention to your fears and protect yourself

Histrionic Personalities (HP)
People who display traits associated with HP are likely to be highly emotional, but behind the emotion may lay few facts. They can often blame others for everything that happens to them. In some cases, this can become highly exaggerated as the event in question may not have even occurred.

People with HP can lack insight and integrate experiences poorly. Their judgment tends to be undependable and highly erratic. They may appear charming to casual acquaintances, but family members, friends and colleagues are likely to soon pick up that they are regularly required to watch a performance and begin to see the person as irritable and manipulative.

Those continually on the receiving end will quickly begin to feel a lack of empathy towards HPs and begin to draw away. The danger for the person with the HP trait is that no one may be kind enough to provide them with some honest feedback. Ultimately, their behaviour can cost them greatly. They like to draw attention to themselves and if they are not the centre of attention they might make something up to rectify this. If you are working with someone displaying this trait, emotions may be used to get your attention in order to make numerous demands upon you and to try to persuade you of something.

In disputes, working with the HP can be hard work. This is because to resolve a dispute by compromise would shatter the HP's illusion that the problems are all caused by other people. Learning to focus on facts and details, and to replace dramatic words and emotions with more realistic ones, can be arduous. Therefore, negotiation and mediation may be difficult.

Histrionic personalities – a summary:
- Always dramatic
- Dramatic and exaggerated speech and stories
- Demands to be centre of attention
- Superficial emotions and relationships
- Will fabricate stories and lie for attention

Tips and techniques for dealing with histrionic personalities:
- Maintain healthy scepticism
- Listen respectfully, and then try to focus on tasks
- Provide structure and focus
- Ask for facts

The future for mediation at work

We are living in an interesting period. For the first time in 70 years the UK has a peace-time coalition government. As an observer, this seems to be presenting both challenges and learning opportunities for comrades on the front and back benches. Those that once traded blows from opposite sides of the House are now forced to work together collaboratively and jointly in the nation's interest. This agreement is symbolic of a new beginning in so many ways. It shows how previous enemies can work on putting their past battles behind them (or at least to one side) and shows what can happen when there are shared interests at stake.

Successful political decision-making and conflict resolution requires speech over silence, collaboration over aggression and creative contention over accommodation. Dr Martin Luther King, Jr. said, *"Our lives begin to end the day we become silent about things that matter."* The political landscape provides an interesting philosophical backdrop for the implied direction the rest of the country should be taking.

Mediation has the ability to touch on both the strategic and operational, the transformational and the transactional machinery of government at both the macro and micro levels. Mediation can have a far reaching impact to help the UK economy get back on its feet following one of the worst periods of recession for many years. The business case is compelling.

As government cuts start to bite and organisations seek new pragmatic ways to solve problems and strengthen relationships, mediation has the potential to perform on the national stage.

The types of areas in which mediation can make an impact are:
- Taking on a major role in restorative justice
- Helping organisations mitigate and reduce risk in line with David Walker's report to government
- Helping to lower insurance premiums when mediation provision is in place
- Supporting the government's initiative to measure general wellbeing
- Helping the coalition to find it easier to work together
- Facilitating conflict resolution principles across the political spectrum
- Supporting the government's plan to overhaul employment laws as part of the Employers' charter

- Improving the nation's health and wellbeing in line with the publication of the Health report led by Dame Carol Black
- Increasing UK skill and key competency levels
- Supporting the UK's objective to secure its place as a leading global player by 2020 in line with the Leitch report
- Increasing the engagement levels of employees across the nation in line with the McLeod report
- Increasing trust
- Helping to reduce the 175 million working days lost every year to sickness
- Helping to reduce the £1.7bn annual cost of absence in the NHS
- Proactively managing the employee relations issues that will surface with the removal of the default retirement age
- Supporting the Office for Equalities predicted increase in tribunal cases that arise as a result of the introduction of the Equality Act
- Providing a method to manage disputes that emerge following the proposed increase in claims for unfair dismissal rising from one to two years
- Becoming a major tool for the potential increase in Class Action cases
- Helping to stem the flow of the 25% year on year increase in legal fees leading to an average of £5.8 million being spent by every major employer each year
- Helping small businesses with limited cash flow find a quicker and cheaper alternative to litigation

In the government paper 'The Path to Strong, Sustainable and Balanced Growth' launched recently by the Chancellor of the Exchequer and the Secretary of State for Business, it was noted that the UK has a lower productivity relative to its peers, with UK workers producing less output for every hour worked. Mediation and conflict resolution help to improve levels of productivity and can support the coalition objective of assisting businesses by reducing costs and red tape. In a climate with little or no fiscal growth, mediation becomes highly attractive.

Chapter 7
Conclusion

A good friend of mine once said that in times of conflict or difficulty one should keep walking. On seeing that I needed a little help with the interpretation of her parable she offered some further clarification. She said that the best thing that anyone can do when in trouble is to keep going. If we stop, slow down, or go backward our troubles are only likely to be prolonged. In a similar way, the stories narrated in this book tell of individual walks or journeys through personal conflict situations. Some found the finish line, some refused offers of help, some retreated and some continue with the journey. Most people would hope that at the end of their journey their story has a happy ending. Unfortunately, it is not always so. Every story is unique. Every story finds its own path. Every story will develop its own dialogue.

Listening to so many stories, I, like other mediators, encourage the parties where possible to not only share their story with me but, critically, to also share it with their opponent. Our view of the world and how we see ourselves can dramatically change when we hear how our actions have made another person feel. Hearing the story from them directly can be very powerful, even moving.

We all have a story to tell. Perhaps as you read one or more of the 12 stories there was something about the story that resonated within you. Maybe you or someone close to you experienced something similar. As a result of reading this book I hope I have prompted you to find someone to tell your own story to, if you hadn't already. Whatever these stories have meant to you, and whichever of the dozens of themes we have looked at has resonated with you the most, the main idea I'd like you to take away is the power of storytelling. As we saw with the headmaster at the start of the book, the longer you hold onto a story the harder it is to shift.

I invite you now to reflect on what you have read. As you do so, think about aspects such as:

- How might the parties have prevented their conflict situations from occurring?
- What could I, as mediator, have done differently?
- What learning points come from the story?
- What would you have done differently and why?

We will all be affected by conflict at certain stages of our lives, and it is impossible to predict how our conflict stories will end. Each of us has the challenge of using the conflict and the stories that emerge from it as an opportunity for insight and change.

My hope for you is that something in this book prompts and inspires you to find meaning in any conflict situation that arises at some point in the future.

Appendix 1

The Mediation Commissioning Process
The following steps are a guide to managing the mediation process

1) Gain the agreement of parties to mediate
Mediation is voluntary, and gaining the consent of the parties to attend is the first stage of the process. It is advisable that a relevant person within the company talks to each individual separately to introduce the concept of mediation. The discussions should cover the reasons for trying mediation, its benefits and how the session will be structured before allowing the parties to ask any questions they may have. As the parties may be unfamiliar with the mediation process, it is suggested that these sessions highlight the following key points:

- Mediation is private, conducted on a without prejudice and confidential basis
- The mediator is a neutral person who is there to assist the parties in their negotiations. The mediator provides impartiality and process management whilst leaving the problem and the decision to settle it in the hands of the parties
- If anyone is dissatisfied with the process, either party or the mediator can terminate the mediation at any time
- Mediation does not affect statutory rights

Once the parties have signalled their commitment to trying mediation, the next step can be addressed.

2) Contact a mediation company to discuss the nature of the dispute
Based on the nature of the dispute, the nominated mediation company will appoint the most appropriate mediator, discuss potential mediation dates and also consider a venue. The mediation session will require a room for each party and one for the mediator/joint sessions. If possible, a neutral venue away from the parties' usual working environment would be advised. The mediation company will need to know who the commissioner of the mediation is (this is typically the person calling to discuss the matter, but may vary dependent on the circumstances). They will also need to know the person that has the authority to settle. This is the individual who can be contacted during the mediation session

who has the authority to sign off any financial settlements or decisions that affect the wider organisation that may be suggested by the parties for a settlement. This person needs to be available on the day of the mediation, although not necessarily face to face.

3) Inform the parties that the mediation company will be making contact with them (or their representatives)

Once the above conversation has taken place, the mediation company is supplied with contact details for each of the parties, the commissioner and the person with authority to settle. Prior to the mediation session itself taking place, the appointed mediator will contact the parties directly to arrange a pre-mediation session.

4) The nominated mediator will have pre-mediation discussions with each party (or party representatives), either face to face or over the telephone

The pre-mediation discussion will involve the mediator having a conversation with each party to find out their point of view on the situation. The mediator will also explain how the mediation session will work and answer any questions that a party may have. The agreement to mediate will be explained to each party at this stage. The pre mediation session allows the mediator to start building trust and rapport with the parties and will help to put them at ease. By the end of the pre mediation sessions the parties will be aware of what to expect on the day of the mediation and feel comfortable with the mediator.

5) The mediation takes place

Following both parties signing the agreement to mediate, it is suggested that one day is allowed for the mediation session. As each case is unique it is impossible to schedule a definite finish time, but the majority of mediations are resolved in one day. The person with authority to settle will need to be available throughout the session.

6) A settlement agreement is drafted and signed

A mediation session usually concludes with a settlement agreement being produced. The settlement agreement consists of an action plan for the parties to adhere to, with the purpose of moving forward. The point of any agreement is that it is symbolic of closure and resolution, it captures the main points of the workplace dispute and provides a document which can be used by the parties in any ongoing review. It is imperative that the agreement reflects an accurate summary of the conclusion of the mediated discussion.

7) The mediation follow-up

In cases where there is an ongoing employment relationship with the parties, a follow up will normally take place with the parties 30-60 days after the mediation has taken place. This will allow the mediation company time to ensure that the terms signed in the settlement agreement are being adhered to. This also allows the organisation to address any further issues that may have arisen.

About the author

Clive Lewis is a leading dispute resolution specialist and Founding Director of the Globis Mediation Group. He is an accredited commercial mediator specialising in helping to solve complex one on one, team, organisational, multi-party and collective disputes. His work covers the private, public and third sectors. He has mediated hundreds of disputes. He is the author of 'The Definitive Guide to Workplace Mediation' as well as numerous published articles on mediation in the workplace. He serves as Hon. Secretary on the board of the Civil Mediation Council, a council which acts as an advisory organisation to government on issues relating to the progression of mediation in England and Wales, and chairs the council's Workplace Committee. His work has taken him across three continents and has included advising governments outside the UK. He is also a trainer, coach and facilitator.

In addition to his day job, he is a non-executive Director for the NHS, a Trustee of the National Youth Jazz Orchestra and another small charity, and a non-executive Director of the Open College Network. His commitment to charity work led to him being appointed as Chair of a government appointed independent panel exploring the rising costs of youth underachievement. The government accepted four of the five recommendations from the report. He is currently studying towards completing a PhD.

Bibliography

Collins, J. *Good to Great.* 2001

Covey, S.M.R. with Merrill, R.R. *The Speed of Trust.* 2006

Cloke, K. and Goldsmith, J. *Resolving Personal and Organizational Conflict.* 2000

Cloke, K. *Conflict Revolution: Mediating Evil, War, Injustice and Terrorism.* 2008

Dutton, D. *The Abusive Personality: Violence and Control in Intimate Relationships.* New York, NY: The Guilford Press. 1998

Department of Health, *Mental Health and Ill Health in Doctors.* 2008

Eddy, B. *High Conflict People in Legal Disputes.* 2005

Ford, C. *Lies! Lies!! Lies!!! The Psychology of Deceit.* Washington, DC: American Psychiatric Association. 1996

Kreisman, J. and Straus, H. *I Hate You – Don't Leave Me: Understanding the Borderline Personality.* New York, NY: Avon Books. 1989

Lineham, M. *Cognitive-Behavioral Treatment of Borderline Personality Disorder.* New York, NY: The Guilford Press. 1993

Mason, P. and Kreger, R. *Stop Walking on Eggshells: Taking Your Life Back When Someone You Care About Has Borderline Personality Disorder.* Oakland, CA: New Harbinger. 1998

Winslade, J. and Monk, G. *A New Approach to Conflict Resolution.* 2001

Office for National Statistics – www.statistics.gov.uk

Insolvency Service – www.insolvency.gov.uk

Employment Tribunals Service – SETA Survey of Employment Tribunal Applications 2010

Sunday Times – 17th October 2010